9

THE SECRET LIFE OF
DANNY KAYE

Also by Michael Freedland

Jolie, The Story of Al Jolson
(originally published as *Al Jolson*)
Al Jolson
Irving Berlin
James Cagney
Fred Astaire
Jerome Kern
Sophie – The Story of Sophie Tucker
Errol Flynn (In the United States,
The Two Lives of Errol Flynn)
Gregory Peck
Maurice Chevalier
Peter O'Toole
The Warner Brothers
So Let's Hear The Applause –
The Story of the Jewish Entertainer
Katharine Hepburn
Dino, The Dean Martin Story
Jack Lemmon

And with Morecambe and Wise
There's No Answer to That

THE SECRET LIFE OF
DANNY KAYE

Michael Freedland

St. Martin's Press
New York

THE SECRET LIFE OF DANNY KAYE. Copyright © 1985 by Michael
Freedland. All rights reserved. Printed in the United States of America.
No part of this book may be used or reproduced in any manner
whatsoever without written permission except in the case of brief
quotations embodied in critical articles or reviews. For information,
address St. Martin's Press, 175 Fifth Avenue, New York, N.Y. 10010.

Library of Congress Cataloging in Publication Data

Freedland, Michael, 1934–
  The secret life of Danny Kaye.

  1. Kaye, Danny.   2. Comedians—United States—
Biography.   3. Entertainers—United States—Biography.
I. Title.
PN2287.K3F7   1986   792.7'028'0924 [B]   85-25122
ISBN 0-312-70163-2

First published in Great Britain by W. H. Allen & Co.

First U.S. Edition

10 9 8 7 6 5 4 3 2 1

FOR SARA

Still my Princess of Pure Delight

ACKNOWLEDGEMENTS

DANNY KAYE IS A BRILLIANT ENTERTAINER, BUT A VERY COMPLEX man, which is why his story is so fascinating. It is also why research into this book was a long if deeply exciting undertaking.

But it was an undertaking that required a great deal of co-operation from a great many people, although I was more than sorry that Mr Kaye himself, whom I had interviewed for the BBC, did not feel able to co-operate. I therefore owe them an equal amount of gratitude. May I then begin the book simply by saying thank you – to:

Ray Anthony; Don Black; Lionel Blair; Saul Chaplin; Allan Cuthbertson; Ivor Davis; the late Diana Dors; George 'Bullets' Durgom; Julius Epstein; Irving Fein; Melvin Frank; John Green; Abby Greshler; Hugo Gryn; Paul Henreid; Wilfred Hyde White; Martha Hyer; Michael Kidd; Virginia Mayo; Bill Orr; Norman Panama; the late Jan Peerce; Bill Platt; David Raksin; the late Leo Robin; David Rose; Jack Rose; Sir Harry Secombe; Marlene Sorosky; Lesley Salisbury; Melville Shavelson; Walter Scharf; Ginette Spanier, Milton Sperling; Jack Warner, Jnr.

Also to those people who are constantly a source of wonder and help to me – the librarians at: the British Library; the British Film Institute; and the Academy of Motion Picture Arts and Sciences, Beverly Hills.

My very sincerest thanks, too, to my editor Mike Bailey. But most of all to my wife, Sara. Without her nothing would have happened.

THE SECRET LIFE OF
DANNY KAYE

THE WONDER MAN

OLD VAUDEVILLE PARLANCE HAD A WORD FOR IT – A DISAPPOINT-ment act. It was the phrase given to a turn on the 'two-a-day' (two performances a day) that stepped in when the star was taken ill. To admirers of Danny Kaye – and some of them, a generation or two ago, would have more considered themselves worshippers – everyone who has ever stood on a theatre stage where Kaye once stood is a disappointment act. Except that the real disappointment has been Danny himself.

When Al Jolson died in 1950, one observer of the show business scene recalled that Jolson, the Mammy singer who had been top of the pops over a period spanning some 30 odd years, had called himself the World's Greatest Entertainer. 'Who is there to take his place?' he asked. 'I can think of only one. And that's Danny Kaye.'

It wasn't a particularly shrewd judgment. Anyone could have told him that Danny Kaye had learnt the art of mesmerising audiences the way Jolson manipulated them, better than any other living performer. He not only made films that achieved respectable reviews, they made a lot of money at the box office. His records didn't just sell well on both sides of the Atlantic, there was hardly a radio request programme at the time that didn't have an overpowering need to play *Ballin' The Jack* or *Anatole of Paris*.

Much more significantly, he performed in theatres and in night clubs. Performed? He dominated them – and in a way that made his already different style, unique.

He sang songs in accents that would have thrilled Mr Berlitz and lyrics that would have amazed Mr Berlin. Sometimes, they weren't lyrics at all – in the accepted sense. One was 'just' a string of Russian composers' names. It was the tongue twister that twisted people around Danny's fingers – expressive fingers that somehow had as much effect on the back of the gallery at the London Palladium as they did on the front stalls.

In New York as well as in London, in Toronto and in Paris, paying customers were eating out of those hands. He moved his hands the way ballet dancers move their feet. Everything that Fred Astaire ever achieved – and Astaire danced with his hands as well

[7]

as his feet – Kaye matched. Even Jolsen at his height would have been grateful to have become that kind of Svengali with so many Trilbys as his devoted subjects.

They were no ordinary subjects either. At the Palladium where Danny Kaye became a monarch of all he surveyed in a manner never previously equalled in Britain's music-hall variety history, King George VI brought his family to see what all the fuss had been about – and stayed to tell this kid from Brooklyn how he had never experienced anything like it before.

He hadn't – and neither had anyone else who booked again and again for black-market seats at the Palladium whenever Kaye played there.

And then something happened. Suddenly, he seemed to lose interest. The only people he really wanted to perform to were children – and indeed the work he did for the United Nations Children's Fund has been outstanding. He wanted to be a new kind of symphony orchestra conductor. Always a frustrated surgeon – those hands again? – he started studying medical techniques. He fancied himself as the best Chinese cook in America. He upgraded his pilot's licence so that he could fly commercial jets. He became a baseball-team owner – and table-tennis champion of Beverly Hills.

That has been his problem, and ours. There were always better conductors than he. Kaye will never be allowed to perform a heart transplant. Chinese restaurants all over the world get on well enough without him. Nobody watching a game of the Seattle Mariners would say the team played better when Danny Kaye owned part of them. Nor are his table-tennis matches likely to go down in sports history. And would you necessarily want to fly the Atlantic in a plane piloted by Danny Kaye? But you would not be likely to forget Kaye on stage – or on film, or on record.

There was – and is likely to be – only one Danny Kaye. These pages explain why.

THE KID FROM BROOKLYN

WHEN HE WAS FIVE YEARS OLD, DANNY WOULD IN LATER YEARS recall, his mother called out: 'Make like Shirley Temple.'

The idea shouldn't be taken too literally. Shirley Temple wasn't even a glimmer in her own mother's eye when the instruction was passed to David Daniel Kaminsky – or should it be Kominsky or even Kominski? It seems to have been a matter of the choice of whoever was spelling it. What is certain, is that it was at that time that David discovered he was enough of an extrovert to enjoy putting on impromptu recitals of whatever was popular in 1918 – before his family and the other people who assembled at their house at 250 Bradford Street in Brooklyn.

Clara Kaminsky much more likely asked her David to 'make like Mary Pickford'. Whatever it was that took the lady's fancy, it was fair to assume that her son could handle it.

A lot was riding on the boy. David was born on a Saturday – always a good omen to religious Jewish families for whom the Sabbath represented a gift from God – January 18, 1913 in Brooklyn's East New York section, an event that would become more significant even than the fact that this was going to be one of the largest centres of organised crime outside of Chicago.

To Jacob and Clara (her husband called her Chaya, meaning 'life') he represented not just a new member of their family whom they were going to love and spoil as only Jewish families could love and spoil the youngest child. He symbolised their new future. Their third son, unlike his brothers who were to be known as Larry and Mac, he was the first to be born in America. And that was much more important to them than might first seem apparent.

People like them expected to move house frequently. There wasn't a Jewish family in Eastern Europe who considered the place they lived in to be their permanent home. So they were always ready to pack their few belongings – usually giving pride of place among their treasures to a feather bed – and go to a town or village that provided the best chance of earning a living, and even more vital, that hadn't for a reasonable time heard the sound of galloping horses' hooves and of Cossacks ready to rampage. The Jews in most parts of Russia had come to expect a pogrom much as they awaited the onslaught of winter.

In Ekaterinoslav (any history of American show business is littered with seemingly obscure place names emanating from within a bagel's throw of the Russian Steppes; Al Jolson was born in Srednicke; the Warner Brothers came from Krasnashiltz) the Kaminskys did little more than exist. Jacob was a horse trader – a business that would have offered few prospects even if they and their people were loved by all and if a constantly shining sun produced a steady crop of vegetables and other produce in numbers guaranteeing that their stomachs would never be empty and their hearts never heavy.

But Ekaterinoslav was in the Ukraine, the granary of Russia and also chosen as the centre for the stories of Sholom Aleichem, one of which later became *Fiddler on the Roof*. It was a life that came to an end with the German invasion of 1941 and the holocaust. Long before then, the Kaminskys decided to make their way to America, which to them seemed like the promised land. It was known as the *goldena medina* – the golden land, so the old cliché about streets being paved with gold didn't seem so outlandish.

Jacob found his way into the usual centre of employment for people like him – in a tailoring sweatshop on New York's Seventh Avenue, where men laboured under a poor light and talked away the hours about the old country, the Yiddish theatre and life at the synagogue.

Rightly, he had concluded there wasn't much chance of selling horses in the 20th century city of New York.

By the time Clara gave birth to their third son, they had come up in the world slightly, with enough money at the end of the week to move to another part of Brooklyn, which was hardly either paradise or even an area of prosperity, but there were trees in the streets and Coney Island nearby had the most exciting stretch of real estate the Kaminskys had ever known. Their two elder sons gravitated to it whenever the weather was hot and they could scrape together the fare for the streetcar.

Having a child actually born in the United States was a wonderful thing for a family like theirs. He would grow up free from any of the fears they had taken so much and so painfully for granted.

More than 40 years later, Danny Kaye would write about the significance to his father of being part of America. In an article in *Reader's Digest*, he told of the excitement in the family on the day Jacob became a citizen and had a certificate to prove it.

'Chaya! Come here,' he called. 'Bring the children.' The children were brought and the certificate was framed and hung on the wall. 'It says,' Jacob told the family, 'that Jacob Kaminsky is a citizen of

[10]

the United States of America! What do you think of that?'

What they thought was that it was the most marvellous thing that could have happened to a poor family from Russia. At last they belonged – and as Jacob told the children, he had just made a most remarkable discovery. He could vote – just like the President of that wonderful country. But much more remarkable was that that President didn't have any more votes than he had. Just one each. It was a demonstration of democracy he had never in his wildest dreams contemplated.

Like all other parents, the Kaminskys knew their David was going to be a huge success. Just how much of a success, however, they could have barely dreamed, even when they told their boy to make like Mary Pickford or whoever.

They had never had much difficulty in persuading him. David would perform at the drop of a potato pancake – or of a hint that he would get a round of applause from adoring relatives and friends for whatever he did. If anyone doubted that this kid from Brooklyn who would one day become Danny Kaye had show business in his blood, he ought to have found a way of going back to Bradford Street, or even to Sutton Avenue where they had lived previously.

Clara had first noted his talents when David was only four years old. She had taken him into a shoe shop – a big event for them both. For Clara it was important because it was the first pair of shoes bought specially for him direct from a store – no more hand-me-downs. For David it was all an eye opener – a whole store full of people and what appeared to be rows of occupied seats, a challenge to a budding showman if ever there were one. David hoisted his way on to one of the chairs and began singing at the top of his voice a tune he had picked up called *Fifty Fifty*. He hadn't a clue what the lyrics meant and it wasn't all that easy to discern the words as he sang them in between the sort of gulps tiny children employ as part of their every-day vocabulary. But Clara was enchanted. She may not have said, 'My boy, the future star,' but that was what she must have felt.

To the boy David himself, Brooklyn symbolised the kind of world in which he thought it was only natural to grow up. With childhood long behind him, he reflected:

'I think I benefited from being born and raised in Brooklyn. That was one of the most cosmopolitan neighbourhoods and that was one of the great joys about it. It's where you learned you didn't dislike anybody because he was an Italian, a Jew or an Irishman or what else. There were great cultural differences, but you stood on your merits as a youngster.'

If it taught him racial tolerance, there was good reason. Small boys are notorious fighters. Understanding each other was the best

[11]

way they had of countering the mutual ultimate deterrent. And in the Kaminskys' part of East New York, they all lived close enough to each other for the Jews to be totally aware of not just Christmas and Easter but of all the saints' days, too, and for the Catholics to realise when Yom Kippur or Passover was on the way.

Kaye would say that his father Jacob was the happiest man he knew, even though he hadn't made it as well as his friends from the old country – who had also worked for Seventh Avenue dress manufacturers and who even in the early '20s smoked big cigars and drove their own cars to and from the smart neighbourhoods where they lived.

It was to Jacob that they would turn for advice – in his own parlour. David asked his mother why they came to the Kaminskys for that advice and didn't meet at one of their own smart residences. She told him: 'I think maybe they left the best of themselves here. They need to come back every now and again.' It was a message the boy never forgot. He knew he had to come back every now and again, too, even if only mentally. David Kaminsky would leave a big part of himself in Brooklyn.

The boys and girls who went to elementary school with him – or to be precise, in the less than colourful language insisted upon by the New York school system, to PS 149 – would leave an equally large part of themselves, and many would stay there for the rest of their lives.

At PS 149, David was – to use the terminology of the day, the kind of phrase that would be to later generations as offensive as the concept of the entertainment itself – a 'pickaninny' in the school minstrel show.

The show's set was a giant water melon – with one of the phoney black children sitting in among the black seeds of the fruit.

David's trouble was that his red hair didn't really go with being a minstrel and his ears were large and very white – and stayed that way when the rest of his face was smothered in burnt cork. But it didn't seem to matter. David Daniel Kaminsky had made his first appearance on stage and loved every minute of it.

He loved, too, going to minstrel shows. At one in a theatre on the corner of a Brooklyn street, he heard a minstrel sing a song that he would never forget. It was called *Ballin' The Jack*. Thanks to that, millions of other people wouldn't forget it either.

Those were the songs they sang in recess time at the Brooklyn schools, too, at PS 149 and when David graduated to the Thomas Jefferson High School, later on.

He was long and lanky by then and his hair had got so red it looked as if a bottle of ink had been emptied on it. David was also a baseball freak – a state of affairs that was hardly to change during the rest of his life.

Because he was tall, he found he could be a pretty good pole vaulter, too. And he could always, but always, 'make like . . .' well, whoever was enchanting the young people in those pre-talking pictures, pre-radio, pre-television days.

When there were school theatricals to do, David Kaminsky went up there on stage with the best of them – except that he always *was* the best of them. For some time, he was not allowed into the dramatic societies and had to content himself with – not reluctantly – playing baseball.

Mrs Kaminsky would have preferred him to go on to the school stage. She liked the idea of her son, even when he was just 12 years old, being an actor. She also appreciated that her own husband was a very good tailor.

Danny would say – and he was ashamed half a century or more later to admit it – that he always regretted that his father didn't show more ambition. In fact, Jacob was in his own way very ambitious indeed. He, for instance, fancied himself as a designer.

He came home with a set of coloured pencils, a huge sketch pad and lots of hope. Clara encouraged him the best way she could. He did his designs and thought they were marvellous. Clara said she thought so, too. He worked on them at night. David heard his father scratching away at the pad. Then nothing more seemed to happen. Finally, David asked him: 'Say, Pop, what happened to those designs you did?'

'Oh,' said Jacob, 'they weren't any good.' But then he added: 'David. A man can't do everything in this world, but he can do one job well. I found out I'm not a good designer, but I am a good tailor.'

David, meanwhile, had found out that he was a good performer at school. It was probably as much as anything a defence mechanism, a totally committed need to get up and perform. Like almost every character Danny Kaye was to go on to play in his first years in Hollywood, he was shy, introverted and frightened to the roots of that red hair that when a girl moved her lips, she might also be trying to speak to him.

As he was to say: 'I was a shy, nervous boy – the sort of guy who always stood behind the guys who whistled at the girls.'

Had the young Kaminsky taken refuge on an analyst's couch – and it would be a few years before he did – the psychiatrist might have concluded that there were deeper reasons for his reluctance to come out and face girls on the kind of terms he wished he knew they would appreciate: when David was 13 his mother died.

Jacob was, of course, hit most of all. He loved Clara deeply and

[13]

she was his adviser as well as his partner. When she was gone, there was a great void left in his life. But even then, in the way of Jewish immigrants of his generation, he was intensely philosophical. Young David couldn't understand why such a thing could happen. Jacob probably couldn't understand it either, but he tried to explain the reason to his son: 'To be happy every day is not to be happy at all,' he said.

The event had precisely the effect on David that could have been predicted. The family sat on the low stools of mourning and believed that the bottom had fallen out of their lives.

It was also the signal (those psychiatrists, no doubt, agreeing) for David, so soon after his barmitzvah – the occasion when boys are suddenly supposed to be men, to take on the obligations of their faith and to realise that maturity may not yet be theirs but responsibility is – to run away from school.

He did it with a friend called Louis Eisen, who joined him in hitching rides to Florida. There, David sang songs while Eisen played a guitar. David also added to the numbers he performed a feature that would before long be his professional stock-in-trade. When he performed his tunes, he used the accents of the people who had been around him in Brooklyn – the Irish and the Italians and the Jewish people like himself.

It may all have been very, very immature and 'busking' in the crudest form, but it earned the pair $8 – enough to get them home after two weeks.

They hadn't spent much during that time. They thumbed lifts and in the evening they appeared at the local police station where they informed the officers that they were hitching home and could they be accommodated in a nice warm cell overnight?

They moved quite a long way in those two weeks. At a small police station in Delaware, however, their hopes seemed to flounder. The policeman rang Jacob Kaminsky and asked if he wanted the boy sent home.

'Oh no,' said Jacob. 'He wants to find out something. He'll come home when he's ready.'

Sheepishly, David did come home, expecting what the neighbours would have called 'a frusk in pisk', or a slap on the face. Instead, Jacob looked up from a newspaper and said: 'There's food in the icebox, David.' He hoped that David had already found out something.

The two Kaminskys, father and son, were finding out a lot about each other. Principally, that they were getting on very well indeed.

Jacob remained the centre of the Kaminsky family. He was adored by all his sons who took delight in the struggles he had with the English language, out malapropping all the others in the neigh-

[14]

bourhood, all of whom sounded like characters out of Leo Rosten's Hyman Kaplan stories.

Jacob, who was now determined to remain a ladies tailor with no further deviations to his career – he had for a time also tried his hand at selling corsets and even saddle bags (a throwback to his days as a horse dealer) – knew there was a word for everything. The trouble was that he sometimes used the wrong word, especially when he thought he was brilliantly taking the correct idiom to say things that didn't sound nearly as attractive in plain prose. When he took his dog for a walk, for instance, the animal didn't merely run straight to the nearest lamp post, he made a 'beehive' for it.

David, meanwhile, had to think about making a 'beehive' for a job. Really, he would have liked to have been a surgeon. There was no doubt about that. He was fascinated by what those people could do to help humanity. When he looked at his own long, expressive fingers, he imagined them clasping a scalpel, and delicately, intricately, working their way around a seemingly inoperable tumour and then with a firmness that was belied by his gentle attitude to those around him, suturing the wound.

Walter Mitty was never simply a James Thurber creation. David Kaminsky was Mitty personified long before Danny Kaye was handed the script of that film.

But medicine in any form, and surgery in particular, was closed for him. Entering a medical school and being kept for the five years or so it took to train a doctor cost more money than his father could muster. David's two brothers had already got jobs in electrical stores and it was fairly obvious he would have to join them.

David wanted work, but he also wanted to do something at which he knew he could be good. Walter Mitty may have required the sound of moving machinery going 'ta-pocket, ta-pocket, ta-pocket' to create roles in his day dreams. David Kaminsky had his own ideas without the assistance of any mystic incantations.

David went looking for work and didn't find it. What he did find was a $5 bill under his pillow every week – a gesture of his father's understanding that times were tough for all in the midst of the Great Depression, but particularly hard for a youngster still finding his feet.

Jacob's friends, the ones who came in their big cars from their big new homes far away, couldn't understand it. 'David got a job yet?' they asked. And when he told them 'No', they proferred the kind of advice they usually came to him for. David was growing into a bum, they said. No, said Jacob, that wasn't it at all.

As Kaye recalled in that *Reader's Digest* piece, Jacob's answer was direct and to the point: 'My son is searching for something he can devote his life to. I can't tell him what it is. He'll never be happy unless he finds it for himself. It may take him longer than others, but he'll find it. I do not worry about him.'

Danny by now knew what he wanted to be. Not a doctor, because reluctantly he had had to rule that out, but an entertainer who was the best entertainer Brooklyn had ever produced. The old friends and neighbours again scoffed. To them that still wasn't a job for a Jewish boy – unless he could guarantee to be another Al Jolson, Eddie Cantor or Harry Richman. They didn't yet know much about Jack Benny or George Burns. And Sophie Tucker and Fanny Brice, well they were something else again, weren't they? The men laughed at the idea.

They enjoyed going to vaudeville shows themselves. Most of all they loved the Yiddish theatres on Second Avenue, which David had heard of and enjoyed too. There they had seen the classics, including Shakespeare, turned into their own language. They also loved their own performers who made sounds that seemed as delicious as a bowl of chicken soup or a plate of pickled herring. Aaron Lebedeff, for instance – who sang a mass of jumbled up words so quickly that they laughed and clapped and tried, always unsuccessfully, to copy him. They didn't know – and Lebedeff certainly didn't know – that that was called 'scatt singing'. Danny Kaye would one day give it all a totally unexpected dimension. But all that was for fun. It wasn't, the way they saw it, for work.

David tried his hand at taking 'real jobs'. Like some character out of a *Saturday Evening Post* story, he became a soda jerk and was told to think seriously about what he would do next. When it was discovered he was dispensing too many ice creams to his friends, that serious consideration was given instant importance. He was summarily fired.

For a time he worked for Dr Fine, the nearby dentist, as his assistant, but found it all too frustrating – and dentistry was poor-man's surgery, nothing like what he considered to be the real thing. He was so frustrated that he didn't even notice that Dr Fine had a dark-haired daughter called Sylvia.

David didn't stay working for Dr Fine for very long. When the dentist caught the red-haired youth using his drill to make holes in a block of wood he, in turn, suggested it might be more productive using it on his head – and also fired him.

Even so, Jacob didn't order David to take jobs. 'He didn't have that ambition of other parents to ruin their children's lives,' Danny was to say years later.

He just hoped that his youngest son would have more sense and make something of himself. For a time, it didn't seem as though David was making much headway in that direction. He got up late

[16]

every morning – in order, it eventually turned out, to make sure it would be much too late to find a job.

Things were admittedly more to Jacob Kaminsky's liking when David joined an insurance firm. Here, there really were good prospects. To the immigrant generation, a white-collar job with a firm that sold insurance represented not merely the opportunities of a good, solid future, but also respectability, the sense that their children had really made it. It was the kind of job that brought in regular money and would keep doing so for long into the future.

By the time David was sitting down at his desk, gazing at all the other desks around him in the grip of a kind of boredom that came close to a stupor, he had to pinch himself to realise he ought to be grateful. Daily, the unemployment lines were getting longer and men's hopes were getting shorter.

Insurance companies, like most financial institutions in those Wall Street crash days, were the most fragile, the ones most likely to go under, the ones from which more former millionaires were throwing themselves out of the upper-storey windows.

Even if 'his' firm were to be one of these vulnerable organisations, it would not prove to be of much concern to David Daniel Kaminsky. An error on his part led to a man who was due to receive $4,000 from the firm in an insurance pay out getting $40,000. The $36,000 discrepancy was discovered long after the recipient had banked his winnings and run, following investigations by a team of private detectives who not only looked into everything David did in his office, but even took him to the cinema in the hope of discovering something about him they hadn't previously known.

What they discovered was that Mr Kaminsky Jnr wasn't terribly good at mathematics. He had added a nought without appreciating the consequences of not checking his figures. His boss meanwhile checked his own figures and decided he could do without his new clerk.

Years later, that boss wrote him a letter after seeing a Danny Kaye show: 'I enjoyed it very much. But when you cost us that $40,000, I thought you were either a thief or a nitwit.'

That event certainly decided David that the time had come to be a professional nitwit.

A SONG IS BORN

IT WAS REALLY THE HITCH-HIKING EXPEDITION WITH LOUIS EISEN that did it – and the period in the insurance company which confirmed the decision.

The fact that David and Eisen got on so well together and enjoyed their stint so much convinced them both to work in show business part time, if not all the week long.

When they could, they entertained at private parties in the evenings, calling themselves Red and Blackie. David, of course, was Red. It was much easier to remember than either Eisen or Kaminsky. As Sammy Cahn was to say about his own partnership with Saul Chaplin, before they changed their names (from Cohen and Kaplan) they sounded like a pair of dress manufacturers.

What Red and Blackie were manufacturing was a means of getting audiences to laugh and clap – although in those early days at the beginning of the 1930s, neither was an easy commodity to come by. They sang songs and told jokes. David found it easier to sing. He wasn't very good with jokes; finding his own formula for making people laugh came later and proved – for those who like assessing such things – what becoming a star was really about.

They even got themselves a radio broadcast, over the local station WBBC – which is not to be confused with a somewhat more important broadcasting organisation with which Red would later have certain associations and which does not have a 'W' at the beginning of its name.

Between them, they decided that their future had to be together as a permanent team. But where would the work come from? In the old days, the answer was vaudeville. A place in an also-ran vaudeville circuit bill wouldn't bring much money, but it could mean a fine training and regular work – performing the same routine, going from one tank town to another as they worked their way across the United States, from a run-down hall in New York State to California.

But vaudeville was already numbering its days. Radio was assassinating the two-a-day and what it couldn't murder, the newly-talking cinema was hungrily taking for its own. Vaudeville theatres were becoming movie houses and one circuit after another was closing down.

For young, ambitious, hard-working Jewish performers like them there was only one answer: a fully-established permanent nursery ready to take their talents and mould them. These were the hotels in New York State's Catskill Mountains which for ever would be known as the Borsht Belt. The name was brilliant. Borsht – a soup compounded mostly from red beets with a generous addition of sour cream – was the life blood of these establishments which fed Jewish New Yorkers as though they had arrived fresh from an organised course in mass starvation.

There were huge helpings of kosher food served at every meal and at every in-between meal, too. They ate chicken and knishes, gefilte fish and bagels and lox in quantities that would today enable the Israeli Army to survive a new Six Day War. The guests got up from their tables knowing that they were well fed only when they were in agony – people like them were rarely merely in pain. When the heat from heartburn convulsed them, they knew that it was good and they were satisfied. That is when they needed feeding with something else.

Acts like Red and Blackie provided this additional food.

It was all part of an honoured tradition. Before them, Eddie Cantor and Jack Benny had done their stints entertaining at the Borsht Belt hotels. After them, Mel Brooks and Woody Allen would tread the same boards, telling jokes with a spicing of Yiddish about the maids at the hotel, the waiters and Mrs Cohen's affair with Mr Greenberg.

The audience loved it – and so did Red and Blackie.

The two of them waited on table and in addition to taking part in theatricals, would do everything they could to entertain – including jumping into a swimming pool fully clothed with straw hats on their heads.

After London's Windmill Theatre, it was probably the hardest audience in the world. Guests who had been exhorted to 'enjoy, enjoy' before each meal, came to the shows in the hotel theatres groaning from their food and determined that enjoy the show they would, too – but only if the entertainment met their own demanding standards.

So Eisen and Kaminsky found themselves 'toomlers' – in short, men whose job was to create a 'tumult'. It didn't matter how they did it. The word sounded like Yiddish, but the sense adapted itself to English perfectly. Both he and Eisen succeeded to the evident satisfaction of everyone.

When there were signs that people were booking out – especially if the weather got bad – an SOS was sent out. 'They're checking out. Get toomling.' Their function in that case was to provide enough instant entertainment for the guests to decide to stay behind after all. Frequently, it worked.

They were exciting times. Blackie played his guitar and Danny regailed the hotel guests with enough highly-accented songs to make their borsht curdle. When they held their sides, it wasn't just in reaction to what had gone down their gullets.

He also learned to dance. 'I didn't know my left foot from my right foot as a dancer, but we made up an act.' And it worked.

The way to these people's Jewish hearts was plainly not always exclusively through their stomachs. It was also equally plain that Red was the more popular of the two. Being a 'toomler' was a summer-only job. At the end of the first summer, Eisen decided he wanted something more permanent and David was on his own. It was a moment for reflection.

As usual it was Jacob to whom he went for advice. His father was always encouraging. When his friends wanted to know what David was doing, he told them his boy was going to college.

Jacob knew that he didn't want to stay in the Borsht Belt and was the first to encourage him to move on.

'There are some people who always have to test themselves,' he told him, 'to stretch their wings and try new winds. If you think you can find more happiness and usefulness this way, then you should do it.'

He decided to continue to work the resorts in the summer – it was literally nice work while he could get it and it was beginning to pay better, too.

'I'd do anything for a laugh,' he remembered at a time when millions of other people would do anything themselves to laugh at him. For years, the pattern hardly changed. Working in vaudeville or cabaret somewhere or other in the winter and spending the dollars he had earned in the summer – sometimes as much as a thousand a month.

The fame of David Kaminsky spread and the managements knew that he brought people to their reception desk year after year, hoping for vacancies.

It was a mutual admiration society. David himself had never been happier. The shy kid in the company of individual girls was a towering extrovert when ordered to perform in public. It was as though he had always been the neighbourhood show-off and was delighted to be well paid for what he would have done more than willingly for nothing. Besides, the food was good – although the near-skeletal Kaye frame looked as if it needed only a rousing cheer to keep it alive, which was practically true.

One of the things he had to learn was how to deal with the big world of show business. He realised that he probably wouldn't get far with a name like David Kaminsky. Changing names was already a big American thing. The melting pot to which immigrants were welcomed when they passed the Statue of Liberty had never really been a melting pot at all. Jews stayed Jews. Italians stayed Italians – except that they were Jewish Americans and Italian Americans and they tried to change their names into something that sounded . . . English.

David's two brothers had changed their names – to Kamen, which wasn't any more English than it could have been called American. David Kamen? Sammy Cahn would have advised that it still sounded like a dress manufacturer – although it might also have sounded like a doctor and that *did* have great appeal. But if this already professional entertainer had any future to look forward to he had to think of commercial success in that field alone.

Walter Mitty Kaminsky had to go into hibernation. The only 'ta-pocket, ta-pocket' he could allow himself was the sound of an audience applauding, which to him already had the stuff of life about it, a magnet to which he found himself being drawn like a sackful of iron filings.

So David Daniel Kaminsky became Danny Kaye, a surname taken by so many people that it became instantly identifiable as Jewish. Hiding his origins certainly wasn't the newly-named Danny's concern. No one could deny that it was more commercial. It also, sounded better in partnership with two other performers with whom he had gone into business – Dave Harvey and Kathleen Young.

This was going to be the beginning of Danny's 'legit' phase. Harvey and Young had convinced him that he ought to join them in a serious dancing act which they would call the Three Terpsichoreans, a strange name for a team who booked themselves into what was left of vaudeville. Few of the customers in the theatres where they played could pronounce the title they had given themselves, let alone knew what it meant. It was the usual vaudeville regime – booking into a theatre early Monday morning, providing the resident orchestra with their music and then going through the routine, hoping the band would either be as good – or better than – the one in the town before.

They lived in small boarding houses, ate around tables where the various acts would gather either to talk about the great things they were going to do in the future or those they had already achieved in the past. Never about their failures at the present. They worked until late at night and slept until late in the morning.

At Utica, New York, hardly a centre of international attention, Danny had a problem. The act were dancing a bolero and Danny's

[21]

role was to move and kiss Kathleen's hand. As he stepped towards her, he fell – flat on his face.

'Wait for the laugh,' said Dave. 'I can't,' said Kaye. 'I've split my pants.' He had – and the audience were splitting their sides.

It was also part of an old tradition and helped the threesome go down very well indeed in Utica.

It seemed too to go down well everywhere else they played. Still a devoted believer in the doctrine of anything for a laugh, Danny played along with it – and fell over and split his trousers at every performance. It was what vaudeville was all about – that and the great vaudevillians who have gone down in American show biz history, of which collectively the Three Terpsichoreans knew they would never be a part.

Nobody pretended it was for sophisticated tastes. Anything that was likely to be received by loud boos from the audience would be met with a long pole with a hook on the end of it, courtesy of the management.

Danny himself got the theatrical if not the literal hook at Detroit. The city more famous for the cars it made than the entertainers it created didn't exactly show a great deal of taste where young Mr Danny Kaye was concerned.

While performing in a show called *La Vie Paris* – vaudeville audiences weren't even considered well enough bred to know that the title was grammatically incorrect – Danny was told that he was fired.

The management of the show, in the shape of one Mr A. B. Marcus, was only willing to pay for two performers, not three. Dave and Kathleen were a lot kinder than many of the people in a business where you fight for yourself because few others will fight for you. They announced that they wouldn't perform without Danny – but would split the two-person salary three ways.

It was known as a 'tab show', not exactly a recommendation for theatrical excellence in 1933.

There were 75 people altogether in the show and they stayed together for the rest of the year and through 1934, doing up to 50 one-night stands as they made their way westward. That was the point when Danny Kaye first realised that his world extended beyond the Borsht Belt and its numerous colonies.

The company – in one of those strange, inexplicable tangents that show business acts take – were booked into the Far East, including China and Japan, countries that were already at war with each other and which couldn't be expected to enjoy the delights experienced by the folks in, say, Duluth (although a rouged comedian peering down the front of a big-breasted girl's dress and saying that he'll take the puppy with the red nose might be considered international).

They were due to begin their tour in Australia – except that Marcus's wife insisted on taking her dog Vita with her and the Australians who had strict quarantine laws were equally determined that she would not. So the show began in Japan.

For Danny, it was an opportunity he would not miss.

The Chinese and the Japanese had mannerisms which he would later add to an ever-increasing library of national characteristics. What was going to be different, however, was that he had no intention of slighting these other nationalities.

He was determined not to be a dialect comedian who insulted people by giving every impression that he considered them inferior. His years in Brooklyn had dissuaded him against any such notion.

That wasn't his idea at all. Circumstances provided Danny Kaye with the perfect reason to develop a style all his own. When he wasn't dancing, Danny was supposed to tell a few jokes. As he could have predicted, the stories that might have pleased the people of Omaha, weren't going down at all well in Osaka.

'Don't worry,' the theatre manager told him, 'it is not polite for Japanese to laugh at visitors.' It didn't convince him.

He was to say he was so maddened by this that he thought 'there was something in this hara-kiri business after all.' Nor was he sure that the Three Terpsichoreans' act was appreciated as a whole by their oriental audiences.

The test of his theories came unexpectedly – when the lights failed at the Osaka theatre. It would have sent other entertainers into prima-donna type hysteria or into unbridled anger. Danny Kaye took it as a chance to show that he was not like the others – any of them. The audiences were mystified – like all Japanese, they were far too disciplined to panic simply because the house was in complete darkness. When they had adjusted themselves to what light there was, they were able to pick out the figure of Danny Kaye, sitting on the edge of the stage, his legs dangling loosely in front of him.

Because they couldn't understand his English, he decided that it wouldn't be right to give himself an unfair advantage. So he spoke a language that none of them could understand – what at the time was best described as Double Dutch and which bore a passing resemblance to what Aaron Lebedeff had been doing a world away. Except that already Danny was doing it in a style that was all his own.

He recited a mass of words that could be found in no language's dictionaries, sprinkling one phrase that sounded Japanese here, another there. If it really *wasn't* polite to laugh in Osaka, they were the rudest audiences in the world. They laughed and they clapped and Danny Kaye had discovered his own way to what show biz liked to call a mob – paying customers who imagined he was speaking in Japanese and couldn't quite make out why they didn't go along with his dialect.

As far as he was concerned, it was as if an earthquake had suddenly hit the theatre – which would not have been all that unlikely. While he was in Osaka, the city was struck by a massive hurricane.

Looking out of his bedroom window, he was practically mesmerised by the sight of a cyclist pedalling madly but with what might have appeared to be an excess of determination against the elements. Danny looked through the glass, still transfixed, and was knocked unconscious by flying debris. But he was back for the next show.

La Vie Paris played in Tokyo and then continued its tour around practically every other Japanese city that had anything resembling a theatre. He was perfecting and honing his stage act, even, at times, commuting between Japan and Shanghai.

Danny learned that he was not just able to make these people laugh, but that he could follow some of their own practices with almost as much ease as they could themselves – and that did not just mean that he had discovered the art of eating with chopsticks, which of course he had.

(It was in Shanghai that he made what he might construe as the most important discovery of his life – his first Chinese restaurant. 'It was overwhelming,' he recalled. 'I was absolutely riveted by the heat, the flames and the technical speed of the chefs.')

When it was necessary to change his clothes in a space no bigger than a foot or two across, change in that space he did – and in about two or three minutes.

In Tokyo, he was called 'Kayesan' which, he said, wasn't bad for a kid from Brooklyn.

The act went on to Hong Kong and to Singapore. By the time they all returned to San Francisco, Danny Kaye felt ready for the big time – even if the big time wasn't exactly ready for him.

He could have hoped that the experience of the Orient would be as much a blooding of Danny Kaye as the Catskill audience sharing with him a bowl of borsht. He arrived back in the States with all the confidence of what future generations would recognise as Anatole of Paris offering his new collection to an adoring assembly of matrons. It was easier designed than bought.

In Japan and China, he had been content with a polite shaking of heads and a salary that rarely exceeded $40 a week. Now he hoped for something more. Within days, he would have liked a chance to be back where he had been. The team were out of work. The management that had been quite happy taking ten per cent of whatever *La Vie Paris* produced was now sure that everything had been milked from their output and had quite clearly lost interest. They were all out of work and Danny was back home with his father – who gave him a great deal more encouragement than he might have thought he had a right to expect. After all, his brothers were earning regular money in the kind of jobs Brooklyn boys believed they were born for – good, small but steady salaries that would rarely change but which would always put bread on their tables in the same two-room apartment in which they would expect to die.

Danny hoped for something more – even though he now had considerably less. But he made Jacob laugh and the senior Kaminsky couldn't understand why he wasn't having a similar effect on the people who decided which acts appeared in the local vaudeville theatres.

Men and women with talent are also men and women with emotions, and emotions frequently lead to temperament – and depression. If the way Danny felt now was any indication of his theatrical abilities, he was very talented indeed.

He felt, he was to say a short time afterwards, as if he had taken one of President Franklin D. Roosevelt's New Deal jobs. And having had the charity, he now needed to find his own feet.

Danny did what everyone else in show business was supposed to do before he eventually succeeded – haunted the offices of the agents and impresarios and tried to persuade them they needed him even more than he needed them.

The trouble, he confessed, was that he was not really an actor, not really a dancer, and hardly most people's idea of a comedian. (The fact that he was larger than the sum of all these parts had not yet dawned on any of them, not even on himself.)

Agents pressed for details. 'Do you sing?' they asked, 'Ye-e-s,' he answered. 'Do you dance?' 'Ye-e-s,' he said. 'Do you do comedy?' 'Ye-e-s,' he replied. And, as he later noted, 'I was finished.'

When he did land jobs they were the kind which performers who valued their status in the world of show business would regard as demeaning. But times were tough. Danny was an assistant to Sally Rand, one of the biggest draws in the world of burlesque, mainly because she had one of the biggest busts in the world of burlesque. She rivalled Gipsy Rose Lee as America's favourite stripper in the days when these ladies were not allowed to more than hint at what they hid under their fans or their fingers. Danny's job was to help her cover her strategic places, but he lost his situation when the fans lost theirs – because a bluebottle buzzed at the wrong moment. Miss Rand was arrested that day.

It is not a chapter that in retrospect gives a great deal of pride to Mr Kaye.

He did only a little better with his next undertaking in the name of the theatrical arts. He became a stooge for a certain Mr Nick Long Jnr, a comedian of sorts – and apart perhaps from carrying fans for strippers, there is not a job which comes much lower in the world of entertainment. For stooges have enormous longevity – as stooges – and rarely have a chance to break out on their own.

He and Long worked at the Casa Mañana night spot and then played for two months with one of America's favourite band leaders, Abe Lyman.

Danny also got to sing a couple of songs, which turned into a bigger opportunity for him than he at the time realised.

British impresario Henry Sherek caught their act and offered Danny a chance to play in London. Perhaps Kaye remembered the loyalty of the Three Terpsichoreans. He decided that he would only go if Sherek took their act. It had to be he and Long together – or neither of them. Sherek took the two.

But he added a couple of terms of his own – Danny would have to perform two solo numbers.

Sherek knew what those numbers should be – for he had already spotted something about this pencil-thin performer with the shock of unruly red hair that would still take some time to dawn on audiences: Kaye was perfecting a way of taking other people's songs and manipulating words as though he were kneading them with his own long fingers.

He would accept Long and Kaye on condition that Danny sang two of those songs he had heard in New York, *Minnie the Moocher* – which he sang so differently from the man who had virtually made it his signature tune, Cab Calloway – and *Dinah* – which Danny pronounced Deenah (or Dena, a name that would within the decade play an important part in his own life.)

The act was booked into one of London's most fashionable night spots, the Dorchester Hotel, less than five years old and in its pristine art-deco glory, attracting audiences equally plush, rich and up to date. London, he was now sure, was about to be his.

It is at this point that one would expect the real Danny Kaye story to begin. The greatest anglophile in the world was plainly at the start of his love affair with what virtually became his adopted city, the place whose population responded to him better than any other anywhere else in the world.

That was not what happened at all. Part of the blame might be laid at the door of 10 Downing Street and the Chancellery in Berlin – because Kaye and Long just happened to open on the night of the

Munich crisis, the evening in 1938 when Chamberlain flew to Berlin to give Czechoslovakia to the Nazis.

While the umbrella-carrying premier was persuading Hitler to sign his piece of paper, and sanctioning a German invasion of Prague, Danny Kaye was trying much less successfully to get the Dorchester audience to approve his own invasion of London. At the end of a mercifully short engagement, it was Kaye not London that surrendered.

The trouble, it has often been suggested since, was that Danny's humour was so American, it didn't travel. That is highly unlikely. The Dorchester cabaret crowd were fairly sophisticated. They were the kind of people who, like the former Prince of Wales, were highly influenced by American entertainment.

But Kaye was way out for them. He later described the posh hotel as a 'saloon', but he admitted it was all his fault. 'I was too loud for the joint. I died the death.'

Being loud wasn't the only thing wrong. 'The atmosphere was wrong,' he recalled 11 years later. 'The pianist kept his back to me for six weeks. I never did get to know what he looked like.'

They were not used to his style any more than were the Americans themselves. And the tricks he had used on the decidedly unsophisticated Japanese were not tailored to go down well with people who, at the best of times, provided difficult competition as they fiddled with their cutlery and clinked their champagne glasses.

Danny was paid £40 a week at the Dorchester and ended up having his contract terminated.

Just occasionally he broke away. He didn't go sight-seeing; the Tower of London was left for another visit. But he did see something of London's environs. He gave a few concerts outside the capital. In Guildford in Surrey that autumn, an audience practically raised the roof of the local theatre in appreciation. It hadn't happened quite like that before. It would again – often.

Danny himself admitted he was a disaster at the Dorchester and that was not belabouring the point. He was to say that he saw it only as a rather unpleasant stopping off place on the way to Paris, which he and Long remembered a great deal more happily.

The problem with being Danny Kaye was that he was in truth aiming a lot higher than he was able to reach. He wanted a Broadway show, but there weren't any Broadway shows yet in the market for an unknown comedian with a shock of red hair, who promised a greater talent than anyone had yet been able to prove existed.

Danny also dreamed of Hollywood. Secretly, because every now and again the message got out that the movies weren't quite respectable enough for products of the legitimate stage – and this was one vaudevillian and ex-Borsht Belt performer who considered himself just that. The fact that he hadn't yet done any legitimate acting was not allowed to affect his own conception of himself.

But needs must . . . and for once there was the germ of a hope that he was on the way.

There was an offer to make films – an offer nobody in his right mind would be able to refuse. Except that these weren't what he considered to be 'real' movies – and they weren't even being made in Hollywood.

It was the age of the film short, a staple part of the average cinema diet at a time when a night at the films always consisted of a double feature as well as the newsreel, trailers and these mini movies. He made one film called *Dime A Dance*, which was considerably more than the value picture goers seemed to put on seeing him at work. But he took up what seemed to be residence at the legendary Astoria studios in New York to make three shorts for the somewhat ambiguously named Educational Film Company run by a gentleman called Art Miller. He starred in one, called *Getting An Eyeful* – and played an extra in the same movie, as if to prevent his getting too conceited. The whole thing was completed in two days and even now, Danny Kaye is less than happy to talk about it.

The picture was followed by two other shorts, *Cupid Takes A Holiday* and *Money Or Your Life*.

His parts in these were so small that if ever a copy turned up – and very few of them ever have – one would have had great difficulty in recognising him.

By this time, he and his partner had gone their separate ways.

But then he met Max Liebman – and a girl called Sylvia.

UP IN ARMS

HE WOULDN'T BE THE ONLY ONE TO SAY THAT UNFORESEEN CIRCUM-stances changed his whole life. The circumstances in this case were that Danny auditioned for a job and ended up with a wife.

Sylvia Fine was playing the piano and writing the lyrics for a show that Mr Liebman was presenting at a tiny theatre on 52nd Street, which was so off-Broadway people hadn't yet worked out exactly *where* it was. (In any case, off-Broadway was an expression that had not yet entered the national lexicon.)

In fact, the auditions were held in the loft of a building on 52nd Street.

Danny had heard about the auditions for the show and reckoned that he could probably land himself a role. He plainly had no idea that the one he would be landing was very different from any he had anticipated.

Sylvia was the pianist at the audition. She was dark, slim and attractive without being pretty. There was something about her that was familiar, but he had to be told. Her father was *the* Doctor Fine for whom Danny had worked as an unqualified assistant.

They talked as Danny got ready to perform. The story he told used as much Japanese as he had picked up on his recent tour. It all seemed a lot funnier than in the original – well, it would . . . considering he used the kind of sounds most Americans imagined were uttered by a war lord about to commit hara-kiri.

As for Sylvia, it was obvious that she wasn't the usual sort of audition or rehearsal pianist either. Not for her to be content to play other people's music and dance to other people's instructions. Sylvia told Danny that she wrote songs herself. They were not the Moon and June type tunes other people dashed off sitting behind a keyboard. She liked to show a biting wit when she went to work. She had a remarkable vocabulary or else a marvellous way of using a thesaurus. Words rhymed to devastating effect. In fact, she told him as they chatted, she was principally involved in political satire. She had even written a song about Sir Oswald Mosley's British fascists, which she called 'Down Downing Street':

Sing a song of blackshirts
A pocketful of lies
Don't you know they've got their eyes
On other pies?

Now Sylvia was writing the songs for the show at which she was the pianist. It was to be called *Saturday Night Varieties* – and the general idea was to do what they could to make it run on other nights, too – and for as long as possible.

It ran for a few weeks. Danny was obviously in love with entertaining – and in love with Sylvia, too. At this early stage in their relationships they had a divergence of interests and talents that made them quite obviously made for each other. Sylvia could write words to songs that needed expressive gestures – mouth gaping, eyes widening, hair standing on end, hands manipulating thin air, all of which Danny was able to supply with a degree of timing she might not otherwise have thought possible. Everything else followed naturally from there.

People came to see Danny perform – among them a young agent called Abby Greshler, who booked him for the Laurel and Pines resort hotel at Lakewood, New Jersey. 'Danny was easily the hit of the season and we brought him back many times,' Greshler told me.

He also set him up for something that would prove even more lasting.

While Danny and Sylvia were engaging themselves out of hours – devoting much of their attention, even so, to their mutual project – Max Liebman was offering suggestions for the coming summer. He was working on the show at Camp Tamiment, and thought Danny ought to join the bill at what was a highly important centre of what could be called junior league show business. Greshler also thought it would be a good idea for him to go there.

To Kaye, the thought was not exactly inspiring. Danny believed he had left all that behind with his last helping of gefilte fish in the Catskills. But Liebman tried to explain that this was different. The camp wasn't the Catskills, but on the outskirts of Stroudsburg in Pennsylvania, run by the Rand School of Social Sciences, which was a leader in the middle-of-the-road American socialist movement.

Camp Tamiment was putting on shows for Jewish working men, not the nouveau-riche or the hard-working master tailors and their families who saved a whole year to go to the Borsht Belt. And the team Danny would be working with was made up of people like himself, aspiring professionals.

Of course, it was not Broadway and not even off-Broadway, but it was much better than starving in a Manhattan garret or even raiding Papa Kaminsky's ice box in Brooklyn.

Imogene Coca and Alfred Drake, two very important names in the American show business story of the following years, were among those on the 'staff'.

Tamiment was in the entertainment business and its principal show was the one that went on every Saturday night presented by Max Liebman. It changed at every performance.

'The shows were terrific,' Greshler recalled.

Liebman first wanted Danny to play the comedian in a Yiddish language version of Gilbert and Sullivan's *Mikado*. What the D'Oyly Carte opera company thought of this obvious breach of what was still very much their copyright was not tested at the time.

Danny did the routine and was a smash. At the time, he thought he was principally going to be a singer, so Liebman let him sing – at first, mostly Yiddish and Irish songs. But Danny Kaye couldn't sing without making his songs sound funny. He sang – and people laughed.

Sylvia, meanwhile, played the piano, earning $50 a week, which was considered at the time nice work if she could get it, and with Danny by her side all the time, she got it.

For ten weeks Danny Kaye led the troupe, convoluting the language, using English the way he had previously manipulated Japanese making it a mass of nonsense most of the time, but inserting the odd word or two, so that whoever was sitting in the audience would know they should have understood what he was saying. They then blamed themselves for not being quick enough.

Sylvia wrote the songs – music and mind-boggling, tongue-twisting lyrics. Then, when Danny was able to perform them on the camp's stage, she played the piano for him too. For eight weeks, they gave out with new material which both they and their audience could have been forgiven for thinking was a mere assemblage of pot-boilers. What they couldn't but hope was that the material was, in fact, the nucleus of a Danny Kaye repertoire that would be associated with him for almost the next half century.

She wrote *Anatole of Paris* – the son of the man who played the oboe, 'which it is clearly understood is an ill wind which no one blows good' – and *Stanislavsky*, later to be refined into *Tchaikovsky*, little more than a brilliant assembly of Russian names, a minefield through which Danny tripped with all the dexterity of a Pavlova – which, incidentally, also happened to be the title of another Danny Kaye song.

The ten weeks at Camp Tamiment went all too quickly. Abby Greshler got the famous Shubert Brothers interested in what he claimed was his major new discovery. He persuaded the head of their New York office, Harry Kaufman to come out to the camp to see the revue. He 'fell in love with the show', Greshler recalled.

He did, however, remark that he didn't think Kaye himself would get very far until 'he learns to keep those cockeyed hands under control'. Which showed how little he really did know. But, as he said, he loved the show.

So much that it opened, under the name *The Straw Hat Revue*, on Broadway at the Ambassador Theatre. Imogene Coca was the listed star, although that September 1939, people were already aware that it would be nothing without the previously little known Danny Kaye.

They came even though it was in the midst of one of the most oppressive heatwaves New Yorkers could remember – and the only air conditioning the theatre was able to offer was in the form of blocks of ice placed strategically under the ceiling fans.

War had just broken out in Europe. But straw hats still gave the impression of a bright, breezy life in which it was always summer or spring. For Danny Kaye, it was very much the spring of his career. The early work had been merely the necessary preparation for what was not going to follow. It was only a place in a Broadway revue of no particular historical significance. But it *was* Broadway with all the attendant value of that street. It meant that the critics came and saw and converted people who previously might not have thought to bother.

Brooks Atkinson at that time headed the list of Broadway 'butchers', who sharpened their axes ready to draw blood every time they placed a new ticket stub in their dinner-jacket pockets. He mentioned Kaye whom he saw as a performer able to 'drop irony into burlesque without overdoing it'. Well, there had been more incisive reviews of players who one day would make a formidable mark on their chosen calling, but it could have been a whole lot worse.

There were some people who complained that even at this early stage, Danny Kaye was showing a certain, shall we say, temperament. Max Liebman was to be quoted on this. 'Like anyone else,' he recalled years later, 'Danny is a mass of contradictions. And there are times when he is hard to get close to, when he is so absorbed with his own problems that he just doesn't listen. There are just a few great stars who have never been accused of having a big head. Durante, I guess is the perfect example. Not Danny. He belongs to the 90 per cent of the group of big personalities of whom it has been said at one time or another that they're high-hat.'

Danny wore his straw hat for ten weeks and then went off looking for more opportunities to display his irony, and drag a few more enthusiastic comments from Mr Atkinson. In the mean time,

[32]

however, he had other business to attend to. Once more, Sylvia joined him in a Danny Kaye enterprise.

It didn't, however, begin like that.

Once *The Straw Hat Revue* had closed, Danny spent his evenings at the Capitol Theatre, to, he would explain, 'get more colour'. Then he would go to the Paramount Theatre, 'to find still more colour'.

Danny was convinced he still had some waiting to do, packed his bags and invested what little cash he had in a trip to Florida to try, as the pulp fiction of the day would have said, to forget.

He decided, he explained: 'If I can't get a job, at least I can loaf with everybody else.'

He wrote Sylvia a letter and she responded reasonably favourably to his suggestions, but said that she didn't feel ready to come to Florida – until, that is, she conveniently found a doctor who said her health needed the balmy air circulating in the Miami area.

In January 1930, they were at Fort Lauderdale. Max Liebman was in attendance. He had to be. They needed his services as a witness to their marriage.

Danny had rung Sylvia and asked her to marry him. Then he put the phone down. As he later said, he didn't have the courage to wait for an answer.

Danny had just $40 to his name, although in which direction he is not quite sure. A few months later, he said he couldn't really remember whether he owned that $40 or owed it. But to Mr and Mrs Danny Kaye it didn't seem to matter.

For no reason anyone was able to work out – other than, perhaps, the complications of getting the necessary blood tests organised in New York – the couple had eloped.

It is an interesting subject for theorising. There was no obvious explanation disqualifying their liaison. Both were of age. Both seemed to suit each other. They were in the same line of business; they shared the same religion. With all of these conditions going for them there seemed very little reason why they needed to elope. The only reason was that neither of them had told Dr and Mrs Fine.

The reason for not telling Sylvia's parents probably had a lot more to do with the fact that Dr Fine still hadn't forgiven Danny for using his drill for purposes that were not strictly curative, and for being in entertainment. Show business, he had decided, was still obviously no job for a Jewish boy.

Whatever the circumstances, they were legitimised less than two months later by a Brooklyn synagogue. With Mr Kaminsky and Dr and Mrs Fine standing under the marriage canopy around them and passing each a glass of wine, they were married according to the laws of Moses and Israel – while Danny broke another glass under-foot in the traditional way.

[33]

The truth of the matter is that the Kayes were in love and the Fines had to accept what the state of Florida had decided they should be allowed to formalise. Why they loved each other is not open to discussion. Even Sylvia couldn't put her finger on it, although she was deeply affected by his ability to make her laugh. She was to admit, however, that he wasn't the most attractive man she had ever met. She was even to call him 'rather ridiculous, with his long hair, high collar and tight suit that pinched into wrinkles at the waist.'

She was also struck by the fact that he didn't walk. He danced. People had said the same about a boy born Frederick Austerlitz, and he grew into Fred Astaire.

But Danny didn't want to become another Fred Astaire or another anybody. He was continuing to develop that style which was his own, a recipe for either super stardom or super rejection. Day after day, night after night, Danny Kaye worked at making sure that stardom was what it would be. He found new words and new nonsense and twisted them around not so much his tongue but every facial nerve in his head. Once more, he seemed to tell his hands that they had to work as hard as his mouth.

His first job as a married man was at La Martinique, a night club that had seen its share of show biz successes. Danny was not at first one of them.

'I was an unqualified failure,' he said in an interview with *The New York Times* a year later. 'No you were not,' said Sylvia. 'All right,' he countered. 'I was a tremendous success.' He was more right the second time, thanks to a certain amount of patience. In fact, his entry at La Martinique says a great deal about the alleged big heart of show business – and, perhaps more, about the problems a management might have in filling in an unexpected hole in its schedules.

He moved into the spotlight, centre stage, while the customers were still chewing – and, worse, still ordering new drinks and clinking their cutlery. The name Danny Kaye meant nothing to them, his first number still less. It was London and the Dorchester all over again. Danny wasn't exactly a failure. He was a disaster.

But there *was* a saving grace. There was a second show two hours later and the people running the club decided he had to have another try. And this time, the audience was a good deal more responsive. Much more responsive. The drinks had had their effect. The company seemed more enchanting – and enchanted. They stayed long enough to clap and cheer. It was enough. He had succeeded where he himself had so recently failed.

It became the fashionable thing to do, to see Danny perform. A surgeon was among the regular crowd there. He was asked why he loved Danny's act so much. It wasn't the act, he said. He came to watch Danny's hands. That was a very intuitive statement indeed.

It was at La Martinique that he introduced a routine that he made famous (and indeed used in his first feature movie) – the Conga. Seemingly out of the blue, he got people to join a huge conga line. The dance had existed before. Danny made it into a definable act, using a stream of words that sounded distinctly Spanish – to everyone, that is, who didn't use it as his native tongue.

Once more, he told the story of the hat designer, 'the result of the twisted eugenics of this family of inbred schizophrenics', *Anatole of Paris*.

He got $250 a week for his trouble, big money indeed. Ed Sullivan, who had yet to make a nationwide reputation through television, was already big enough fry as a newspaper columnist to be not only noticed but taken very seriously indeed – which was precisely how he took Danny Kaye.

He wrote about Danny: 'He can do anything and do it well. He can sing, dance, squeeze the last laugh out of a situation and he's boyish enough and attractive enough to play romantic leads.'

It was a view clearly that Sylvia shared. She wasn't now claiming for her husband any of the Adonis-like characteristics she had previously denied were his. But she could do something about the way he looked. She liked his hair to be, she said, 'medium', touching the back of his collar, which very few men wore at that time. She liked him in loose jackets – the kind that doubtless made him seem to have a little more meat on his bones than he actually possessed. She told him to wear sober ties, not the long, wide and loud 'kippers' that Americans seemed to take to as though national pride were at stake if they wore anything smaller. (He told her he didn't like her to wear either ear-rings or veils, so she changed her dress taste as he adapted his).

Money seemed to be made as regularly and as easily as at the national mint. He went into restaurants with Sylvia and ordered the most expensive items on the menu – at every course. It was Sylvia who decided that he needed as many lessons in keeping cash as he did in keeping his musical notes. When Sylvia told him she had seen a necklace she loved almost as much as she loved him, Danny rushed to his bedroom, found an old pair of sports shoes from which he dug out a collection of smelly dollar bills and a few coins. 'Your necklace,' he told her. She decided to keep charge of the family exchequer and give Danny a controlled income.

It wasn't just in economics that her influence on Danny became important.

In years to come, he was to describe himself as a 'wife-made man' – and then added laconically: 'She has a Fine head on my shoulders'.

[35]

It was in the La Martinique period that the Fine head really began to fit snugly on the Kaye shoulders. She nurtured his self pride, she smoothed the anguish, she worried for him. She worried so much that she also worried Ed Dukoff, who was next to the star the most important man in the club – he was in charge of publicity.

After the Dukoff treatment and with more notices like Ed Sullivan's, Danny was a triumph night after night.

Sullivan liked him every time he went to the club. His second notice declared: 'Last night, Danny came out on the floor and went into a serious line of talk. He was elegant and he was sincere. Suddenly Danny emerged from the extremely literate philosophy he was expounding and went into a completely insane routine. The transition was so swift, the high comedy touch so expert, that your reporter rolled under the table. I've never seen a star so completely fracture an audience.'

The audience stayed fractured – thanks to Sylvia almost as much as to Danny himself. But especially thanks to Danny's ability as a listener.

Sylvia would play him her latest composition and he would react instantly.

Thanks to Eddie Dukoff – who before long would join Danny as his personal manager – and comments from people like Sullivan and the other columnists, the most moneyed and most influential people in town came to see him.

Among those who stayed at La Martinique for 65 hard, brittle minutes was Moss Hart, one of the most respected and talented directors on Broadway. He went to the show on the recommendation of another legendary Broadway name, Mack Gordon, who thought Danny was wonderful.

Abby Greshler did too: 'He was brilliant,' he said.

Hart liked what he saw and said that he was now planning to put on a revue, simply because it would give him an opportunity to feature young Mr Kaye. Three days after making the promise, Hart phoned the Kaye residence at the top of 52nd Street. Sylvia took the call. Hart was offering her husband the chance to appear in a new show with Gertrude Lawrence.

LADY IN THE DARK

GERTRUDE LAWRENCE WAS THE STAR, BUT IT IS DANNY KAYE WHO IS remembered when people now talk about *Lady In The Dark* – even though the music was by Kurt Weill with lyrics by Ira Gershwin, an impressive roster if ever there were one.

Lady In The Dark needs to be recorded in the annals of show business along with Jolson's first performance at the Winter Garden and Ziegfeld's first Folly (or, for the purists, his first Follies).

Danny only had a small part. Once more, it was an opportunity for him to sing Sylvia's songs. Once more, they included *Anatole of Paris*, which by now seemed to be his signature tune but which he was now singing in a much sweeter, more trained voice.

The New York Times was to record a 'bedlam of frantic applause', greeting the still basically unknown Kaye at the Boston out-of-town opening – an occasion sometimes not altogether different from a session with the Spanish Inquisition.

Lady In The Dark opened in New York with no one at all in the dark about its new star's reputation. He had found a way of mesmerising audiences, sitting on the stage as he did it, or wrapping himself up in the fantasy of songs they had never heard before.

The show became a legend in its own time and Danny was the most legendary part of all. He was such a hit that even Dr and Mrs Fine approved of the idea of having a son-in-law in show business. As for Jacob Kaminsky, it was as though the world had moved from Brooklyn to Manhattan and the world was a sweet place where wars and pogroms never happened any more.

Gertrude Lawrence is on record as saying how pleased she was to be in on the birth of a major new entertainment personality. She would, however, have been less than human not to ever so slightly resent his apparently instant success, which took all of 13 years.

The success was consummated with *Tchaikovsky*, now firmly out of the mould of *Stanislavsky*, and presenting for the attention of his audience the greatest tongue twister of all time. He proved what any entertainer would want to prove more than anything else – only he could do it. Not only could only Danny Kaye rattle off a

[37]

collection of names – and what names! 'Sapellnikoff, Dmitrioff, Charpnin, Kryjanowski . . .' As he said, 'I *love* Russian composers' – only Danny Kaye made it sound entertaining, brilliantly funny and exhausting all in one go.

It also became something of a battle of wits which at times resembled a ping pong match. While at Boston, he sang *Tchaikovsky* and brought the house down.

As the house was tumbling around him, Danny had one thought in mind: 'I'm dead.'

The next number was Gertrude Lawrence singing *Jenny*. There was no way she wouldn't with one chorus erase for ever the memory of that moment of *Tchaikovsky*. Or if she didn't achieve that, there was no way that hit of his would be allowed to remain in for the rest of the run of the show. Miss Lawrence would see to that. It was an actor's intuition based on an inherent belief in the inhumanity of one performer to another.

Miss Lawrence sang *Jenny* and it was sensational. So sensational that she showed no animosity to Danny or his hit tune.

But as the weeks went on, and so the show transferred to Broadway, Danny noticed that *Tchaikovsky* wasn't going over quite as big as its original promise seemed to indicate. Why? It was as good a feast as ever. He was singing it as well as ever – better perhaps. And, even as he sang it, Miss Lawrence was contently swaying behind him, sitting on a swing.

After those weeks and those performances, Danny dared to do what he had been afraid of doing all the time up till then. He broke stage rule number one and looked over his shoulder.

That was when he realised what happened that night and had happened every night since the opening in Boston. Miss Lawrence was sitting in her swing, delicately making little flicks with her scarf.

She had been deflecting attention from him. It was a moment for revenge. When next she moved forward to sing *Jenny*, Danny sat on the swing behind her – and did nothing. Except twitch his nose and raise an eyebrow. *Jenny* didn't get its usual ration of applause that night.

Not a word was spoken between them about that. But Gertie never twirled her scarf again and Danny refrained thereafter from twitching his nose. The result was they both got their applause. And a niche in the Broadway story.

Few people admired the show more than Ira Gershwin, who on opening night betrayed the true sentiments expressed by many another show creator: as the curtain went up, and he heard his first lyric being sung on stage, he chickened out and ran away in the direction of the nearest bar. As he left the theatre, he could hear the crashing sound of applause. When he came back, the audience were still cheering.

Everyone was aware that something rather special had happened. Kaye was as aware as any of them – although it only really reached home when one of the chorus youngsters banged him on the back and said just two words, 'Boy! Danny!' Boy! Danny! it was.

The part Danny played, Russell Paxton, a chauffeur-cum-magazine photographer, turned out to be even more important than Moss Hart imagined when he wrote it.

All this might give the impression that Danny Kaye was now the happiest of human beings. He wasn't. Jack Warner Jnr, who, before Sylvia came along had been on a 'double date' with Danny, met him again at this time. 'He was the most depressed, dejected person in the world,' he told me. It would be a continuing paradox in Danny's life.

If Gertrude Lawrence was far from thrilled about the competition Kaye offered, her husband Richard Aldrich was even less sanguine.

He actually did suggest excising either Danny or his *Tchaikovsky* number from the show. But she decided against it. In his biography of his wife, 'Gertrude Lawrence as Mrs A', he quoted her telling him: 'Danny is a talented performer and he's entitled to his chance. Don't worry about me. I can take care of myself.' It is doubtful if she really was that generous.

But the audience certainly was. Night after night. Now Danny was being courted by other managements – including the night club owners who at first hadn't been so sure about him.

The Martinique invited him back – to play at the club every night when he finished at the theatre.

There were dozens of precedents for that sort of thing. In days gone by, the girls from the Ziegfeld Follies would be expected to play in at least one other Ziegfeld show the same night, rushed from one theatre to the next by fast cars given a police escort with sirens wailing.

Danny, with Sylvia's encouragement, was ready to talk business. She wrote him new songs and he sang them at the club within an hour of the curtain going down for *Lady In The Dark*.

It wasn't always an easy experience, although it was usually an uplifting one. And his night-club audience had no idea of the troubles that had gone into making those apparently meaningless words string together.

In those days, Danny was a fairly good listener and a good rememberer at rehearsals. Sylvia would play him her latest composition and he would react instantly. She would suggest bits of 'business' and he would take them. He memorised harmonies she played which she herself instantly forgot. He had no trouble with her lyrics, words she couldn't remember once she had scribbled them on to a yellow pad.

Danny's problem came on the stage or the night-club floor when the spotlight was on him. Between the two of them, they could have rehearsed a dozen or more different numbers and routines the day and night before. Each Danny knew and improved upon. But when he was actually at work, he had only about three numbers ready for the audience, a state of affairs Sylvia described at the time as 'murder'. Just before he went on stage, both she and Max Liebman had to, as she put it, 'redescribe' the work to him. It was, she said, 'like a cat trying to bark like a dog'.

If that cat did have trouble barking, it didn't have any difficulty at all with its saucer of milk at La Martinique. In his second week at the club, his salary was doubled. The following week it was trebled. Finally the management gave him a percentage of their gross take – a tribute not lightly handed out.

It was the place to which taxi drivers knew instantly they had to take their best 'fares', anxious for a night out that featured only the most riveting entertainment. At the club itself, the *maitre d'* and his assistants could be sure of $50 tips – again a figure that was almost astronomical in 1940 – if they could successfully guide clients to tables that mysteriously found themselves getting closer and closer to where Danny was to perform.

Then, when Danny left *Lady In The Dark*, managements were once again figuratively in line with their cheque books open. The one that won was at the famous Paramount Theatre.

It was Danny's own decision to leave *Lady In The Dark*. Really, it had been a question of who would go first. Without Gertrude Lawrence, there *could* not be any show. Without Danny Kaye, there probably would be a sudden lessening of demand for tickets. Gertie was an established star who would always be able to land a star job. Danny was a 1940 phenomenon about whom the popular papers were begging to find out what colour socks he wore and what he ate for breakfast.

He left the show and Moss Hart went around Broadway saying that his bright new discovery had let everyone down – for the show closed soon afterwards. Danny was so upset about this that he sat on the floor outside Hart's apartment, waiting for the writer to either return or leave the flat so that he could tell him how sorry he was. It was an untypical act of humility on Kaye's part. Eventually, they made up. Hart knew that Danny was a spectacular talent he would hope to be able to use again – even if

[40]

only at rates that would look distinctly inflated compared to the price he was paid in *Lady In The Dark*.

Meanwhile, Danny Kaye, the contract for the Paramount under his arm, knew he had arrived. He ordered a black Cadillac – even this luxury division of General Motors had taken Henry Ford's dictum to heart and believed that black was beautiful – and drove to Brooklyn. He thought the neighbours would be impressed. They weren't. Later, it turned out that Jacob Kaminsky had got in before his son – and warned them not to encourage his David's vanity. Danny didn't do that sort of thing again.

He was concentrating now on building his career and helping other people to build theirs – notably the Brooklyn Dodgers. He followed the progress of his home town baseball team with all the devotion other men in his new income bracket reserved for the stock market. He and Sylvia had moved to a magnificent new apartment now on Central Park South. It matched his status and was a suitable place to give those interviews before moving off in the Cadillac to the Paramount.

At the Paramount, there were five Danny Kaye performances a day. That took some work, even for a former Borsht Belt 'toomler' who had had to find a way to get audiences at Osaka to understand what he was doing. But it was worth the strain for as long as he could take it. At the end of every week, there was a $20,000 cheque awaiting him, which could be conservatively estimated to be worth perhaps $300,000 at today's rates.

'Gee,' said Danny, as he walked on stage. 'I'm so glad to be back on Broadway.' It sounded nice and modest – although modesty has never been a charge that could be levelled against him – and his audience roared its approval with a fuselade of cheers and claps. At the first performance on his first day Danny received an even louder response than was to greet that statement at later shows. No sooner had he said the word 'Broadway' than a battery of pneumatic drills working on a building site nearby opened up. 'Never mind the cannon, fellows,' said Kaye. 'Just tell 'em I'm glad to be back.' The audience roared too. That was showmanship. Precisely what he should have done.

It was the kind of remark which separated the men from the boys. The stars from the also-rans.

To anyone not used to the Danny Kaye brand of humour, he must have seemed like a fellow biding his time while waiting for the men in the white coats to come and pick him up. He didn't tell jokes, he didn't just sing songs. There was *Minnie the Moocher* and there was *Anatole of Paris* – with *Tchaikovsky* thrown in for good measure. There was an impersonation of every Nazi rabble-rouser the tough New York audience had ever seen on a cinema screen –

at a time in history when to most Americans the Nazis were no more than considerably ridiculous figures of fun. One minute he was a German, the next an Italian. He portrayed a British Army officer and the people out front could have been forgiven for thinking that he had just graduated from Sandhurst.

Above all, there were those hands – still spinning, caressing, painting the characters he was portraying without a costume or a flake of make-up.

And then there were the words of his songs. He had to savour them, swill them around his tongue like a tester in a French vineyard. When the words did taste right, they were teased out of his mouth. When they were wrong, they were spat out as though they were an indifferent vintage or a blend that was missing a certain ingredient.

What made Danny Kaye so special was that he himself was that certain ingredient and a perfect judge of what he needed to go with it.

When it worked, it did so, even in those early days, beautifully. 'It's a great thrill,' said Sylvia, (for someone who) 'must necessarily determine what is funny by intellectual and mechanical means, to see someone arriving at the same conclusions – and even top it by sheer and unerring instinct'.

It sometimes took them 40 or perhaps 50 attempts to get that far. But both of them knew that if it happened, it would work.

When Vinton Freedley, a producer whose track record included some of the greatest and earliest Fred Astaire successes, came to the Kayes for a new show, it was going to be a great opportunity to demonstrate how they could fit their individual speciality to an otherwise ready-made production – called *Let's Face It*.

It was a musical that looked as if it were going to have everything that Danny wanted – and it did. It was a Broadway show, with Danny Kaye as its undoubted star and it was set to be the kind of production future generations look back upon and remember as one of those experiences they will describe to their grandchildren.

The real reason it all went so well, however, had very little to do with the show. Except that Danny was the star. Later, when it went to London without Danny in the cast, the production was a flop.

In 1941, however, with Danny in the lead, it was everything anyone could possibly expect. It was not just bang up to date, it had a distinct air of prophesy about it. The show was about life in the Army – a matter of only months before the Japanese Air Force struck at Pearl Harbor.

The main score was supplied by Cole Porter and Herbert and Dorothy Fields, with extra numbers by Sylvia. She took the title to heart. She faced it.

[42]

Danny went on stage and told the story of the three bears – which gives some idea of the importance of the Kaye interpretation. Al Jolson used to boast that he could knock people over reciting Little Bo Peep. Danny did it with his – and Sylvia's – *Three Bears*. But if knocked over they were by his trip to the nursery – reciting the rhyme like a five-year-old – they were virtually flattened, then rolled sideways, by a little thing called *Melody In 4-F* – 4-F being the grade he thought should be awarded him, or rather the character he played, by the draft board's medical team.

This might not have looked so great on paper, either – even though it began promisingly enough like a Negro spiritual: 'Oh, they passed a law down in Washington, DC . . .'

Plainly, a lot of waving arms and bending bodies were called for here. But after the first couple of lines . . . gibberish again. 'Words' that would sound like 'git-gat-gay-say' had sprinkled among them odd groupings that *could* be found in the dictionary – like 'mailman – ring – questionnaire' and 'a fine specimen', which might have been referring to the inductee or the bottle the doctor asked him to fill. Once we get the idea that Danny has taken his physical exam, saluted the doctors and been pronounced now 'A-1', we know that the medical men decided after all he is fit – and that he can be safely introduced to the more exciting parts of Army life – like being involved in war games and peeling potatoes.

On stage, it was hilariously funny. And that was the Kaye art. You only had to sit in an audience and listen to all that nonsense to understand the story from beginning to end.

The show ran for 16 months, with Danny himself now the toast not only of Broadway, but of everywhere else in America where he could be heard on radio. He was pressed to make more movies, but the memory of his 'short' career was still too vivid.

And he was still not nearly as self confident as his outer appearance would seem to indicate.

What he was doing, he told Sylvia, was trying to consolidate what he had achieved, because he could never be sure he would ever come up with anything quite so exciting or successful again.

Sylvia saw some truth in this attitude. But the public didn't, and Max Liebman who had remained part of the team and who with Sylvia was daily trying to dream up new numbers for their joint prodigy couldn't understand it either. Least understanding of all was Jacob Kaminsky who was spending his winters in Florida, thanks to his successful son.

If he didn't want Danny himself to appear boastful to the neighbours in Brooklyn, there was no law that said a Jewish father couldn't brag a bit. As he told his David, when he heard about his stage successes, he could 'qvell', which anyone familiar with Yiddish knows could inadequately be translated as filling with pride, although that says only half of it.

People around Miami Beach at the time were able to report the amazing sight of two elderly gentlemen 'qvelling' jointly as they talked about their sons in show business. One was Mr Kaminsky. The other came from a similar background and had a similar name. Mr Kabelsky had a son called Jack Benny.

There was no open sign that Sylvia wasn't equally proud. She was doing everything she could to convince the general public that all Danny did was going very well indeed. The heartache was mostly on her side.

As she told *The New York Times*: 'The hard work starts from the moment I pick up a pencil and face a leering piece of blank paper. This ensues a period of anything from two to eight weeks, during which time I chew and swallow eighteen pencils, twenty-nine cups of black coffee, argue with my collaborator, Max Liebman, and am very careful not to let Danny see a single word.'

There was good reason for this 'screening' of the star from his material. Given a first look at a song or a routine by the two people who knew him better than anyone else, Danny Kaye as an audience was like the entire clientele of La Martinique in mid-winter before a bottle had been opened. He made it very clear he hated everything they produced and that he was not prepared to be amused.

Artistic temperament? Much more probably, it was that sense of insecurity again, the kind that frequently goes alongside colossal talent. In other words, he knew how good he was, but would he also ever be able to convince his audience – to say nothing of the critics?

It was an unusual collaboration, this. He wasn't like the conventional stand-up comic who could buy material from any one of a dozen or so writers or from the kind of joke factory that, say, Bob Hope would soon have working for him. Neither was he an ordinary singer who would happily use any of the popular songs of the day. He was a 'speciality' act who had a 'speciality' writer working for him who just happened to be his wife. They needed each other. Danny needed the material that was tailored for his needs just as individually as were his suits or the sports jackets he wore on stage. Apart from Sylvia's married relationship with Danny, as a creator she needed him as assuredly as he needed her. Her stuff was very good – exceptionally good – but there was no way in which she was able to present it on a stage herself.

It wasn't just Mr Kaminsky who felt pride. The whole of Brooklyn was cheering their 'kid', and with them most of New York. At the same time, the still partly-immigrant American Jewish community felt a tinge of extra special joy at one of their own yet again being fêted among the greats of their country's show business. Jolson, Cantor and Sophie Tucker had a new heir and their people were ready to pay homage. The scoffing had finished. Yes, their boy was as big as any of them.

So what was there about this man Kaye? He wasn't yet at a stage in his career where he could risk seeming to be immodest himself. Interviewed by a newspaperman, he'd say he was finally getting a luckier break after some dozen years or more of frustration.

But things were never as simple as that. Inwardly, he knew he had made it and no one doubted that he had a right to feel an air of triumph as he turned the key in the latch of that Central Park South apartment.

Ironically, Marshal Tojo's decision to order the bombing at Pearl Harbor had its positive side as far as Kaye and his show were concerned. It had to be faced that *Let's Face It* couldn't have been more topical had it been commissioned by the Department of War as a public relations exercise aimed at increasing the number of volunteers for military service.

Danny himself was among the first to volunteer for the Army. But he had to content himself with the khakis he wore on stage. The doctors, who put him through the kind of routine he so graphically displayed in his *Melody In 4-F*, declared that Uncle Sam could do without his help. Still nurturing, despite all he was achieving on stage, his innate belief that his real talents lay not so much in a Broadway theatre as an operating theatre, he found their conclusions illuminating. Mr Kaye, it seemed, had a malfunctioning sacroilliac, which would be likely to inhibit his usefulness to the Allied war effort.

He immediately decided to follow the example of the various entertainers who had spent most of World War I entertaining troops and selling war bonds. Danny began his bonds drive practically the moment there was a war to sell bonds for.

He still recognised the fact that he was a wife-made man – and so did Sylvia, albeit reluctantly. Everyone who had ever read the credits on a sheet of music or who closely examined the small type in a theatre programme knew that all Danny's specialist numbers were provided by his wife.

'People think I'm a very clever girl,' she said during the *Let's Face It* run – when she was still accompanying him on the various night-club sessions that enabled him to supplement the not-so-small fortune he was now eking out for himself.

Maybe, she conceded, she was a clever girl, even a very clever girl. Yet it only looked that way on paper, she insisted – 'after

[45]

weeks of hard work. But when I go out people expect me to make like Dorothy Parker.'

He was the first to recognise how much he owed her at this early, still formative, time. 'At home,' Sylvia told *The New York Times*, 'Danny's the boss – definitely. But at the theatre I'm the boss. And I tell him and he takes it.'

He wasn't always so sure that he did take it – not all of it, that is. He didn't terribly care for Sylvia's bringing him down to earth, while the echo of an audience's thunderous applause was threatening to undermine the theatre's foundations.

'Boy, did you stink!' she told him. 'Did you louse up that number!'

That was a kind of love, too, but it could take some living with.

Sylvia and Liebman were in their own manner still feeling their way in this new career which Danny had given them. There was a case for thinking that perhaps things were getting a little easier when it came to preparing material for him. Danny, Sylvia declared in another one of her deprecatory definitions of pure truth, 'doesn't know anything'. She meant well and even her husband knew what she was less than kindly saying.

She and her partner had one reaction when Danny laughed at anything they produced. They looked at the paper again, screwed it up – and then threw it into the wastepaper basket. 'If he doesn't like it, we're pretty sure we've got something. He hardly knows what he's going to do with a phrase till he begins to work on it, but we can guess how he'll do a phrase somewhere else. But sometimes all of us get surprised.'

No one seemed much surprised after a trip to see *Let's Face It*. The show was all that any critic or anyone else, for that matter, had said about it.

Not that things were ever as easy as they looked. It wasn't just Sylvia who, to use her phrase, 'sweated blood' over a number. Danny was never the kind of entertainer who had to be pushed on stage, whose stomach was so knotted before a performance, he could count all the butterflies chasing each other inside.

He had his attacks of nerves, but he was superbly confident. Even so, he knew there were times when he had to work at what he was doing.

Sylvia wrote her Three Bears routine – in true super-star fashion, Danny would vary it from performance to performance – because it took advantage of the habit he had developed of reverting to baby talk whenever they were having a gentle tiff in the kitchen or bedroom. The habit would, professionally, serve him very well indeed in the years to come.

If it always brought stupid domestic issues down to a sense of

[46]

reality at home, it did not always work that way on stage. 'You feel so silly up there, a big hoke of a man talking itsy-bitsy,' he confessed.

If he were not talking 'itsy-bitsy', he was adapting the scat-singing of *Melody In 4-F* to situations off-stage as well as on. Doctor friends couldn't keep them away from discussions on the latest medical problems or the newest discoveries that were going to revolutionise their science.

More frequently than the hospitals concerned would care to admit, Danny watched a surgeon he knew operate. The man who had gone so regularly to La Martinique to watch Danny's hands couldn't have realised that here was a case of mutual admiration. The women involved might not have been all that happy to realise it, but the activities he watched, hidden behind a surgical mask and gown, included more than one case of childbirth.

The doctor who allowed the watchful Kaye eyes to peep over his shoulder had a quid pro quo in mind. He was an ardent jazz lover. At the end of a complicated day operating they would retire to the surgeon's apartment. The doctor played the piano and Danny gave out. He went through all he had seen in the hospital, throwing in a mime of every procedure and the odd scat word to the doctor's accompaniment. It was a different *Melody In 4-F*, but it was probably a similar event that had prompted Danny to suggest the idea to his wife.

What pleased Danny most about *Let's Face It* was that he was obviously to all concerned the number-one star. Even if he had made such a startling impression in *Lady In The Dark*, he was number-eight in the cast list. This time, the theatre marquee said it all in lights – 'Danny Kaye in . . .'

The original $1,000 a week specified in his contract with Freedley had additional clauses entitling him to a percentage of the gross, and that percentage was now showing all signs of tripling or doing even better than that.

What brought him that money was the satisfaction of knowing that he was, in the words of *The New York Times's* Theodore Strauss, one of the survivors of a breed of entertainer who were 'extinct as the dodo' – the performers who could hold an audience from the front of the orchestra to the back of the 'dollar seats'.

It was an extraordinary ability. Even harder, in its way, however, was to be able to do that when faced with the apparent limitations of a 'book' show with a complete cast decked out in costumes and surrounded by sets that could so easily distract. With Danny in front performing his acrobatics that wasn't possible.

What there was inside the seemingly so light Kaye frame – he

[47]

moved so frenetically that it appeared almost transparent at times – was an energy that needed to escape as much as steam needed to be pumped from a contemporary railroad engine. Without that facility, both would be likely to explode.

Danny expended his surplus energy on stage. Sylvia did it sitting at the piano – playing not her own music but that of the principal composer of the show, Cole Porter. Danny was the first to recognise the symptoms. 'She's nervous and tired from working on the show with me. I can always tell when she plays like that. Me, I'm up and I'm down, but whatever it is I get it out of my system. Sylvia's different. She's quiet outside and like a wound-up spring inside.'

Three months after the show's opening, Danny proved that merely appearing on stage was not enough to prevent those explosions. He still went on, but he spent his nights and part of his weekends at Mount Sinai Hospital – suffering from what was diagnosed as 'nervous exhaustion'.

His intestines at this time must have resembled the taut springs of an almost-overwound clock – which was one reason why the hardest day of the week for Danny Kaye was Sunday. After eight performances a week, there was nothing for him to do on Sundays but loll on a couch with *The New York Times* at his elbow, his feet and everywhere else he touched.

The one day on which he was able to relax was in such a contrast to the excitement of the days that had preceded it – days when he knew he was dominating every member of the audience in sight and the thousands on the other side of the spotlight whom he could not see – that it was easy to unnerve him.

None of this obviously upset the Kaye on stage. To some people, it was merely the way they expected a star to behave.

If that was recognition of having arrived – a number of big stars would register the same complaint – there were happier signs of his success. That month, the Newspaper Guild made him their 'Page One Award' for being 'the outstanding comedian of the year.'

Sylvia, meanwhile, got an award, too, for her part in preparing Danny's material.

There were now practically regular offers from Hollywood. It was an accepted part of the route for entertainers of his stature. Make a name for yourself on Broadway and the studios wanted to share in the pickings. But Danny, the overnight success for whom it had all been a very long night indeed, was still not ready. Even a contract offer from the most prestigious 'musical' studio of them all, MGM (is it possible that those initials didn't stand for Makers of Great Musicals?) couldn't drag him away.

The MGM offer was worth a fortune, $3,000 for every week he was either standing before the cameras or in some way working on whatever part they gave him. Whatever part that *was* simply wasn't enough. 'I would work for much less, believe me,' he said at the time, 'if they would give me character roles and let me learn how to act. But I know they would just put me into a speciality spot here and there and one bum picture would put me back two or three years. I'm very young. I've got lots of time.'

Sylvia undoubtedly had something to do with that. The female head on his shoulders wanted him to consolidate what he had achieved thus far and not to run quite as wildly as some of those lyrics he sang before he was able to walk – in time with his success.

He didn't say that he was unsure of the company of Hollywood people, but he was certainly happiest now with the musicians he met, men like Artur Rubinstein and Isaac Stern, as though he were chasing an area he had not yet made his own, but one day would.

His own stature was assured, so the people in his peer group didn't provide the challenge of those outside it.

Danny was also suffering from the problem faced by a thousand other comedians. People meeting him at a party would almost bully him into playing the comic off-stage as well as on. As the Hollywood musical director Walter Scharf told me: 'Danny is not a funny man to meet socially. He talks very seriously and very quietly.' So his fellow guests were invariably disappointed.

He was doing his share of benefit concerts, too. Many of these were for Jewish charities at a time before the true meaning of the holocaust-to-come could even be imagined. He 'gave out' with the accents he had mastered on stage in *Let's Face It*. They were part of his stock-in-trade. But he wasn't willing to tell Jewish jokes or get into what today would be called the 'ethnic' business.

Years later, he would say, 'I have never once, by word, inflexion, or gesture proclaimed what I am. An entertainer belongs to all the people in the theatre, not to one group. There are a lot of Jewish and Catholic and Negro entertainers whom I don't like – merely because I think they're bad entertainers. I am not interested in racial or religious distinctions. I simply ask how well they're qualified, talentwise.'

A few years after that, during the Six Day War in the Middle East, he would revise that judgement slightly, but the dialects he rejoiced in on stage were not those relied upon by other comedians who came from the same Brooklyn neighbourhood as he.

When *Let's Face It* finally closed, Danny felt ready for the idea of Hollywood. And so it seemed did Hollywood. The film rights to the show were sold to Paramount and the Kayes were sure they were ready to accept the offer to repeat the Broadway performance on the big screen. Except that the film was made without Danny Kaye's special material – no *Melody In 4-F*; no nursery song. It was also without Danny Kaye. Paramount starred Bob Hope and Betty Hutton in their movie.

There was little time, however, for recriminations. Another offer was in the pipeline at the same time and this time Danny and Sylvia felt ready to accept. Sam Goldwyn was sold on the idea of a film that would be dedicated to the American serving man. He was even more sold on featuring the young man he had read about in the New York papers.

KNOCK ON WOOD

IN A WAY, WHAT SAM GOLDWYN DID WITH THE FIRST FULL-LENGTH Danny Kaye movie was precisely what Paramount did not do with *Let's Face It*. It was the story of a young hypochondriac in the Army who isn't sure if he is supposed to be fighting the Japanese or the Defence Department. The film was *Up In Arms* – which fairly accurately describes what movie audiences were to be about Danny Kaye in 1944.

He may have been the pride of Broadway, but the people who went to New York stage shows were from a very limited section of the American population. They were invariably regular theatre goers for whom a live performance was as much a part of their lives as breakfast in the morning and dinner at night. Most of them came from New York itself or from the surrounding districts; practically all of them were middle-class. Thus, a whole stratum of American society never paid money to sit in a theatre at all and practically all of them had never heard of Danny Kaye.

Outside America itself, the name rang no bells at all – until, that is, they sat in dark cinemas in England and Australia or India and saw the young blond performer with the somewhat long nose, manipulating the English language in a way that might have been guaranteed to send lexicographers hunting for the phone number of the nearest psychiatrist.

Danny's hair was blond for reasons best known to the make-up department at the Goldwyn studios. They thought that it would photograph better than the natural red Kaye plumage. His nose was long simply because he wouldn't shorten it. Goldwyn was not one of those Hollywood moguls known to make unreasonable demands on his actors, but he seemed embarrassed by Kaye's nose.

It was a time when the Hollywood movie czars were out to demonstrate the power of their devotion to the American dream. The war was a perfect platform on which they could declare their unbridled love affair for the country that had adopted and nurtured them. America was the land of the free, where a person's background or religion didn't seem to matter – except to the people

[51]

who came from that background themselves. Wasn't Danny Kaye's nose just a little too Jewish? Did it perhaps draw too much attention to his racial origins? Would it look quite nice on the screen?

Danny, who believed that hospitals were places where he was able to study the techniques of doctors who, as far as he was concerned, were the finest showmen of all, wouldn't accept the premise that they could also be places where noses, Jewish noses at that, could be shortened.

He said no to a new nose, but yes to an entirely new career. *Up In Arms* wouldn't be the best Danny Kaye film, but it would set the pattern for the rest of the bunch that followed.

Up In Arms was Sam Goldwyn's secret weapon. The film mogul who used the English language the way laundries treated wringing-wet clothes had always liked mixing his output of quality stories with comedy. In the 1930s, Eddie Cantor had been the pride of his independent studio's output, a larger-than-life comedian who sang in his own style – if owing a little to Jolson – but who wouldn't be distracted by the curving lines of his contribution to national morale, the Goldwyn Girls.

Danny Kaye must have seemed an obvious candidate for the role of the Cantor of the 1940s – and not simply because his background was so similar, born in New York of poor Russian-Jewish stock, and left motherless in childhood. Both had been sensations on Broadway despite the fact that neither of them had anything resembling obvious sex appeal.

Sylvia was not alone in deciding that there had to be something more to her husband than captivating good looks. Goldwyn knew that when he joined the other Hollywood studio chiefs in rushing to do a deal to bring this unusual talent to the screen. But he was the only one who now saw the Kaye image projected through a lens.

None of them had taken the trouble to view the shorts he had made previously, which is fortunate for all that would happen in the years following 1944.

But for the moment, the problems were obvious, even to men who, unlike Goldwyn, hadn't come to Hollywood in the early years of the century and made the first film to be shot in the California sun, *The Squaw Man*. Before he started, Sam had to get across the message that Kaye would be a performer to have audiences riveted to their seats – that is, when they weren't falling about in the aisles. After all, Sam Goldwyn wasn't the illiterate clown his own publicity made him, the best-known manipulator of words since Mrs Malaprop. He was universally respected throughout the industry as being the most caring producer in the film town, a man who would rather jack a completed movie than allow a product he considered inferior to go out under his name.

Above all else, Sam Goldwyn was a creator of stars and a user of stars. He it was who once rang Louis B. Mayer – a man whom he disliked intensely, as only one mogul could hate another – and said: 'We have a great problem.' 'What?' asked Mayer. 'I want Clark Gable and you have him.'

Well, in 1944, Clark Gable was an internationally known star. Danny Kaye wasn't.

Goldwyn was never one of the studio bosses who believed in playing it safe, but for the picture, he fell back on the formula that had proved so successful in its more primitive way with Cantor – surrounding his new star with lots of women, not all of whom today seem as beautiful as he undoubtedly thought they were in 1944.

President Roosevelt was among the first to be convinced. He saw *Up In Arms*, invited Danny Kaye to Washington – it was just before the election that would confirm him in office for a fourth term – and submitted to the Kaye treatment. 'Bark like a dog,' ordered Kaye and the President of the United States barked.

There was no way that Goldwyn could get audiences merely watching a film – even with Danny Kaye – to bark. With any luck they would be convulsed. But what if they weren't?

The Goldwyn Girls, World War Two vintage, were Sam's backstop, just as they had been the last time he made a musical with Cantor.

He even took a Cantor story as the basis for *Up In Arms*. It may not have been easily recognisable but there were close similarities to *Whoopee*, which Eddie made in 1930.

Even if Sam thought he had a prospective hit on his hands when he signed the contracts for *Up In Arms,* he would have been gifted with rare insight indeed to really project the effect that picture would have. It gave the world a new star and Goldwyn a new bankable asset.

To the film industry, it showed for the first time how Danny and Sylvia Kaye worked – for it was almost as much Sylvia's film as it was her husband's. The story was by Don Hartman, Robert Pirosh and Allen Boretz, but Danny's own musical routines came from Sylvia, with help once more from Max Liebman.

Melody In 4-F was transplanted to the screen as a big production number on the deck of a troop carrier – while Danny is supposedly in the process of running away from his commanding officer (Louis Calhern) and protecting the girl he wishes were his (Constance Dowling). As in most musicals of the time, the story was not allowed to get in the way of the numbers, although the hypochondriac private screwing up his eyes in preparation for what looked destined to be gallons of tears was every bit as effective as it had been on the stage in *Let's Face It* – and a great many more people saw it.

But the most memorable scene of all was when Danny and his room mate (an early and much lighter than usual performance from Dana Andrews) take Miss Dowling and Dinah Shore (the nurse who loves Danny, although he prefers Dana's date) to a cinema.

As they line up for the movie to start, they eat their popcorn, talk to their neighbour (a tiny cameo rule for Margaret Dumont, more familiarly the foil for Groucho Marx) and wonder how long it will be before the movie begins. Which is where Sylvia took over with *The Lobby Number*.

Danny, the shy introvert who believes the world is involved in a mass conspiracy to infect him with every disease known to man, suddenly becomes a thing demented. The bore of waiting for a movie to start, the wading through a succession of credits made to satisfy the egos of a score of technicians and executives as well as stars, now became a moment of cinema history.

'Manic Depressive Pictures present . . .' he began – and accompanied the introduction by the sound of a lion roaring. Neither Mr Goldwyn nor Mr Mayer was on record as complaining. We found out who wrote the screen play, who did the recording, even the 'nicknackery by Thackery' and the 'Dickery by Dock'.

When the picture started, there was 'Carmelita Popita, the Bolivian bombshell' as well as a man with a name no one but Danny Kaye would dare to try to pronounce whom we knew was the 'dangerous German spy'.

Of course, Sam Goldwyn couldn't argue. All the tongue-twisting terpischore – for that's what it was, Danny Kaye's tongue danced – that had enchanted the people in the night clubs and sitting in Broadway theatre seats was there to do nothing less than bamboozle film audiences. It didn't take too much imagination to realise that that was precisely what people paid their money to hear and see.

Whether or not Sam Goldwyn at that stage was prescient enough to realise it, *Up In Arms* was the first casting of the die, the start of the cutting of the pattern. Danny played what in Brooklyn he would have described as a 'schlemeil', an innocent abroad in a world that seemed constantly set to confuse him. No one appeared to see anything strange in this child among men suddenly being awarded the great gift of wit and vocal dexterity shown so clearly in his songs. That was what happened when two totally separate sets of writers got busy in putting words into the extraordinary flexible

Danny Kaye lips. The two were put together in the expectation that no one would even notice. Well, you could see the join – but it didn't matter.

What you could also see as Danny went through his paces on the set at the Goldwyn studios was the evidence of tension between Sylvia and her husband. That, too, would become part of the pattern.

Danny performed his numbers and Sylvia told him to do them again. When there were complaints to be made to the director Elliott Nugent, it was Sylvia who made them. When there were suggestions to make about how a number would be performed, it was to Sylvia that they were addressed. None of this mitigated Danny's own contribution. It was one thing to put words on paper, to put the head on Danny's shoulders. It was another to shake that head, to mouth those words with the expression that so appealed to people, almost none of whom had any idea of what to expect.

Dinah Shore was officially the female lead in the picture, mainly because she had a voice that attracted customers into the record shops. It was four years away from *Buttons and Bows*, but Goldwyn had the idea that she would help get people into the theatres – even if she was hardly anybody's notion of a movie beauty.

Her voice was the kind that GIs wanted to hear and so did many of the members of the Academy of Motion Picture Arts and Sciences. *Now I Know*, the number written for the picture by Harold Arlen and Ted Koehler got an Oscar nomination.

It wasn't originally going to be a Dinah Shore starring vehicle. Nor was Constance Dowling, who had done very little up to that date and did not do much more afterwards, slated to share the billing with Danny. Goldwyn had originally decided on another girl whom he was grooming for Hollywood stardom – and one who had previously worked with Danny, Virginia Mayo.

Her path had crossed Danny's on at least two previous occasions. At one time, they worked on the same vaudeville bill in a small theatre in Baltimore. She was ring mistress to 'Pansy the Horse', played by two men whose subsequent show business fate is unknown. 'We got to know Danny very well,' she told me.

Then, when Danny was starring in *Let's Face It*, she was appearing in the theatre over the road, Billy Rose's Diamond Horseshoe, which was to be immortalised a couple of generations later in *Funny Lady*.

'I told Danny I was leaving to go to Hollywood,' she remembered. 'He said that he was, too. I said I was going to work for Sam Goldwyn. He said that was who he was going to work for. Then we both mentioned *Up In Arms*. It was quite a coincidence.'

She, too, went through the trauma of having her work on screen subjected to Sam Goldwyn's approval of her screen test. For a time she wasn't quite so lucky. He decided she was still too raw, too inexperienced for the lead role. Instead, as observant audiences can now see for themselves, she became temporarily a Goldwyn Girl who did little more than look pretty and heavily made up, climbing the gangplank to the troop ship, and then sitting on deck, administering more lipstick. Bigger things were in store for her – as they were for Danny.

He, however, was immediately recognised and hailed as a new star, the big discovery of 1944. The troops were among the first to appreciate him. The final card on the film was a notice saying that Mr Goldwyn was offering *Up In Arms* for free showing in military theatres. Before long, Danny Kaye singing Sylvia Fine entered the homes of people on both sides of the Atlantic – *The Lobby Number* was an immediate success on the hit parade. The record – slightly changed, part of the original lyric was incorporated in a different song – was being spun on radio turntables all over the world.

Now, by anyone's reckoning, Danny was an international star. Sam Goldwyn certainly thought so. He couldn't wait to get him into a new film. It was a matter of mutual attraction. Sammy loved what Danny did for his picture, a film he was proud to call one of his, too – the message that a Sam Goldwyn production spelt quality was not lost this time round either. Danny, for his part, was quite smitten with Sam. He was more than just grateful for what the picture was doing for his career. He also liked his boss.

It wasn't difficult to make fun of Goldwyn. It wasn't just what he said or what people said he said – the rumour was that his publicity people churned out 'Goldwynisms' by the hour – but the way he said it. If he did ever let drop that he feared his head was 'in a moose', he did so with a high voice that made his Russian-Yiddish accent embarrassingly hilarious to hear face-to-face, for the first time. Danny could impersonate Goldwyn so that even the mogul's wife Frances would be confused. More than that, at the drop of a script, he would copy the Goldwyn facial expressions.

Goldwyn knew that he did it and, if only not to cross the goose that was laying the golden egg, gave every appearance of loving it. Danny would 'do' Sam and Sam would collapse in a heap on the floor. What no one could understand was how Kaye could be a 'visual' comedian 3,000 miles away from his audience. Once, Danny phoned Sam's Beverly Hills home from New York. 'Sam,' he said, 'I'm doing the fish face' – and Goldwyn collapsed in the familiar heap.

That was talent.

Now, there was another Danny Kaye–Sam Goldwyn film on the stocks. Danny was playing a double role in *Wonder Man*, which the cynics among his friends were already suggesting was no less than one might expect from a man with a double personality.

A double personality? Certainly by 1945 there were already two faces of Danny Kaye evident for those whose path he crossed. One was the face the ever-widening cinema public was getting to love. The other was that of the man who sat on the edge of a film set looking as though a black cloud had deliberately sought him out and was menacingly hovering over him as a personal affront.

At one time only Sylvia knew about that cloud. Now even Virginia Mayo, cast at last as his leading lady, could see it. 'Danny is very moody,' she told me. 'He would not have too much cheer.'

He was Pagliacci come to life, except that every now and again the clown would put on his red nose (if not his red hair) even when the cameras were not turning. 'He did loosen up a bit. He would kid around a lot on the set of *Wonder Man*. We got very close and very friendly.'

It wasn't difficult for people to know that Kaye was there at the Goldwyn studios. Everywhere he went, he made his mark. 'Danny was in the make-up department early in the morning,' Virginia remembers. 'The make-up man had a thick German accent. Danny was always mimicking him. Everyone used to laugh.' Whether the man with the German accent laughed quite so loudly, is a matter for conjecture.

Wonder Man was the perfect vehicle for the new Danny Kaye, film star – the story of a kindly, scholarly young man who is never happier than when he can sit in the public library, making notes – writing with both hands simultaneously, because it saved an immense amount of time. He didn't appear to have a great deal of personality, but the shapely librarian played by Miss Mayo didn't worry about that. She liked him – although she was totally puzzled when that personality changed out of all recognition. And no wonder – Danny was infused half the time with the mind of his twin brother, Buster.

Now Buster – or Buzzy Bellew – was the spitting image of the brother Miss Mayo knew as 'Mr Dingle.' (Surprise, Surprise – Buzzy had changed his name) give or take a quiff of blond hair and his lack of the iron-rimmed spectacles worn by his brother. But there the similarity ended. Buzzy was a night-club entertainer, murdered after unwittingly getting himself involved with a set of mobsters.

He 'materialises' after the killing, but only to his brother – which provides some superb opportunities for highly predictable comedy situations which the genius of Danny Kaye made even funnier than writers Don Hartman and Melville Shavelson could have planned. Danny's perfectly reasonable asides to his brother were, of course, highly upsetting to the policeman on the beat in the Brooklyn park where they met. And as for the two lovers on the park bench. . . .

This seemed Danny Kaye at his best – although there was even better to come, thanks once again to Sylvia's brilliance. There was, for instance, the Russian singer who sneezed every time he came near a vase of flowers – it was a routine Danny had dreamed up and performed for Sylvia while they were still contemplating that elopement to Florida – and the phoney opera singer, who tries to escape from the gang by disguising himself as a member of the opera company. Of course, the tights look too loose, the hat doesn't fit and the false beard and moustache fall off, but there was a lot more to it. Danny had to seem as though he were improvising the libretto in response to the suitably well-built coloratura soprano at his side. And improvise he really did. As Melville Shavelson told me: 'We merely wrote that he would use the music as a means of passing a message about the gangsters to the district attorney who happened to be sitting in a box at the opera. Well, Danny did the rest.'

'The rest' was using an Italian accent to sing 'Me scaredo, me afraido . . . Mr District Attorney.' It was a brilliant finale to what was to be one of the best of the Kaye vehicles, still as funny today, 40 years after it was first performed.

Virginia Mayo was well aware of how brilliant he was. 'He was enjoying being wonderful – when he was plainly having a wonderful time.' Which was no more than anyone could hope of a film called *Wonder Man*.

It was that in spite of the sort of horrendous happening that dogs the nightmares of most film producers – to say nothing of insurance companies. Right at the beginning of the movie, Danny as Buzzy Bellew performs the *Bali Boogie* with dancer Vera-Ellen, his fiancée. Near the end of the dance, Buzzy jumps into the centre of the huge drum which formed the centrepiece to the routine. Vera made it perfectly. Danny broke his ankle. His work was completed eight weeks later – with one part of the dance actually put into the camera two months after the one a second before.

Danny certainly had gained the supreme accolade – the undying affection of Mr Goldwyn himself. In *Wonder Man*, he was allowed to wear his hair almost the way God had intended – considerably less blond than it had been in *Up In Arms*.

Danny Kaye was Sam Goldwyn's new star, as big as any he had had in his career up to then and both Kaye and Goldwyn liked it that way. And so did critics on both sides of the Atlantic.

In *Picturegoer* magazine in Britain, Wilson D'Arne wrote: 'A good comic is as welcome in this country as a miner's meat ration. You have arrived. We want you to stay.'

That seemed to be the reaction of everyone who came into contact with him. Goldwyn certainly felt that. He had in mind a third Kaye film which was going to be a remake of the Harold Lloyd picture about a milkman who becomes a boxer, *The Milky Way*. Appropriately, this would be called *The Kid From Brooklyn*.

Meanwhile, Danny was busy doing what today would be called commuting between the West and the East Coasts of the United States. He was now important enough for magazines to consider it worthwhile to take him back to the Brooklyn this particular kid remembered. He was photographed at the local drug store talking to the proprietor and the neighbourhood postman both from the same Jewish street, who had attended the same school. He also went back to that school and was shown talking to the principal in the kind of pose he would never have dared affect a generation earlier. Happiest of all, it seemed, he was talking to another old schoolfriend – in his doctor's office.

Going back to his roots was another opportunity for him to share a bagel and smoked salmon and cream cheese with his father, who seemingly was spending every moment of his day talking about 'My son, the actor' to his cronies as they gathered at the delicatessen or sat in the synagogue on the holidays.

But he was also in New York to work. It was a time when every successful entertainer had to shine in at least three media before he could be said to have made it – in films, on records and on radio. In 1945, Danny signed to make a series of radio shows – sponsored by a brewery – on the CBS network.

He was paid – and the figure seems breathtaking, considering the value of the dollar four decades ago – $16,000 a week for *Blue Ribbon Time*. 'I'll spend it to make good on the air,' he said at the time. Which sounds amazingly modest for a man already hailed by some as 'the new Jolson'. Since, however, it was the age when Jolson was all but forgotten by most Americans, it was something of hollow praise. Danny, however, knew it wasn't going to be so easy.

And as for that $16,000. . . . Out of it he had to pay his own orchestra, actors and writers. That still left plenty for Kaye to 'make good' – and even if it didn't, he hardly had to queue up at the nearest soup kitchen. Goldwyn had paid him $125,000 to make each of *Up In Arms* and *Wonder Man* and by the time the first year of *Blue Ribbon Time* was up, it was being authoratively reckoned that he was worth something like half a million dollars a year, the sort of figure at which more established performers like Bing Crosby or even Clark Gable wouldn't have turned up their refined noses. But then, Kaye did have so much more going for him.

Danny was the first to realise that an entertainer like he wasn't a perfect subject for a radio series, which in that pre-TV age was the most important of all the branches of show biz as far as exposure was concerned. Crosby, for one, only had to open his mouth to have people begging for more, and to only slightly mix the metaphor, eating out of his hand. Bob Hope needed nothing more than to put his joke factory to work and he was a radio natural.

But how would Danny come across without those hands, which one writer said were 'the most expressive since Eleanora Duse'? And without those faces?

Danny, thanks to Sylvia's head on his shoulders, was using that head every bit as intelligently as anyone who knew them would have expected. It wasn't enough for him to begin his show, week-in, week-out, with what fans of his two movies would have accepted as 'typical Kaye' scat sounds of 'git-gat-gittle'. He brought in a team of writers whom both he and Sylvia thought were the best they could get, headed by a bright youngster named Goodman Ace, who ten years later would be best known as the creator of the Sid Caesar TV shows.

On radio, he did it all – *Tchaikovsky*, *The Lobby Number*; an Irish tenor here, a Japanese general there, a Russian – always a Russian – when there was no one else. Seemingly, the occasions when there looked as if there would be no one else were very rare indeed.

Sylvia decided, as before, what was good for her genius husband and what was not good – and wrote more and more material. It should, on paper, have been yet another episode in the rapidly rising Danny Kaye success story. But neither of them was really happy with it. Danny not only needed to be able to display visually his incredible abilities, he yearned, too, desperately for the kind of rapport he felt he only got when he was able to play to live faces. In the movie studio, he escaped this difficulty by pretending the cameraman or some other technician was an adoring fan – for like Jolson again, his relationship with an audience was more a love affair than a business arrangement with people who bought tickets. When he broadcast, even a live studio audience was no compensation for the realisation that the people he was really playing to were sometimes thousands of miles away. To some entertainers that is a pacemaker, to Kaye it seemed an embalming process.

The critics weren't all enthusiastic either. *Time* magazine demonstrated just how powerful Danny Kaye now was in the world of showbusiness by awarding him their supreme award in March 1946, a cover story.

'Unlike great clowns of the past, he does not wear funny clothes, fall on his prat, throw custard pies or even borrow ancient jokes from Joe Miller,' the writer of the piece recorded. 'His chief comic assets are a nimble brain and an even nimbler tongue. . . .'

The radio series, however, seemed an aberration in what the magazine described as a career of 'six years of breath-taking

[60]

success'. As the anonymous critic noted: 'Better seen than heard, Danny Kaye is never at his best on radio. Listeners miss the vitality of his clowning, the humour of his mugging. Not a good straight man, Danny flounders as he lugs the weight of dull dialogue.'

And the magazine noted there were too many variations on one joke: 'My sister married an Irishman!'

'Oh, really?'

'No O'Reilly.'

Now, one didn't expect to go to Danny Kaye for that. Or even for 'My sister comes from the South-west.'

'Oh really?'

'No, Oklahoma.'

As *Time* pointed out, 'Now hardly a word beginning with "O" is safe.'

Despite all this, *Blue Ribbon Time* seemed to be a hit. *Radio Daily*, as important to the industry as were the *Hollywood Reporter* and *Variety* to movies and stage shows, put Danny's show level with Jimmy Durante (who had been at it for at least 30 years) at fifth place.

Strangely, none of Danny's inhibitions about his radio show were echoed by his enthusiasm for recording. He was decidedly choosy about what he did record – *The Lobby Number* hit from *Up In Arms* was undoubtedly perfect for a disc, but he refused to record *Melody In 4-F* or the sneezing number from *Wonder Man*, which he thought were much too visual, but there seemed a huge, insatiable demand for anything else he would make – and he was more than happy to agree. Each record meant more money, more exposure – and more opportunities to twist that tongue.

Tchaikovsky was ideal. So was *Minnie the Moocher* – complete with vocalised support from the orchestra. There were smoother numbers, too – the kind of songs that people who only knew Danny Kaye from his movies wouldn't automatically have associated with him, like *St Louis Blues*, which backed that old, old vaudeville tune, *Ballin' The Jack*.

He also turned a number which had been a nice foil for the duo of Fred Astaire and Gene Kelly in *Broadway Melody of 1940* (and had much earlier been a stock part of the repertoire of Fred and his sister Adele), *The Babbit and the Bromide*, into a charming solo opus. When Danny sang *Danny Boy* his sales rocketed – and not just in the Irish quarters of New York or in Ireland itself. Instantly, he turned what had always previously seemed a standard strictly for the wearers of the green into something to delight people who played records anywhere they could be bought.

But Danny the record maker was no easier to work with, as some had by then discovered, than was Danny the film star, the radio personality or live-show stopper. Johnny Green – as he then was;

he has since dropped the final syllable of his first name – discovered this when he recorded a set of Gilbert and Sullivan numbers with Kaye.

Now Green subsequently became a close friend of the Kayes, and a great admirer of 'that miracle of gift which is his musicality, which screams at one. It has nothing to do with musical knowledge or supreme music ability. He radiates the elements of music from every pore. Every move that he makes is music. If anyone is poetry in motion, Danny Kaye is that in spades.'

But he was also difficult in spades, too. The recording of the Gilbert and Sullivan discs took place at the Decca studios on Melrose Avenue in Los Angeles. It was early in 1946, long before tape was in use. In three hours, four sides had to be recorded direct on the disc.

'If you didn't manage to get four sides in that time,' John Green told me, 'you were in big trouble – or at least just one guy was in trouble, the orchestra leader.'

In this incident, John Green got into trouble – and to this day blames it all on this 'miracle of gift', Danny Kaye.

'Danny,' says Green, 'is an irreverent fellow – to anything except his own whim. He has enormous reverence for his own whim of the moment – and is irresistibly funny. Nobody can take that away from him. And when Danny Kaye decides that, no matter what it costs, he is going to make the orchestra laugh, he'll make the orchestra laugh. To hell with Decca, to hell with the Kapp brothers (who owned Decca), to hell with Johnny Green. "I'm going to have fun tonight . . ." That was his behaviour.'

For the first couple of times that Danny broke up the orchestra – to say nothing of the recording session – Johnny Green laughed too. 'How could you not laugh?'

But finally, he pointed to the studio clock. 'I said, "Danny, shall we?"'

'He got very put out by me.'

'"I can tell time," he said.' Green looked to the control room where Sylvia was sitting. He was hoping to get help from her. All he got was a shrug of the shoulders.

To an old pro like Green, it all looked like the worst kind of unprofessionalism. 'Danny Kaye allows for only one star – himself. His little old buddy Johnny Green on the podium at that moment was there to serve him – and I was not to think about my own relationship with Decca, and I was a Decca artist myself. Well, have you any idea how much a horse's rear end I was at that time?'

At the end of the first of the three hours of that session, there was nothing on disc. Johnny Green put down his baton, went to the hat rack in a corner of the studio, took his hat and his coat, walked right

[62]

out in front of Danny Kaye, in front of the orchestra, out of the room, towards the parking lot, got into his car and drove home – and, it seemed, out of Decca for good. No recording organisation expects its artists to walk out in the middle of a session for which they have committed other expensive performers.

'I didn't hurt Danny at all. Me I hurt. I may not have loused myself up for ever. But I didn't do myself any good. I just got fed up with Danny being a clown with the orchestra, telling jokes, doing his dialect stuff, that sort of thing.'

Green ate a hearty meal of humble pie, apologised to all concerned, and finished the album – one which, alas, is too much of a collector's item these days, the copies are as rare as finding an associate of Danny Kaye who will admit only good things about him, who sees only one side of his hitherto secret life.

Part of the infuriating thing about being with Kaye was just that – never knowing which part of him you were with. It wasn't just because of his moods. Sometimes, it was simply because you never really knew who you were dealing with. There was nothing sinister in that, simply that he himself didn't always know when to stop playing the great entertainer.

Sylvia tells of the occasion when she opened her front door to greet an old man, speaking with a thick Russian Jewish accent and dressed as though he had just stepped out of the Steppes, via the steerage section of an immigrant ship which everyone would have thought had put into dock for the last time sometime before the 1917 revolution.

He said his name was Kaminsky, was Danny's uncle, had never met him, but was filled with pride at the great success his younger brother Jacob's son had achieved. Sylvia was kind and considerate, even if the man smelled as though he had never seen a bath tub.

She told him that her husband was out. The old man smiled indulgently. Yes, he would have a glass of tea – coffee wasn't his cup of tea at all. Yes, perhaps a bagel. But what he really wanted was $30,000. That was when Sylvia got angry – until she realised that old Mr Kaminsky was 33-year-old Danny Kaye.

There was more trouble with servants over Danny's abject refusal to conform to most people's ideas of convention than over anything else.

A side of Danny Kaye few knew, however, was the Kaye of compassion. John Green experienced that aspect of the man, too. He has never spoken of it before and, indeed, it sounds not unlike a page from a Raymond Chandler novel – although Chandler would never have dreamed of bringing Danny Kaye into a Philip Marlowe tale.

This time, it was the elegant John Green, at the end of a marriage

[63]

and in the midst of a steamy affair with a beautiful, extremly well-known lady living in Beverly Hills, who needed help. The woman's husband had threatened to go after Green with a gun.

'It was an hysterical affair,' Green told me. 'Never having a chemical necessity for alcohol, but as a stupid, dramatic gesture, I was doing a lot of drinking. Never at work. But if I finished work at 6.30, by 7 I was smashed. It took a toll on my health.'

And it took Danny and Sylvia to get him better. 'They came one night when I was ossified. They took me to their house and hid me.' Not that the normally fastidious John Green looked anything like the man either of them would have easily recognised. His hair was unkempt, his clothes askew – and he hadn't shaved for two days.

Green's job as head of music at MGM was, to use his own words, 'down the drain'. The Kayes saw it as their mission to bring him back to life – and work again. Consequently, they locked up every cupboard and cabinet containing hard liquor in the house, the only part of the mansion at San Ysidro Drive to which the family had moved – it is just round the corner from the celebrated Beverly Hills Hotel – where their friend John Green was denied access.

'But I conned the key to one of these cabinets from the butler,' he recalled.

'It was morning and Sylvia had gone to the beauty shop. At about 11 o'clock that morning, I fell on the floor unconscious and was rushed by ambulance to the Good Samaritan Hospital.'

He recovered consciousness about two hours later – to find both arms paralysed. As he said, 'That was great for a piano player!'

He hadn't shaved now for about five days. Danny Kaye came down to that hospital – and demanded a razor, a shaving brush and a stick of shaving cream. He then proceeded to shave his friend – in the course of a typical Danny Kaye one-man show, although, as audiences in various parts of America were now beginning to find out, there was really no such thing as a typical Danny Kaye anything.

Before the 'show', there was a moment of seriousness as he called, too, for a basin of hot water. 'This is not our Johnny,' said Kaye. 'I'm going to shave you and you'll look like Johnny Green again. Then you'll get up out of that bed and be back at Metro in two days. The doctors can't do it for you. But I can.'

The lecture over, the show began. Danny adopted his favourite Yiddish accent. Suddenly, he was big star and big friend no more. Instead, he was the little barber in the shop at the corner of the street in Brooklyn where Jacob Kaminsky would go once every two weeks.

'For God's sake,' he said, 'vy de hell you lyin, in de bed? Vat de

[64]

hell mit you? You mit a beard like dat. You goin' to grow a beard, grow a beard. Don't mess arahnd mit a stoupple like dat.'

As the man now regarded as one of the most distinguished names in Hollywood, patron of the Academy of Motion Picture Arts and Sciences and of ASCAP – the Association of Composers, Authors and Publishers – told me: 'I felt so ashamed of myself! Within a couple of hours of his shaving me, I started moving my hands slightly. I wasn't back in the studio in two days. It took three or four and I was on a cane for a couple of weeks. But Danny Kaye got me better.'

Danny liked the trappings of success, like having those servants to help clean both the Beverly Hills house and the plush apartment they had filled with antiques in Manhattan. He enjoyed having people to ensure that the bespoke suits he now wore were always pressed, serviced for missing buttons, stuck zips and other unfortunate occurrences. But regretfully, he usually answered his own telephone – even if the callers didn't always realise it.

There are a score of top playwrights, musicians, Hollywood directors, producers and writers who can testify to the number of times they have had to wait at the other end of a line while a Russian piano teacher, a Japanese houseboy or an Italian manservant – to say nothing of an English butler – called Mr Kaye to the phone, with Mr Kaye always remembering to change his accent in time.

Once he posed as another vagrant – and was thrown bodily out of the house by the cook, who wasn't exactly amused when Sylvia tried to pacify her by explaining the situation.

'It makes it darn difficult to keep a maid,' she said at the time.

But Danny playing Danny playing a film or stage role could move mountains – and audiences of all kinds. Artur Rubinstein was no more doubtful about the immense Danny Kaye talent than hundreds of others have been subsequently. That *Time* magazine piece reported him saying: 'I feel most often about him what everyone else felt about Chaplin. I am not so much amused as I am moved.'

Consequently, the offers came flooding in – and from equally unexpected quarters. The Blue Ribbon beer company and CBS may have Kaye booked up for radio and Sam Goldwyn's contract with him for movies was completely watertight, but there were daily offers for things he couldn't yet consider. Gabriel Pascal wrote offering Danny the title role in a new version of *Macbeth* and the Metropolitan Opera suggested a Danny Kaye *Figaro*. He wasn't yet ready to accept. A generation or two later, it would be precisely the sort of thing to get the Kaye juices going, but for the moment, he was busy consolidating what he had already.

THE SECRET LIFE OF WALTER MITTY

HE HAD ONLY MADE THREE PICTURES WHEN A MAGAZINE ASKED THE
question: 'Where does Danny Kaye go from here?' It wasn't asked
out of sour grapes, born of the idea that yet another new screen
performer had come along and once having arrived . . . so what?
Everyone, but everyone, recognised that everything about Danny
Kaye was extraordinary.

Up In Arms had been sensationally good. *The Lobby Number* and
Melody In 4-F had people holding in their sides while, at the same
time, trying to find a free hand to pull their open mouths back into
shape. *Wonder Man* was even better. *The Kid From Brooklyn*, while
displaying what most people now accepted as the typical Kaye
charm, was, on the other hand, less exciting – although he trained
for six weeks in a real-live boxers' gym, and there was a gem of a
routine called *Pavlova* made to measure, as usual, by Sylvia, which
did for the ballet what *Tchaikovsky* did for music. Again, Danny said
it wasn't a number he was going to record.

It also became increasingly apparent that the two lives of Danny
Kaye were never more clearly separated than when the movie
cameras were trained on him. For much of the movie, he was
playing again what his neighbours in his own section of Brooklyn
would recognise as the *schlemeil*, the well-meaning, unworldly
individual who got into scrapes always of his own creation but
never of his own intention. Within that framework, all his movies
could seem interchangeable. His acting was competent. But when
he did his speciality numbers, he was a totally different man. He
came alive. He dominated. In short, he was unique. No one had
ever sounded or looked like that on a movie screen before. The pity
that was beginning to register with audiences was that these two
personalities *were* so separate.

In an interview with *Picturegoer*, an unnamed writer/producer
was asked what was wrong with Danny Kaye. He replied, 'Well,
y'know a Gregory Peck lasts through the picture.' It could be
surmised that Danny Kaye himself was laughing all the way to the
bank. Each of his pictures was taking more money than the one
before and even Sam Goldwyn, a man not easy to please was

satisfied enough to want to talk about the next venture before the last one was finished. And Goldwyn, unlike the big factories that were the other studios, was an independent producer who made sometimes no more than one film a year.

Still, he was in as big demand as ever. A week's night-club engagements could still bring him $4,000, and audiences were paying him the supreme compliment of knowing the things he did as well as he did himself. Danny returned the compliment by adopting the language of his fans. It was the age of the bobby-soxer; the conversation emanating from the clubs and dance halls where they gathered was strictly jive talk. When he saw one bobby-soxer clapping wildly, he pitched a finger in her direction. 'Shoot the pinky to me, Stinky,' he declared and the house – as it usually did at a Kaye performance – collapsed.

His radio show had a totally committed public eagerly looking forward, every time he signed off, to the next broadcast seven days later.

Songwriter Dorothy Fields said her baby daughter was already a devoted fan. 'For everyone else she vomits. For Danny, she laughs.'

She wasn't the only baby learning to laugh at Danny Kaye. In 1946, Sylvia gave birth to their own baby daughter. She would prove to be their only child, and the joy of her father's life. Anyone knowing Danny Kaye would not find it surprising that they chose a name for the child straight out of his song repertoire. She became Dena – pronounced, as in the song, Deenah; very definitely, not Dinah.

Meanwhile, Danny was still very much Sylvia's boy. 'When I look at a bunch of words strung together, they don't mean much to me,' he was saying at this time. 'I've no idea how they're going to sound in my mouth. But Sylvia knows and Sylvia is almost always right.' The 'almost' there could have sounded ominous.

When Danny *was* providing his own material, it was for the off-screen and off-stage moments that still got Sylvia confused – and sometimes annoyed. At about the time *The Kid From Brooklyn* was showing in her neighbourhood theatres, Mrs Fine, Sylvia's mother, had a phone call from the kind of gangster who appeared in the movies: 'See here,' said the dismembered voice, 'Dis is der hangout of Marblehead Moe and I'm warnin' yer. Lay off callin' here or I'll get de mob to take yer for a ride. Understan'?' Of course, it was Danny.

She made him ring Mrs Fine to apologise – although he said it spoilt the joke. As the years went on, he allowed less and less to spoil his jokes.

What concerned the Kayes' lawyer Louis Mandell at this time

was that Danny seemed to regard funniest of all one of the most serious things of all – his money.

Few queried the clothes that Danny bought – they were all business investments; a big star couldn't be expected to wear anything but the best. The same went for Sylvia's dresses, and for some of the expensive things they had in their houses. But Danny was extraordinarily generous with tips, spent lavishly buying things that no one could think he really needed. Mandell decided that the way to curb his excesses was to give him an allowance of $50 a week.

One thing Danny talked very little about at this time was politics. If he had come out and nailed his political colours to any mast, they would probably have been shaded pink. But on one occasion, he fixed them for all to see – as did Gene Kelly, Humphrey Bogart, MGM's future boss Dore Schary, mouth-organ virtuoso Larry Adler and a string of writers.

They called themselves the Committee for the First Amendment – and were protesting against the subpoenaing of 19 writers who had been summoned to appear before the House Committee on UnAmerican Activities – the forerunner of the McCarthy hearings – run by a man named Parnell Thomas, who ended up in jail himself. (The First Amendment of the American Constitution guarantees freedom of speech.)

Together, they chartered a plane to take them to Washington – and were thereafter condemned by the Hearst Press for being a planeload of fellow-travelling Communist sympathisers, after which most of them gave up. The first to withdraw his support was Bogart, who declared that he hated Communists more than most. Danny withdrew his support, too. The whole event left a great deal of bitterness. As Larry Adler put it to me: 'It was definitely not a Communist front organisation. I was never a Communist – although I saw no reason why anybody should be made to say so – but I cannot easily forgive those who did give up.'

One of those in the First Amendment Committee was Mel Frank, who later wrote three Kaye films. What he remembers about this trip to Washington was the flight back to Hollywood by way of New York.

'This was the time when it was virtually impossible to get a hotel room in New York and this whole group of wonderful Hollywood personalities were stranded at La Guardia Airport – and you have never seen such a miserable lot of people in all your life.'

It would have been a lot more miserable without Danny along. 'First of all, he goes into the pilot's booth and comes out with the pilot's hat on. He played a drunk pilot trying to explain what the trouble was. He was just incredible. And then on the journey back, lightning struck but Danny was just hilarious.'

(There was another adventure on the trip when a group of the protestors *did* manage to find a room – at the Waldorf Astoria Hotel, a suite owned by Howard Hughes, who kept a young lady there. The trouble was, he didn't tell the lady that the Hollywood set were coming. They arrived to find her 'entertaining' in the bedroom. 'Just think,' said Ira Gershwin who was one of the unwelcome visitors. 'There are another ten amendments.')

Nothing would stop Danny being hilarious – when he was in his own spare time and when he was being paid for it.

Early in 1947, even Mr Mandell couldn't worry about any slight excesses on his client's part. He was back on the live stage – and getting $68,000 for the seven days he did at the RKO Keith Theatre at Boston, where the marquee proclaimed: 'On Stage – Danny Kaye – In Person!'

The money was plainly seen as an investment by the management. The performance followed an engagement in Chicago, where the theatre grossed in his week there precisely $179,000.

It was the virtuoso performance the people queuing for hours for tickets would have expected. There was none of the lack of command that the film critics had occasionally noted. The stage was his every time Danny appeared in front of the curtain.

Most performers at the theatre – there were films to see, too – were on stage for no more than 20 minutes. Kaye was there for 65 – alone. Alone, he pranced from one end to the other and then along the aisles. Alone, he sang. Alone, he told stories. Alone, he jumped into the orchestra pit.

When he was joined on stage it was by the tiny singer Georgia Gibbs – whom he proceeded to demolish by imitating everything she did. She loved the demolition act as much as anyone else.

He didn't know what he was going to do until he actually mounted that stage. Monday's show was different from the one on Tuesday. No performance was ever the same. He would sit in his dressing room, a small red piano ready for any last-minute experiment and contemplate not just the performance ahead, but the career he had made himself.

He wore a Terry-towel robe – which had inscribed on its back, 'Property of the Sherry Netherland Hotel'.

One night he saw that his microphone was loose. He called for a screwdriver and Danny worked on it himself, right in front of his audience.

'I could have died right there,' he said. 'But the audience loved it. Then, when I finally got the thing fixed, I realised that the impact of my introduction was lost. So I asked for a new intro, and the crowd howled.'

As he said: 'I've got a strong gambling instinct. Outside of my business, I wouldn't risk a dime on the turn of a card or the role of the dice, but on stage I took chances. If you don't vary your stuff, you're sure to bore the orchestra – and why should the paying customers laugh when the musicians are sitting around with long faces?'

Look magazine spotted that he was in his element. He admitted that he preferred the stage to making movies. 'I don't hate the movies,' he quickly reassured the writer of the piece. They're a great medium. But I have more pleasure from playing to an audience.'

And the audience clearly had more pleasure being played to – not that each and every one of the people in that Boston crowd wouldn't have been willing to produce a written guarantee that they would be lining up at the box office for his next film. And it would be worth the wait.

The film they saw next was undoubtedly the best in his entire screen career. *The Secret Life of Walter Mitty* seemed to embody the dreams of everyone who has ever imagined that instead of sitting at an uncomfortable desk in a humdrum office he was out riding a horse in the Wild West or sailing a ship through uncharted waters in the midst of a storm.

The film was based on a story by James Thurber who, despite what a number of literary purists subsequently said, was to tell me he thought Danny Kaye was precisely the Walter Mitty he envisaged. The basic idea was retained. Walter Mitty was a daydreamer. But then Thurber's short story was just that – extremely short. In one edition, it took up no more than four pages – and of the episodes so beautifully told by that master of short-story writing only one was retained, the tale of the surgeon who saves a patient's life on the operating table by using a fountain pen to replace the faulty piston on the anaesthetic machine. Danny Kaye wouldn't be seen dead rejecting that – on or off the table.

Instead of flying a naval plane, he was an RAF flyer – someone at the Goldwyn studio knew a thing or two about the impeccable English accent Danny used when mimicking an executive there. He was also a Mississipi gambler, that Western hero and the sea captain who when asked whether he could still man the helm with an injured arm, replied that, of course, he could . . . it was just broken. He wasn't the gunman on trial for his life who could fire at anything at 300 ft with his right *or left hand*. Instead, he was the dandified figure in the cut-away morning coat who designed hats – Anatole of Paris, of course. If this wasn't enough, Danny also

[70]

played a gunman involved with the IRA. But 25 years after the end of the first batch of troubles and 20 years before the start of the next lot, it was considered a little too sensitive and the episode was dropped from the final movie.

Thurber only had time in those four pages to postulate that the day dreams came to Mitty while driving with his wife on the way to the stores. In the film, he had no wife – if he had, it would have made it difficult in those still prudish days of 1947 Hollywood to bring in Virginia Mayo, who was again cast opposite Danny.

Now, his mind was allowed to wander as he drove his mother in her car to the station, from which he travelled to his work in town as an editor working for a firm of pulp-magazine publishers.

He played an ideas man whose ideas were constantly being purloined by his boss – again the sort of character he played in *Wonder Man*, the uncommon mind who could have done with a little more common sense. Then, there was the case of the German spy . . . all super Danny Kaye stuff.

Walter Mitty hears the constant sound of 'ta-pocket, ta-pocket, ta-pocket' racing through his mind. But it and the incidents producing it came in the midst of those Kaye-Fine routines – after shooting down his hundredth German plane when he just happens to be asked by the men in the RAF officers' mess to impersonate the Central European Orchestra conductor, and best of all when he plays *Anatole of Paris*. The crowds at La Martinique never heard or saw it done better.

The credit, of course, went all sorts of ways – to Danny and Sylvia, naturally, and to the director Norman Z. McLeod. But then there was the musical arranger on the picture, David Raksin, still fairly fresh from his experiences as the writer of probably the best theme music ever for a Hollywood thriller, *Laura* – in which the music seemed even more important than the action on the screen. That wasn't the case with *Walter Mitty* although his work in this was vital.

Sylvia played the piano for the playbacks. Raksin's job was to 'make it more extravagant, expand it.' As he told me: 'Sylvia played and wrote in a very simple way. There was a lot of her music that was going up half a tone at a time with diminished chords.'

For the Western scene, he arranged the familiar ballad, *The Streets of Loredo*. For the sea-captain routine, he adapted the music from *The Flying Dutchman*. In the riverboat gambling scene, there was a compilation straight out of the Stephen Foster songbook.

Working on *Walter Mitty* was an experience Raksin will not forget in a hurry. 'Danny was always funny,' he remembers. 'If not impossible. People working on Danny Kaye pictures, with all affection and deference to Danny and to Sylvia, grew old a lot faster than they would have done otherwise;' he told me.

'But I have a lot of respect for them both.' (Later, David Raksin worked on a number of committees with Sylvia. 'She impressed me very greatly with her sense and her intelligence.')

One of the troubles people always had on the sets of Kaye pictures was that Sylvia frequently gave the impression of doing Danny's dirty work. When there were jobs to be done that plainly Danny felt uncomfortable doing, it was Sylvia who did them for him.

To outsiders, however, there seemed that nothing could possibly upset the way things were going for the Kayes. Everything in their garden seemed rosy. Danny had signed to take his stage show to London. The Palladium promised to be an unusual additional dimension to his career – although just how unusual no soothsayer could possibly predict. For the present, it looked like no more than a risk that he was going to take. As it was, he had already taken two other risks – both of which stunned everyone who knew the off-stage, off-screen Danny.

He was leaving Samuel Goldwyn – and he was also leaving Sylvia.

LET'S FACE IT

THE NEWS STUNNED THE KAYES' FRIENDS, BUT IT WAS THE KIND OF stunning that comes when a close relative dies of an incurable disease which he had had for so long. The illness had been part of him for so long that people just wondered *when* it would happen – and when it did, it left everyone numb.

There had been rumours of a parting of the Kayes for months. The verbal battles on film sets were no longer private property. The moods were visible on private occasions as well as public. Everyone else lived with it, so why shouldn't Danny and Sylvia? And, after all, their partnership wasn't confined to the bedroom or the kitchen.

When the news did finally break, it was the talking point all over Hollywood, in the studios, in the restaurants, in the delicatessens, in the lines moving their orderly way into theatres – where a session of *The Lobby Number* would have been very welcome to ease the atmosphere.

As the rumours multiplied, so did the reasons alleged for the split. One of them was that Danny couldn't bear the sound of baby Dena crying. He put his emotions to Hedda Hopper to try to kill that one. 'The truth,' he said, 'was that hearing the baby cry and not knowing whether she was ill tore my heart out.' He emphasised that their breaking up was not intended as a gesture of finality. 'Our separation is an attempt to salvage our marriage, not end it.' Then came an explanation that was not new to the film capital – and which many a studio habitué would have appreciated: 'For the past eight years, I have been working hard to get ahead. In the process, our personal relationship suffered.'

But was he still in love with Sylvia? He was as honest as he used to tell his theatre audiences to be. 'If you refer to that rapturous feeling we had when we first married as love, I suppose I'll have to say no. What people can retain that for eight years? But if you mean by love those basic principles that brought us together in the first place, I'll say yes. I'm still very much in love with her.'

Sylvia wasn't giving any answers herself, but the mind boggled at how this wife-made man, who carried her head on his

[73]

shoulders, would cope. He worried, too. 'If our marriage ends, Sylvia won't work with me. And even if she would, I don't think I'd want her to.'

Memories flooded back of the days at Camp Tamiment, of La Martinique and *Let's Face It*, when they sat together on the couch of their Manhattan home planning the future Sylvia always said was in store for her brilliant husband.

'Don't think I fail to appreciate Sylvia,' he told the columnist who knew more about the love lives of most Hollywood stars than they knew about themselves. 'She was perfectly content to work through me, let me be the Big Guy. Perhaps she would have been content to live through me, but I didn't want things that way.'

Danny was letting matters drift off into various tangents.

'Success has brought me a form of personal happiness and I've been able to pass that happiness on to my father. It's not merely that I can buy him anything he wants. The biggest kick he can get out of life is being the father of Danny Kaye.'

He was probably right. What is not so certain is that Sylvia was quite as sanguine about her own role as the wife of Danny Kaye.

It didn't please her to read statements like the one in which he said: 'A man cannot exist when he feels he is a puppet in the hands of his wife.'

Her own doubts settled on strange facets of his behaviour. She it was who had interested Danny in opera. They were close friends of Jan Peerce, then at the height of his career with the Metropolitan Opera and whom the Kayes knew as Pinky. When Peerce overwhelmed the audience at the Met, Danny decided he had to know more about it. He bought all the Peerce records he could get.

'It became an obsession,' Sylvia reported. 'He didn't just listen to the music, he learned the words. All of them, from every opera he could get hold of. I suddenly realised,' she said, 'that I had created a Frankenstein.'

It was a feeling that didn't only apply to opera. He was just as certain in his own mind that he was doing right by Sam Goldwyn, too – even though the mogul responsible for his *international* fame was offering him a newer and more tempting contract. Danny protested that he was not ungrateful to Goldwyn. But he was taking Warner Brothers up on an offer they were making him, which would allow him to make pictures for other studios as well as their own. For Jack L. Warner, head of production at the organisation bearing his name, stealing a top star still at the height of his box-office drawing powers from another studio was the sweetest, headiest delight he knew. If someone did it to him, he would do everything short of calling in the Mafia to administer another form of contract on an erring ex-employee, but turned round this way, it was his favourite sport.

Danny saw no moral issue involved there. 'Let me say I consider Sam to be a great producer and to admit that he has been wonderful to me. No matter what he does, Goldwyn has a certain ever-present dignity that commands admiration and respect. I think it's because we all know how much he lives and loves pictures. He doesn't want the Goldwyn name attached to anything mediocre. But however much I like and admire Goldwyn, I have my own career to think about.'

Neither was he giving Sam all of the credit most people seemed to think he deserved. 'I don't think Sam gave me my first break out of charity. He took a gamble with me and the dice came up eleven. We both profited by our relationship. And I'm sure that if my pictures had lost money, he wouldn't have kept picking up my options. He's a realist, too. I believe that Goldwyn made an honest attempt to find something different for me in every picture we made. But there was a certain sameness about them and I felt that if I continued to do similar films people would get wise to my tricks and to my mannerisms.'

The same thing had been said by the critics, but the public were constantly proving that they liked the Goldwyn formula – and *Walter Mitty* was a deserved box-office smash. Yet Danny took to heart what people told him. The one thing he believed he couldn't allow was to be type cast. He wanted to lose the *schlemeil*.

Goldwyn had offered him a flattering new contract. But one clause was missing – the chance to make pictures for another studio. Sam had created a blue chip and he was going to keep it that way.

Danny denied that he had said he would never make another Goldwyn film, but he *was* now tempted by other people's offers. Warners had come up with the idea of starring him as Don Quixote. Now that was the kind of part that he wanted. 'The question of outside pictures was my big beef. My first contract provided I could make one outside film a year. I never took advantage of that. So I felt that if my destiny was to make only musicals, I wanted to do only a few pictures, maybe just one every two or three years. I can always go back to the stage and night clubs.' Which was precisely what he was going to do, but this matter had to be sewn up first.

Warners were offering him what he acknowledged was a 'wonderful deal'. And indeed it was. He was being granted the kind of opportunity that came only to top stars – to choose his own director and leading lady as well as the story. And he would do it for all five pictures he was scheduled to make.

He would find that more difficult to achieve than seemed likely at the time of signing. But then, he was a top star, he was still young, and he had the thrill of the London Palladium to come.

THE COURT JESTER

The Palladium was known as the greatest variety theatre in the world. Top American stars looked to the Palace on Broadway as their Mecca, but they would admit that given the choice, the Palladium had to come out on top.

A number of American stars had already appeared at this vast theatre in Argyll Street, just a stone's throw from Oxford Circus. So many of them – Judy Garland, Carmen Miranda (Hollywood stars didn't come much bigger than this now almost forgotten Brazilian dancer who wore more fruit on her head than most British families had seen on their tables in nine years), Dinah Shore and Betty Hutton – that it looked as though part of the British Empire (and not just Moss Empires, who owned the theatre) was being given away; perhaps in exchange for America's contribution to post-war recovery, Marshall Aid.

Before the war, it had been the home of the greatest music hall performers in the land. George Robey had appeared there. The Crazy Gang had made their mark in the theatre. It was the house where the King and the Royal Family came once a year for the annual event still known as the Command Performance.

When Val Parnell announced that Danny Kaye was going to be his next attraction at the theatre, the American conquest might have seemed complete – except that he followed on Mickey Rooney, who was the first flop the theatre had known for years.

Rooney, at the time still best remembered as the child star of the Andy Hardy films and the Judy Garland musicals like *Babes In Arms* and *Strike Up The Band*, had arrived in Britain as brash as the tough-guy kid who had made tears run down the cheeks of film goers in *Boys Town*. This time, however, the tears were of amazement and anger. He as good as told British newsmen on his arrival that he was entitled to conquer London and the Londoners should be grateful for it.

They weren't grateful and Mickey Rooney was the biggest bomb to hit the British capital since the last V-2 raid three years earlier. The news was cabled to Los Angeles. Danny was not pleased to hear it.

There is a tradition at the Palladium – on a star's last night at the theatre's number-one dressing room, he or she paints a message on the mirror for the person who will occupy that room the following week. It is a symbolic gesture and Danny got the message before he even saw the Palladium building for the first time.

Nothing about his arrival in town was terribly auspicious for him. Not only was there about as much advance interest at the box office as would have greeted the arrival of the North London Brass Band, but Val Parnell, the theatre's boss was doing little more than filling in after Rooney.

What few people realised was how tough a time it was for Danny. His involvement with the Committee for the First Amendment had done nothing to benefit his image with America's solid right-wing bloc, who were going around singing 'The Only Red We Want Is the Red We've Got – In the Good Old Red White and Blue'.

The UnAmerican Activities Committee was casting strange, unfriendly gazes in Danny's direction, and now Westbrook Pegler had chosen him as his principal candidate for vituperation. In his 'Diehard' column, Pegler was saying a lot about Danny, all of it extraordinarily unflattering – so unflattering that there were whispers around Hollywood that it would take a brave man indeed to give Kaye a job of any sort once his current contract obligations were exhausted.

London seemed the perfect escape channel. At least, an agent called Harry Foster seemed to think so. It was he who suggested Danny to Parnell, when he rang the American asking for suggestions to replace Rooney.

'What about Danny Kaye?' asked Foster.

'Is his act good?' asked Parnell.

'I don't know,' said Foster. 'But we've both seen his films.' Which says a very great deal about the position Kaye held in show business at the time. He was known as a prodigious film performer, but nobody any more seemed to remember how he could react on stage.

Parnell said he was willing to experiment. 'Find out how much he wants,' he told the American.

What Danny wanted was never disclosed at the time. But it certainly amounted to not much more than a bag of peanuts, compared with what he would command immediately afterwards.

For him it was an opportunity to get away from America at a time when he was beset with problems, Pegler and his insinuations on the one hand, and Sylvia and Sam Goldwyn on the other.

Anyone about to open in a strange theatre has two principal concerns – how sure he is of getting his act across to the equally strange audience, and whether he is going to be better than the man who was there before him.

Normally, the hardest thing is to improve on a sensational success. But suddenly, the difficulty changed course. It was going to be even harder to be good when his predecessor had been bad.

How much was Rooney's failure due to the audience being so difficult? He couldn't tell.

All this, of course, only served to emphasise the sense of insecurity Danny felt as he got ready for London, less sure than ever that London was ready for him.

In London itself in that grey February of 1948, he found himself plagued by both his doubts and his determination to rise above them. Unlike most performers of his kind, he was not worried about superstition – one of the worst of all, to rank with saying 'Macbeth' out loud in the auditorium and to whistling in the dressing room, was that you didn't go into the theatre and see another star at work. But he went to see Mickey Rooney and was terrified at the way this major star was failing to communicate.

Could that be his fate, too? He felt that all too easily it would.

He was there in the theatre for the Wednesday matinee that Rooney cancelled, pleading the affects of the vaccination he had been obliged to take before crossing the Atlantic. The theatre was empty of everyone except the Skyrockets Orchestra, which under its leader Woolfie Phillips was just about the best band a variety theatre had ever boasted.

Since they were there and being paid for being there, Danny suggested to Val Parnell that he use the available time, space and manpower for a full rehearsal.

Parnell may have decided it was an act bred out of total insecurity – verging, perhaps on hysteria, but there seemed no real reason to say no. So he said 'yes', and as a result of saying yes felt as though he were a child again in the business in which he had spent virtually his whole life. Watching Danny Kaye at work was an experience he had not known before. He was beguiled by the red-haired figure on stage. So was everyone else, from the pro- gramme sellers and the ushers to the stage hands and door keepers who also had been brought in for an afternoon's work only to find that they had, instead, become an audience for a show, the like of which none of them had witnessed before.

He really need not have been quite so anxious. The audiences who had already seen *Wonder Man* and *The Secret Life of Walter Mitty* were to provide him with a degree of affection that was almost bankable. He should have realised that the place was a different city, living in a different age, from the one he had played to on his last appearance in London – at the Dorchester. Admittedly, the

[78]

Palladium audience were not the society set who sat in starched shirts at the plush hotel. Not yet they weren't anyway.

But he might have noticed that the welcome seemed a lot warmer, as though the frustrations of post-war austerity were going to disappear, simply because a brash young American had come along and told them they were all going to be friends and enjoy themselves.

It still didn't guarantee a full house. News of the impromptu rehearsal should have telegraphed itself to the public, but then telecommunications in the late '40s were a lot slower than they are today. And anyway, there were nine days to go before Danny's own official opening. Mickey Rooney didn't go on stage at the Palladium again. He was replaced by the much respected British comedian Sid Field – who every night would point to the box where Danny sat at each performance and introduced him as the next guest star at the Palladium.

The box office didn't provide all the answers to his prayers. It wasn't all sold out in advance of the opening as he expected. In fact, his insecurity was such that Parnell sent men out to actually give away tickets – just in case the star he had come to regard as a 'find' would be put off by the sight of empty seats.

What neither Danny Kaye nor anybody else connected with show business on either side of the Atlantic could anticipate was what happened when he first went on that stage for the second half of a long variety bill and sang the opening notes of *Ballin' The Jack*.

Actually, it happened a few moments before. Danny was introduced by Ted Ray, at the time one of the most popular comedians on BBC radio. He said, simply, 'Ladies and gentleman, Danny Kaye' – and waited for the star, dressed simply in a brown sports jacket and lighter brown trousers, to appear.

Danny didn't.

He was introduced again.

He stood – glued to the floor in the wings. Charles Henry, the theatre's production manager, had seen that sort of thing happen before – and knew what to do. He quite literally pushed Danny on to the boards of the stage proper and into the glare of that so inhibiting spotlight. The audience was his as soon as he said a bunch of words, few entertainers had dared pronounce before: 'I'm shaking like a leaf. Honest.'

What no other performer had ever experienced before was happening to Danny Kaye visibly, palpably, in those earliest moments on stage.

The earliest moments were the hardest moments. If in Chicago and Boston he had extended a twenty-minute act into one lasting twice as long, here he was doing something no one had ever expected. It was like Jolson at the Winter Garden again. There was, it seemed, an electric current going from Danny's mouth and his expressive hands to every seat in the auditorium, from the boxes at the side to the front and back stalls, the royal circle and the gallery, too.

At 11 p.m., nearly an hour later than expected, he almost had to be helped off stage. The story was to be repeated for the next six weeks, but history was made that first night.

The newspapers told the story, probably none more graphically or accurately than the *Evening News*. Its critic wrote: 'It really seemed as if the roof must go sailing over Oxford Street at any moment.'

When that roof did go sailing over Oxford Street, the news spread like a contagious disease – which really was precisely what it was. Kaye fever had hit London with epidemic proportions and the only cure was a seat at the Palladium. Which was now easier said than arranged.

In the *Daily Express*, Leonard Mosley said: 'I think personally it's Danny Kaye's complete and utter craziness. He's a comic with a madman's mind, a sort of schizoid kid that appeals to the lunatic fringe in us all.'

It was a demonstration of the greatness of Danny's performance that language like that was intended to sound – and was effectively taken as such – as a compliment.

The *Daily Telegraph* was convinced that the month-long planned Kaye visit could be extended for a whole year, and the *Daily Herald* said that Danny was a 'superb artist'.

To the *Evening Standard*, he was nothing short of a 'superb sorcerer' who cast a spell on those around him. As for his act, it was 'a mosaic of calculated craziness that left the audience more breathless than the performer.'

Well, as we shall see, not quite.

The only doubt was expressed by the then influential but some-what stuffy *Manchester Guardian*.

It noted: 'One has seen many finer music-hall artists, and indeed, the supporting bill contained one comedian, Ted Ray, who is quite the equal of this renowned visitor. But it is the cinema and the cinema alone which makes the big reputations today.' The paper's critic did, however, allow himself a certain amount of praise:

'Yet another American film star came to London last night to vindicate in the flesh the vast reputation won in advance by his screen shadow. Mr Danny Kaye, a blithe, leggy young comedian, did not make the mistake of supposing that the Palladium audience, however curious to see him, would take a mere smile and a bow as evidence of his talent. He rushed rather to the other extreme and provided a turn lasting nearly an hour, in which he essayed almost every department of music hall art from fantastic (and very witty) dancing to imitations and sentimental ballads. In nearly all he was a success and was able to gloss over any thin patches with a display of debonair and coltish charm much to the taste of the audience.'

In the *Evening Standard*, Milton Shulman had no inhibitions at all. 'In the comedians' Hall of Fame,' he wrote, 'there are niches for the shuffling walk of Charlie Chaplin, the frozen face of Buster Keaton, the barbed wit of Beatrice Lillie, the youthful exhuberance of Harold Lloyd. There will undoubtedly be a niche as well for the "git, gat, giddle-de-reep" of Danny Kaye.'

What Mr Shulman, one of the most respected critics in Britain for more than 30 years, liked was the sheer versatility of Danny's act. 'In addition to a nimble tongue, he possesses a superb sense of parody.

'Thus he can successfully portray a Russian singer with hay fever, a coloratura who misses her top notes, a child at the zoo, a harassed GI, a baritone off pitch, a conga dancer and a cinema cowboy.'

Nobody now was having to give away seats. Any spare tickets the Tuesday morning after his opening were hungrily gobbled up by touts who the next morning were selling £1 seats for £20.

It was the same story not just once a night, but at every performance. This was the time of twice-a-night variety at the Palladium with shows at 6 o'clock and 8.30 and what Danny did in the first show, he generally did not do at the second. On Wednesdays and Thursdays, there were three shows for him, as there were for every Palladium performer. (The idea there was to provide matinees that coincided with early closing day both sides of the 'Water', the River Thames. Shops shut on Wednesday afternoons in South London in those days and on Thursdays in the North of the capital.)

It was an exhausting schedule. Danny would go on stage direct from his dressing room at every performance. Unlike other players, he didn't linger in the wings or chat with the technicians. He wasn't being unfriendly. He was simply exhausted.

In his book *Every Night at the London Palladium*, Patrick Pilton recalled some of the wheezes employed by people to get into the theatre – including two otherwise respectable old ladies who produced apparently valid tickets and were shown to their seats, only to be told shortly afterwards that two other people claimed the same spots.

Both sets of tickets plainly listed the same date, time and exact location of the seats. Except, as became apparent only after careful

[81]

scrutiny, the old ladies' seats were for the Prince of Wales Theatre, not the Palladium.

Princess Margaret, then only 17, went to the theatre and was plainly overwhelmed. She told her sister and went back to the Palladium with Princess Elizabeth, the future Queen, to see the show over again. Then she went again, and again, and again. On February 26, the King and Queen, their two daughters and the Duke of Edinburgh went too – sitting in the stalls because the Royal Box had already been booked.

It was the first time a reigning monarch had attended a variety show that was not strictly a command performance. And it was also the first time one had sat in the stalls, even if a group of ticket holders had had to be turfed out. (One of them replied to a request that he forego his ticket in return for another night, 'Not bloodly likely. The only person who will get me out of this seat is the King.' It took some persuasion to convince him that the King it was.)

The King smoked three cigarettes in the course of Danny's performance, but one of them went out while the royal hands were too busy wildly applauding the Kaye performance. Neither the King nor the Queen called out the scat nonsense lines that formed part of *Minnie the Moocher*, but both Princess Elizabeth and Princess Margaret did.

By this time, Danny had developed a routine which, unlike other theatre routines, always seemed real, original and fresh. Someone would shout from the wings and ask if he wanted a cup of tea. Then, near the end of his number, a girl called Olive would come out from behind bringing him a steaming cup of the brew he had told people out front that he found more refreshing than anything else. Olive's appearance always seemed to take him unawares. She came out the night the Royals were in the stalls. As always, she didn't say anything, she simply glided behind him. The King was intrigued by this. 'Danny,' he called from his seat, more willingly than whenever he made his Christmas Day broadcast or addressed his subjects at the launching of a ship, 'Danny . . . your tea, your tea.'

That was indeed the seal of approval. From that moment on, all Danny Kaye needed to convince people he was the Royal Family's favourite entertainer was a 'By Appointment' warrant to wear in his hat.

The King and Queen and their children paid him the supreme compliment by calling round at his dressing room after the performance.

The King asked him back to the Royal Box, which had been prepared for the party after the show.

'Would you like a drink?' the King asked him.

'Thank you, sir,' Danny replied.

'What would you like?' the King asked next.

'Well, Sir,' said Danny, 'Scotch would be nice.'

'Scotch?' retorted the King. 'God, we don't even get that at home.' But Danny got it that night.

He had extended his usually extended act by ten minutes because of the royal party.

The King even told Danny some of his favourite stories, which also gives an idea of the amazing Kaye feat of making people feel at home in his presence. The King suffered from an appalling stammer and the idea of public speaking was anathema to him. Telling jokes to a perfect stranger was something kept for very special occasions.

That visit, too, was following Princess Elizabeth's example. When she and Philip went to his dressing room, they asked him to join them for dinner. He pleaded a previous engagement. Later, he confessed there was nothing else in his diary. He was simply too scared to accept.

One of the reasons could, of course, have been that he didn't have Sylvia by his side. The trip had proved one thing: he could more than cope in front of an audience without the insurance policy of knowing that Sylvia was either in the wings or sitting on the piano stool at his side. But even if for the moment her head wasn't still on his shoulders, he still felt the wife-made man, singing her material, doing other songs and routines the way he had planned them with her. And he didn't have her at his side to bolster his confidence at moments like the meeting with royalty.

If there *was* a lack of confidence, it was anything but apparent on stage – where Danny went through the gamut of his repertoire, and then some. There was *The Lobby Number* and *Molly Malone*. He was the RAF pilot and the German orchestra conductor. He was Chinese and he was Italian. He was French (*Anatole of Paris*) and he was Russian (*Tchaikovsky*).

The only thing stopping him was the limits that existed to the energy of even Danny Kaye. The choice was his – get off while the going was still so very good and, in true show business tradition, leave them gasping for more or carry on until the exhaustion showed itself to the point of making him *have* to get off. He chose a middle course. When the sweat poured off his brow down his cheeks, and his heart was pumping almost alarmingly, he sat himself down on the edge of the stage and with his feet dangling down into the orchestra pit, he talked.

He smoked a cigarette and he called for that cup of tea. And he talked. It didn't seem like part of the act because he wasn't really talking to the audience. He was having a one-to-one conversation

[83]

with a single person in that audience. His genius was that every person in that huge 3,000-seat theatre was convinced that the single person was himself.

It was a new theatrical style – yet in the same tradition as Jolson's getting down on one knee or Will Rodgers twirling his lasso. No one had dared do it before. Because Danny Kaye did dare, more than the Palladium was his. Britain believed he was theirs – all of them, the people who were lucky enough to get seats for his performance, the ones who were trying and even those who knew they didn't stand a chance.

Buying a seat for the evening wasn't the same as getting a ticket for a Danny Kaye show. Seats were literally like gold, but it *was* possible to get into the theatre for one of the standing-room-only places. There were up to 300 of these at every performance. They were available every time Danny went on stage for the simple reason that they couldn't be booked in advance. Anyone wanting a standing place would have to come along to the theatre before a performance began and hope he or she could get one.

That, of course, was easier said than done. Sure the places were there – inside the theatre and outside. Kaye worshippers, for that was surely what they had now become, decided that the only way to be certain of a place was to queue for it. So they queued all night.

Bill Platt, now chief electrician at the Palladium and a junior on the electrics staff at the theatre, newly out of the Army, at the time of the Kaye onslaught on London, remembers it well: 'There was never anything quite like it. I don't remember ever seeing it before. We would leave the stage door at about 11 o'clock every night and there would be queues, of young girls mostly, all the way from the box office round the corner into Great Marlborough Street – people queueing for the following night's show. Now that was sensational. In my lifetime, I've never known anything like that happen.'

Getting tickets for *seats* for a Danny Kaye show was as much of a challenge as being able to get a pair of nylons or a packet of cigarettes.

Songwriter Don Black remembers the time Danny Kaye was in London for the pleasure it brought to his fairly poor home in Hackney, East London. His mother had just recovered from a dangerous operation. She had had a brain tumour removed. The family were so grateful to the surgeon that they wanted to buy him a present. He made it known that the only thing he wanted was the fulfilment of the one quest on which he had drawn a blank. The man who could remove brain tumours, couldn't conjure up two tickets for the London Palladium.

The young Don Black, then at school, wrote to Danny Kaye at

the Palladium to tell him of his predicament. Two tickets came by return of post. Today there is one leading figure in the entertainment industry who will not hear a word against Danny.

It was the same story every time Danny Kaye appeared. If it wasn't so genuine, it could be argued that the Royal Family had become part of the most sophisticated public relations stunt of all time – except, except. . . . Except that genuine was precisely what it was.

A seat at the London Palladium was indeed the right place to be and to be seen to be. But it wasn't like an evening at the opera or ballet for distinguished government visitors. People were begging to be part of a theatrical experience, the like of which no one had ever known before.

The Royal Family told their own friends of what it was like seeing Danny Kaye perform – even if those same people had not read all about it in the papers themselves. The Marquess of Milford Haven, nephew of Lord Mountbatten and cousin of Prince Philip – and as such, best man at his wedding three months before to Princess Elizabeth – queued up for a three-shilling seat in the gallery (but then went backstage afterwards to meet the star dubbed by all Britain's newspapers thereafter as The Wonder Man.)

Writing in the London *Daily Mail*, Maurice Wiltshire wondered about Danny's secret. And then he concluded: 'Even he scarcely knows it. You would get something of the effect in a dream. Kaye reduces life to the nonsense he feels underlines all of it.'

The really lucky ones were those who managed to get into *two* Danny Kaye performances. They were the ones who realised just how different he was from one show to the next. Even Danny himself wasn't sure what happened between performances.

'The gibberish comes out different every time, though I try to work to a kind of pattern. I don't know what the secret is. Maybe it's that I get the feeling over that the audience are invited to a party.'

It was a party that the whole world was getting to know about. Particularly the folks back home. Jacob Kaminsky was the pride of the neighbourhood in Brooklyn – Danny was now finally persuading him to move – not merely because he knew all about his son's success from his letters home, but because the papers were full of it, too.

'Danny Kaye, making his first personal appearance in London last night as the star attraction in the vaudeville bill at the Palladium, scored the greatest success seen in the British music hall in many years,' *The New York Times* had recorded and it tried to explain what everyone else had found simply inexplicable.

'It took two minutes of Mr Kaye's inspired craziness to explode the myth that the British audience had gone sour on personal appearances of Hollywood stars. On the stage for nearly an hour, he held the audience for every second of his act with something vital and entertaining.'

One of the most trying roles in this miraculous story of Danny Kaye at the Palladium was that of a member of the supporting bill. Each and every one of them knew they were there simply as a warm up for the star attraction – who was so much more than any other star who had ever appeared with them, even on that stage. Being a supporting act to Danny Kaye was like being a comedian at a strip show. He knew, and everyone else knew, that he was there simply to fill in time.

At the Palladium this time, the situation was even worse. People with tickets secure in their wallets didn't even bother to come along to the theatre until Danny was just about to go on.

One elderly comedian of whom it might have been said he had seen better days (although he probably hadn't) wasn't shy of saying how frustrated and angry he felt. One evening, however, his usual perfunctory applause was followed, as soon as he had retired to the wings, with what sounded like a thunder clap. It was a performer's dream and he was as puzzled as anyone. Danny hadn't slipped in on stage without anyone knowing. There he was at his side. No one else was there either. At last, he thought, his big moment had come. He was encouraged by the others standing next to him to take the bow they all agreed he had by now deserved. He jumped out on stage – only to discover the real reason for the overwhelming reception. Winston Churchill, then Leader of His Majesty's Opposition, had quietly slipped into the theatre, but remained at the back out of view until after the man's act had finished. He didn't want to upstage him. Little did he know until he took his seat in the front stalls, just how much upstaging he *had* been responsible for.

Kaye was, of course, as flattered by the great statesman's attention as he was by the visit from Their Majesties and the Princesses. What he didn't realise at the time was that Churchill, admiring though he was of Danny's performance, had been studying technique. He saw his own appearances on the platforms of the world as a kind of showmanship – a charge levelled by his enemies for years, but one that was stoutly and genuinely denied by his supporters as well as by himself. But he confessed to Danny that he was in the theatre as a sympathetic soulmate.

Later, he went round to the star's dressing room and explained just how closely he had been watching what Danny had been doing.

'That little business you did before,' said the former war leader who had been haranging 'audiences' for 50 years and was himself then 73 years old. Danny wasn't sure what he meant until he pointed out the routine when for a brief moment he had turned his back on the audience, paused – and then managed to get across his next words with much greater emphasis.

'It was well done,' said Churchill, puffing his cigar, and offering one to Danny who said no. 'It's a good trick,' he added. 'I first used it myself on a speaking tour of Canada 20 years ago.'

Danny, of course, knew it had been a good trick. But he only wanted to use it on stage – a fact that tended to please Churchill. 'Young man,' he told him, 'you have a tremendous grip on a crowd. You would make a formidable adversary in politics.'

No one in London was regarding Kaye as a formidable adversary – although Danny did tell him about the time he got President Roosevelt to bark like a dog.

They seemed to get on like a couple of guests at dinner at 10 Downing Street. The photographers who clustered around them certainly thought so – although Danny said he was a little put out by the attention they were paying the old man. 'Hey,' he shouted to them, 'come back here. I'm the star of this show – and a guest in the country besides.' Churchill was not unamused.

The entertainer's links with the Royal Family continued apace. As the weeks went on, his inhibitions with the great of the land melted somewhat. When he was invited to an after-show party that the younger Royals were attending he accepted. From midnight until five in the morning, he and Princess Margaret were singing duets together. The princess only agreed to call for her mink coat and go home when her brother-in-law, the Duke of Edinburgh pointed out that protocol was such that nobody could leave until she had gone, too. And there may be some people present who weren't quite as keen to sing with Danny Kaye until his next show that evening. That is debatable. What is not debatable is that from that time on, Danny and the princess became firm friends.

Danny was telling British newspaper readers not to over-estimate him – which probably, as in most other cases of top entertainers invited to be modest about themselves, really meant nothing of the kind.

In an article supposedly written by him for the London *News Chronicle*, the most intelligent popular paper of the day, he declared (literally): 'I am not a sociologist – economist – statistician-politicianbiophysicistlaryngologist or even a ground nuts expert.' (It was the age of the calamitous if brave British government attempt to make a fortune by growing peanuts in East Africa. Danny was as aware of its failure as anyone else.)

'I'll match my ignorance with any man.'

What he had been good at was sizing up his audience. He knew he shouldn't make the mistakes he made the last occasion he was in Britain.

'This time, I read in a book and learned that there were 44,790,485 people on the island. That's a lot of people. I figured if I could get a sizeable crowd of them together we might go places.'

Then he dismissed the ideas he had heard about British people being reserved. 'From my experience, I would like to know what happens when they let themselves go. Do they pick up the island and swing it around their heads?

'I haven't any fancy theories about humour, and the quickest way to put an audience to sleep is to give them the applied psychology of laughter. But in my trade you either learn how to sense the mood of people who are looking at you, saying "show me", or you go home.'

Danny was not going home for that four weeks he was booked into the Palladium. In fact, he was not going home for a lot longer. His stay was extended by another fortnight – since the Palladium was not able to take that newspaperman's advice and work things out for all concerned for him to stay there for a year. Suffice it to say, no one had ever known anything like it.

The magnetism that was Danny Kaye extended itself in other ways, and in other ways Danny was showing a kind of generosity that had not always before seemed apparent. It was as though he was so grateful for success that nothing was going to stop him showing that gratitude – for he recognised that nothing, but nothing, that had gone before was quite as important as this.

When a popular British radio comedian called Reg Dixon appeared on stage in the provinces singing the signature tune which he had composed himself, *Confidentially*, Danny rang him personally to ask if he would mind if he himself recorded it.

Of course, Reg Dixon was enormously flattered, not only that Danny wanted to sing his tune, but that he considered it important enough to ring him up to ask permission to do so. The result was that people at home in Britain – who would now buy absolutely anything that Danny chose to put on wax – heard him singing:

'Confidentially, I like to talk
Confidentially, with a girl like you.'

He sang it at the Palladium and he now sang it in people's homes, along with all the more usual Kaye standards. It suited perfectly, Danny's light but extraordinarily tuneful and soothing voice.

Then there was the British toy manufacturer who gave Danny an expensive doll – one of the few luxury toys being made in Britain at the time – for Dena. Danny asked him if he minded his not accepting it, because Dena had plenty of toys and he thought it would be much nicer if it were given to poor children. That impressed people, too – particularly those who had been expressing for years their dismay at how the really nice things went free to the very people who usually could afford to buy them.

Perhaps most important for people in his business, Danny had a rapport with newspapermen in Britain – a breed of whom he had been as suspicious as they had been of him. The same reporters who had been so anxious about him at first, later became regular visitors. There was no side between them and the star. He knew them all by name, and there was a bottle of whisky ready to pour for them every time they came. None was on better terms with Danny than the doyen of British theatrical writers, Hannen Swaffer, who looked like something out of a novel by Dickens.

He wore a black suit flaked with white – the ashes dropping from the ever-present cigarette which was taken out only when replaced by a new one. But he knew more about theatre than practically any other man in Britain.

'My boy,' Swaffer told him. 'I have been going to the music halls for fifty-odd years and I have never seen a greater personal triumph.' It was the judgement of an expert which had to be respected. Except that he added: 'Mind you, you don't make me laugh.'

He had, however, made sufficient people laugh for him to be virtually an institution in Britain. That other institution, Madame Tussauds thought so, too – and took advantage of Danny's presence in the capital by taking his measurements for a wax model and by asking him for an old suit he could let them have to dress it in.

The Archbishop of Canterbury, Dr Geoffrey Fisher, met Danny, too – and told him that he also used to be a funny man, which was not part of the curriculum vitae normally recorded for the Primate of All England.

Danny was introduced to him outside the House of Lords. An MP had shown him around the neighbouring House of Commons. Dr Fisher plainly was quite impressed with the young American – until, that is, he stepped out in front of the car carrying the MP and his guest.

'Young man,' said the Archbishop, shaken but not stirred by having his life so very nearly in the hands of an American comedian, 'you very nearly achieved some real fame.'

Most people believed, however, that he really had achieved that fame. And more than that. Having been courted by the highest in the land, it was not unreasonable that the highest Americans in the land would pay him just as much court.

Lewis Douglas, the United States Ambassador who wore a black eye patch – covering the result of a mishap with a fishing hook in a Scottish stream – told him: 'You are a better ambassador of goodwill to Britain than all the sedate personalities or officials.'

Walking past the Palladium box office in Argyle Street was like standing outside Harrods at sale time. One couple queued for 26 hours when they heard that, contrary to expectations, there just happened to be the possibility of a few vacant seats.

And so it went on. The Grand Order of Water Rats, British Variety's number-one fraternal organisation, inducted him into membership, which meant that he was now regarded as being one of the theatre's greats.

The Student's Union at the London School of Economics, then as now, not the least iconoclastic group of individuals in Britain, elected Danny their honorary president.

And he did a few unorthodox things, too. He became friends with doctors and surgeons in Britain as he had at home in America. And just as at home, he persuaded one of them to allow him to view an operation in practice. It wasn't as easy in England as it had been in the States. The hospitals were in the first flush of government control as part of the National Health Service, so questions were asked in Parliament about Mr Kaye's visit. The ministerial answers seemed to indicate that something had to be said for international goodwill.

The most important Danny Kaye events were still, however, happening on the stage of the Palladium. Like the time he borrowed the orchestra conductor's baton – and inadvertently broke it. He didn't know it at the time, but it was the start of a whole new career for him. Suddenly, in the course of his variety act he had discovered the almost aphrodisiac qualities of the power a conductor had over an orchestra, even when clowning around.

What does a conductor do when he breaks his baton? Frankly, he looks silly. Danny decided to look silly and make people enjoy laughing at him being so ridiculous. He pretended to stab himself with the jagged ends of the sticks. Anybody else doing that on stage would probably make people search for their watches or politely stifle a yawn or two with their hands. Danny had them rolling around in agony.

His pianist Sammy Prager, who was with Danny at every single performance, wasn't slow on the uptake and struck up something from grand opera. Danny appreciated that. It was the kind of timing that he demanded of people whom he recognised were as important to his act as he was himself.

He told his audience that night that at last he was going to find out how an opera star could sing at the top of his voice for 45 minutes after supposedly being stabbed to death.

Since everybody else had sometime or other wondered the same thing – to say nothing of the fact that by now they laughed at whatever Danny wished to dish up for them; grand opera or grand larceny of a nursery rhyme – they collapsed once more.

Later, he realised the value of those particular lines. The next morning, Boosey and Hawkes, suppliers of musical instruments to the profession, had an order for 100 new batons – one for the orchestra leader to replace the stick that had been broken and the rest so that he could use them in his act. That was going to be one piece of business – or *schtick* as show business would get to call it – that *would* be repeated.

But he did continue to experiment. There was, for instance, the song that he had heard on his car radio in California a very short time before leaving for London. It sounded just the sort of relaxed, easy-listening that was forming as important a part of his musical repertoire now as his scat singing and his dialect pieces always had been.

He asked Eddie Dukoff to get hold of it for him. In London, he sang it one night in a Hillbilly style – it was before the days of Country and Western ⌐ and thought it was no more than OK. The next evening, he sang it straight and the applause rocked the Palladium chandeliers. The song was *Candy Kisses* (the kind that were wrapped in paper). The reaction convinced him that this was a number to record, even though some of the more typical Kaye songs were still not being waxed. The result was that the song became one of his greatest hits.

Finally, the six weeks were up. As on all other nights, the audience there on his last night packed the Palladium from front to back, upstairs and down for as much as the London County Council's fire regulations would allow.

What was scheduled to be an hour's performance, and which practically everyone knew would be two hours and finish at around 11 o'clock, went on until well past midnight – which in the London of 1948 presented innumerable problems. Not simply that the orchestra and the doormen and practically everyone else were on overtime, but much more significantly, there were such things as last buses and trains. Few had come to the theatre by car in those days, but no one seemed to mind.

Not a seat was unused from the moment he first appeared on stage that night until the house lights came on, signalling it was all over.

The atmosphere all night would normally have been called electric – except that it was that every time he appeared behind the

Palladium footlights. Now the electricity was supercharged and, as far as anyone could gather, was supplied by some kind of nuclear energy that must have been discovered at about the same time as the atom bomb tests were held at Bikini Atol a couple of years before.

As the evening wore on – or drifted away, for no one seemed to notice anything else happen – Danny looked at his own watch and decided it was time to draw attention to the fact that it was now half past eleven.

'Does anyone want to go home?' he called. 'No,' came the answer, as well orchestrated as one of the choruses in *Minnie the Moocher*.

'And your last buses and tubes?' 'We'll walk,' someone called – and once more the place collapsed. It was encore time – but Danny had given no impression of ever expecting to leave, let alone wanting to go.

'What time it it?' he asked.

'Early,' shouted someone in the balcony, to huge applause from everyone else.

That night of March 13, 1948, he had gone through all his usual routines, seemingly leaving nothing out. 'I'll stay for as long as I can make an intelligible noise,' he said and then explained to his audience that his 'pipes' were going. The public on this occasion wouldn't have cared if he had them relagged there and then. They wanted to hear him. It was a perfect example of that incredible force which distinguishes a great star from an unusually talented performer. There are opera singers whose voices have been better who can still hold audiences in a stupified state, while others with perfectly tuned larynxes that might sound splendid on record, can't keep the attention of six people in an empty room.

Long past midnight, the audience itself had taken over as Danny stood alone on stage, wondering what had happened. A few chords of 'For He's A Jolly Good Fellow' from the front of the house were taken up behind and within seconds, the whole auditorium was singing it to their hero. When they had finished with that, they followed on with 'Auld Lang Syne'. Danny stood, bowed to his public and then found himself bending low, shaking hands seemingly with all 3,000 people in the theatre at once.

The *Sunday Express* noted that in the six weeks he had been at the theatre, he was 'the most sensationally successful single performer to appear in London in living memory'.

A quarter of a million people had been to see his show. In today's television terms, the figure loses some of its impact. But as a response to a live show, it was nothing less than staggering – simply because if Danny had wanted to, he really could have gone on for that year.

People saw all kinds of messages in what Danny had achieved.

The Conservative *Daily Graphic* was convinced that he was a great demonstration of private enterprise at work, something to counter the effects of what they saw as the dreadful Labour Government.

'Danny Kaye could not compel his enthusiastic audiences to spend their money on seeing him. He had to deliver the goods. He had to attract the buyers by the quality of his performance. It was a perfect example of free enterprise in action – the willing buyer meeting the willing seller.'

Politics was not what Danny Kaye was selling now. What he *had* sold was himself and everyone seemed to be grateful. London hadn't known a Danny Kaye before. And Danny Kaye had never known a London. It was a show business phenomenon. Something for the history books.

THE INSPECTOR GENERAL

LONDON MADE AS INDELIBLE AN IMPRESSION ON DANNY KAYE AS Danny Kaye made on London. He still talks about those heady days of 1948 and Londoners still talk about the effect he had on them.

From the night of that last show onwards, Danny has been the yardstick by which every other entertainer's performance at the Palladium has been measured.

He could be forgiven for flying into the then tiny Los Angeles Airport in March 1948 feeling very pleased with himself indeed. If there were any problems on his mind, they were all connected with his life at home, the place where he was still a star, but where he had to take note of what other people wanted, as he did in a theatre. There was Dena whom he was extremely anxious to get back to . . . and there was Sylvia. It was time, he decided, to end the separation. And he did. As Sylvia said, 'He just came home.'

That doesn't mean it was the totally happy ending to the story of their break up. They were in the house together again, but rumours have persisted for the past 37 years that their marriage has been hardly a happy one. It was not to be the last parting of the ways.

Meanwhile, the story of the Palladium triumph was the talk of the town – and the offers started tumbling in once more. There was the first film at Warner Brothers to be made – to be based on Gogol's story *The Government Inspector*, although the studio hadn't got round to calling it anything yet – and one title being banded about was *Happy Times* – after a song in the movie which subsequently became Danny's big hit of 1949.

Since Danny and Sylvia *were* back together again and their friend John Green was in charge of the music, the times seemed happy indeed. And then there were the other offers that he was having to think about – like the notion that he should play Frosch, the drunken jailer in *Die Fledermaus*. He wanted to do that, but the time just couldn't be found.

For the moment, however, he had to reflect on public reaction to another of his projects. It wasn't exactly like the Palladium – to say

[94]

the least. *A Song Is Born* really ought not to have been born at all. Cynics who knew anything about the film industry could be excused for thinking that it had all the stamps about it of a movie made for one reason only – fulfilling a contract.

The picture was innocent enough, but people didn't want their Danny Kaye innocent. They wanted to laugh at him, to be impressed by the aggressive Kaye style, to fall about as they marvelled at the tongue twisting through routines they knew no one else could do. Instead, they saw a film that was innocent – and one they had seen before, in fact only six years before. Only then it had been called *Ball Of Fire*.

In 1942, Howard Hawks had directed Gary Cooper in a film about a professor who falls in love with an uneducated girl (Barbara Stanwyck), although at first he is more in love with the way she talks than the way she moves her hips.

Now in 1948, Howard Hawks directed Danny Kaye in a film about a professor who falls in love with an uneducated girl (Virginia Mayo), although at first he is more in love with the way she sings popular songs than the way she. . . .

Both films had the professor living with a group of other professors, all much older and even less worldly than he. Both seem to have used the identical set for the large house where they lived and studied – words in *Ball Of Fire*, music in *A Song Is Born*.

Ball Of Fire was notable because it was one of the earliest pieces of work by the man who has since become regarded as probably the greatest writer of comedy in Hollywood history, Billy Wilder, who wrote the screenplay with Charles Brackett. Sam Goldwyn rightly believed that the film was one he could be proud of – even if there were discernible similarities to the Snow White story.

What possessed him to remake it, and as a Danny Kaye vehicle, is anyone's guess. He didn't have Wilder this time – Wilder was to tell me that he always regards it as a mistake to try to remake something that had proved so successful in a former incarnation – but chose Harry Tugend to provide a pancake-like script that took no account of the distinctive Kaye talent.

Interestingly enough, Gregg Toland was cameraman on both pictures. Alfred Newman was in charge of music on the first film – which was not a musical. His brother Emil had the role in the second, which was. In fact, it was the music that did save the movie. It seemed as though anyone who had ever beaten a drum or tooted a horn was there to see the somewhat indifferent songs born in this picture – including Louis Armstrong, Benny Goodman, Charlie Barnet, Lionel Hampton and Tommy Dorsey.

Danny hoped for more from Warner Brothers and what was now going to be called *The Inspector General*.

[95]

The original Gogol play had been written in 1836, an extra-orinarily brave thing to do in a country which was no more free as far as speech was concerned then than it would be a century or more later.

Danny saw that it wasn't going to be easy. 'The whole problem,' he said at the time, 'is to integrate the musical numbers with the story. The balance must be held just right. And I like to use the music to help the story and actually make plot points in song, just as I like the plot to make the numbers seem inevitable.'

Jack Warner took Danny Kaye under his wing as everyone knew that he would, if only because of what he represented, booty extracted from the competitor he admired – and resented because he admired him so.

There was the select treatment that Warner allowed only for stars whom he regarded as particularly important at a certain time. Bette Davis would never be allowed into his private dining room. Nor would Errol Flynn (apart, that is, from times when the mogul had distinguished guests to impress – like Albert Einstein to whom he said, 'I have a theory on relatives, too – don't hire 'em' or Madame Chiang Kai-Shek, the Chinese leader who made him remember, he said, 'It's time I took in my laundry'.)

He didn't like stars in the dining room because it prevented his talking about them, or more important, discussing money. But Danny Kaye and the acquisition of same was something to show off.

More than that, he took him home with him – or rather invited him to dinner. Usually, the Warner dinner parties were moments to savour. Jack's own private chef was brought in to cook meals that appealed to a gourmet pallet, served off the finest china, eaten with the most expensive silverware. And most important of all, Jack Warner held court – telling the most outrageous jokes, using the most obscene language and hearing everyone dutifully laugh, scream and clap wildly.

That wasn't what happened the night Danny and Sylvia went along to the house at Angelo Drive. Bill Orr, later to be head of production at the Warners' studio and Jack's son-in-law (The Son-in-law Also Rises dictum didn't only apply to MGM) was there that night.

'It was the most incredible experience,' he told me. What made it so incredible was Danny Kaye. For Danny got up to make a speech – and then proceeded to imitate every single person who had spoken before him.

Among them was Laurence Olivier.

'He was so brilliant that if you shut your eyes you would imagine it really was a replay of what happened before. It was as though a

[96]

Left: The Danny Kaye most of his fans would like to remember.
NATIONAL FILM ARCHIVE, LONDON

Below: The *Wonder Man* as opera singer. The words weren't right, but it sounded a lot better like that.
NATIONAL FILM ARCHIVE, LONDON

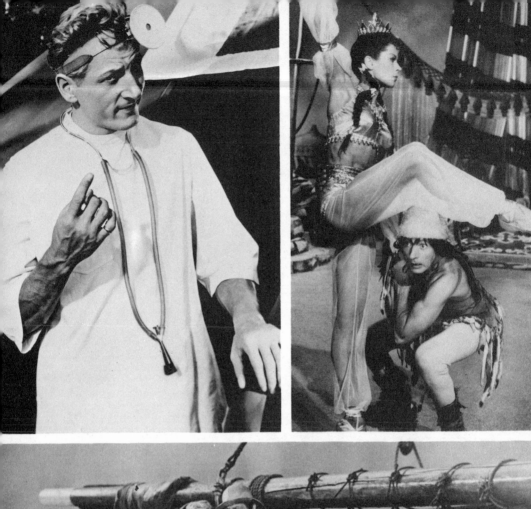

Above: With writer-directors Norman
Panama and Mel Frank on the set of
Knock On Wood. NATIONAL FILM
ARCHIVE, LONDON

Top left: A real Walter Mitty pose this
– except that it was in *Up In Arms*.
But he would have liked to have been
called Doctor Kaye. NATIONAL FILM
ARCHIVE, LONDON

Top right: His ballet wasn't bad either
– in *Knock On Wood*. NATIONAL FILM
ARCHIVE, LONDON

Bottom left: Walter Mitty, the sea
captain. He's told Virginia Mayo not to
worry. His arm is only broken.
NATIONAL FILM ARCHIVE, LONDON

Right: Only Danny Kaye could sound
and look as much like a mad Russian
conductor as in this episode in
The Secret Life Of Walter Mitty.
NATIONAL FILM ARCHIVE, LONDON

Top left: This is the story of Minnie
the Moocher. It was enough just to
look at him. BBC HULTON PICTURE
LIBRARY

Top right: Why should he keep his
feet on the ground? In 1947, Danny
Kaye seemed to do it all with his
hands – and his mouth. BBC HULTON
PICTURE LIBRARY

Bottom left: Never happier than with
the greats of music. This was with
Artur Rubinstein at the Royal Albert
Hall. BBC HULTON PICTURE LIBRARY

Right: Squadron Leader Walter Mitty
– with a little persuasion from Virginia
Mayo not to take his day dream too
seriously. NATIONAL FILM ARCHIVE,
LONDON

Top left: Danny as daddy, with Dena and Sylvia. Music seemed to be in the blood. NATIONAL FILM ARCHIVE, LONDON

Bottom left: An early political stand. With Paul Henreid, Lauren Bacall and Humphrey Bogart on their arrival at Washington Airport as part of the Committee for the First Amendment delegation, protesting against the House of UnAmerican Activities Committee's probe of alleged Communism in Hollywood. BBC HULTON PICTURE LIBRARY

Right: With Glynis Johns, an ageing Court Jester. NATIONAL FILM ARCHIVE, LONDON

Below: With Kurt Jurgens and Nicole Maurey in *Me And The Colonel*. It was Danny's first serious role. NATIONAL FILM ARCHIVE, LONDON

Left: Socking it to 'em – at his favourite theatre, the London Palladium. BBC HULTON PICTURE LIBRARY

Below: With Bud Flanagan and Chesney Allen on the stage of the London Palladium at the 1948 Royal Command Performance. BBC HULTON PICTURE LIBRARY

tape recorder had been switched on.' Except that no tape recorder could have made it sound so funny as well as so real. 'To my mind, he was never so funny or drole on stage or on the screen. Quite marvellous. Nobody had ever seen him do that sort of thing before.'

In the studios, the Kayes' relationship with Messrs Warner was somewhat more fraught. As Bill Orr remembers, 'Danny and Sylvia gave us a lot of problems – particularly with Sylvia, who did most of the talking at our meetings. The script was by Philip Rapp and Harry Kurnitz, who were the best, but Sylvia kept saying that they weren't satisfied and we'd have to go to William Morris because we needed to get an extension of the start date. It never seemed to work out.'

There were at least three or four versions of the script presented, before Orr, on behalf of Warner Brothers, felt he had enough.

He told the giant agency: 'We are ourselves satisfied and want to start. In our opinion, the changes are not getting any better.'

It was now a complicated situation. Danny and Sylvia were ready to go too – but with the last script they presented and which Warners didn't like. There were contractual reasons why the film had to start immediately – or else the Kayes and everyone else would be on excessive overtime. Now it was Warner Brothers who wanted an extension – but on their terms.

Finally, terms *were* arranged by virtue of a magnificent piece of skullduggery for which Mr Orr is still justly proud.

Sitting in his office, Steve Trilling, who was Jack Warner's number-two in the studio (but best known as his hatchet man – Warner always deputed the job of sacking executives to Trilling; the boss would go away and everyone knew a firing was in the wind, until someone else was given the job . . . of firing Trilling himself) was anxiously trying to find a way of resolving the problem. It was Orr who thought he had the answer.

What inspired him was seeing the couple plan a routine involving three mirrors. It was highly complex, and involved a great deal of double photography. He knew that neither Danny nor Sylvia was ready for work on that scene.

'Right,' he told them, 'we'll start on Monday – with the triple mirror scene.' That got him his six-weeks extension. 'And it was probably the highlight of my career.'

Orr, too, was struck by how much Sylvia was the one who appeared to take the decisions – and if not to take them, then to convey them to studio executives or to other people who could make life difficult for them.

'She would be the front person who would do the complaining,' he recalled. 'Danny would always be the very attractive and cute one who would agree that he wasn't happy with things, but Sylvia would know all about it . . . that sort of thing.

'But once the script had been formed and he was launched, he did the work.'

Whatever he did at this stage, however, seemed to merit the approval of Jack Warner, which was no usual thing. When Danny told the boss he needed a week off, Jack ruminated and came to the wholly reasonable if unexpected decision that giving Kaye the time could mean very valuable publicity for the studio in general and for *The Inspector General* in particular.

The reason was that Danny was going back to London. And this time, the presence of the King and Queen was not entirely coincidental. Once more he was going back to the Palladium, and this time he was to go at the end of a bill containing a number of other entertainers. The difference was that now, the bill was longer, the other entertainers were a lot more important and he would be expected to entertain for a somewhat shorter period. If the other entertainers were more important, the same could also be said for the audience. For this was the Royal Variety Performance and Danny was being invited to appear in the undisputed role of star of stars. It was, of course, the time for more worry – except that he did have the comfort of knowing that Sylvia would be there with him, sitting on the plane with him, working over his material with him in their hotel room and, most significantly of all, waiting in the wings, watching every movement, willing him to be brilliant.

It was to be an evening, on the whole, of veterans of variety. Bud Flanagan was heading the Crazy Gang of his old pals, Nervo and Knox and Naughton and Gold, which meant that a night of mayhem could be expected. With them would be some performers who appeared in music halls when a seat at that kind of theatre meant also swigging a glass of beer and smoking a pipe or cigar – magic names in their way like Nellie Wallace, Talbot O'Farrell, Ella Shields, G. H. Elliott and Randolph Sutton, some of them stars before the Kaiser moved into Belgium in 1914. But Danny wasn't the youngest performer. That distinction went to a pretty 13-year-old in pigtails named Julie Andrews.

The papers in London were agog that Danny's reappearance at the Palladium had cost his (or rather the brothers Warners') studio £15,000 or $60,000, as the dollar rate then was. Today that sum would barely cover the catering bill in the studio commissary for one lunch time.

Rehearsal time was an excuse for a Danny Kaye performance Charles Henry hadn't expected. Henry Hall, one of BBC radio's top orchestra leaders, was taking the entire cast through his interpretation of *There's No Business Like Show Business*, Irving Berlin's paean to the theatre, a tune which then was barely two years old, but which was already regarded as the trade's international anthem.

Standing in the midst of the assorted British variety talent assembled for the occasion, Danny, in the floppy khaki hat which a few years later would be a trade mark, did something shocking and previously unheard of.

He said he didn't like the way Mr Hall was conducting his orchestra. Since the said Mr Hall was known as a musician with whom one did not trifle – the very outfit he wore in the pit, immaculate tail coat, stiff white shirt front, inspired a respect mingled with not a little fear – it was a brave, not to say foolhardy or rude thing to do.

Even worse was what Danny did. He stepped down into the pit, borrowed Mr Hall's baton and conducted the orchestra himself the way he wanted to hear the tune played.

The conductor didn't like it very much and there were a few mumbles from other members of the cast – that here was an American upstart behaving in a rather unprofessional way in the holy of holies, the greatest variety theatre in the world. But none of them could deny that whatever might happen on the evening itself, that rehearsal alone was a great show biz occasion. None of them would have known that they were part of a Kaye routine which before very long would be as important to and as identified with Kaye as *Tchaikovsky* or any of his scat songs.

The invitation to come to the show caught many English people by surprise, and with delight. As soon as his prospective appearance was announced, the box office was inundated with requests for tickets. One man offered £100 for a single seat in the stalls – now a customary price to pay but at the time an incredible amount.

Danny himself was not at all surprised to be asked. The invitation had first been mentioned on the evening the King and Queen called at the star dressing room. Val Parnell informed them he intended to ask Kaye to star. 'That would be very nice,' said Queen Elizabeth (now the Queen Mother) 'I think we could stand it,' said the Duke of Edinburgh – to which Danny added: 'I would crawl on my hands and knees to come.'

He didn't have to do anything of the kind, although officials at London Airport, now Heathrow, said they had never known a welcoming crowd like it.

The variety business as a whole welcomed him. He was a marvellous advertisement for the stage. Like every other distinguished entertainer from abroad, Danny was invited on to the BBC's prestige interview programme *In Town Tonight*. In those days, the programme was live – and scripted. It began with the sound of flower girls on the steps of Eros in Picadilly Circus (which also gives some idea how long ago 1948 was) and the cry of 'Stop'. Once more, the announcer intoned, the sound of London traffic was halted to find out who was *In Town Tonight*.

That was not the sort of show to impress Danny Kaye. Once he had satisfied himself of the fact, the BBC were to be less than pleased they had invited him in the first place.

It was sabotage. A guest on *In Town Tonight* was expected to go through his paces as the script said. But Danny Kaye wasn't going to do that. Nor was he going to allow anyone else to go through their paces either. He made faces at a bird imitator who was struggling to tell the world why a sparrow sounded different from a robin. It was quite unpardonable if you were a bird imitator, but the best kind of entertainment in the world if you were sitting behind the window of the control booth with him.

When motor magnate Sir William Rootes was being interviewed about the state of the British economy and that week's Motor Show, Danny took a powder compact from one of the BBC girls and started dabbing his face, so that the poor industrialist didn't know if he were talking about cars or carrots.

As Danny waited his turn, he sat himself down at the studio piano, which he wasn't supposed to do at all. Then he begged a cough drop (it was the time of sweet rationing and that was the only confectionery off the ration) from a member of the Luton Girls Choir, who were 'on the bill' too.

When it was his own turn to go on at last, he feigned sudden nervousness. Until two seconds before he was due to go on the air, he pretended to be too frightened to enter the studio. Then he grabbed a bunch of scripts from the presenter and the engineers and proceeded to pretend he and the papers were shaking with fear.

The so-called interview over, he proceeded to read the announcer's closing lines, together with all the printed fade-out cues that weren't meant to be read at all.

Writing in *Picture Post*, Ronald Frankau gave the impression that everyone was more grateful for the Kaye performance than the sweat on interviewer John Ellison's brow seemed to indicate.

Said Mr Frankau, himself a radio comic of some note: 'He has immense moral courage, complete self confidence, entire lack of inhibition and a happy-making memory for faces and names. And yet he is entirely free from conceit – and never, even under most trying and tiring circumstances (and he is being incessantly mobbed, asked questions, telephoned to, surrounded and heckled) is he irritable or unkind. But he is working. One feels that he has said to himself. "I am a servant of the public. They – and nobody else – pay me. I will do my job." He is doing his job all the time.'

They were generous words indeed from a writer who said he didn't want to be thought a sycophant. So much so did he not want to be thought one, that he forgot to ask for Danny's autograph – which he wanted for a child, of course.

All this was by way of warm-up for the show itself. Once more, the eyes of America were on what their new 'Ambassador' would do. *The New York Times* was ecstatic that he fulfilled his task admirably. 'Kaye Stops Show For British Rulers,' headlined their story. 'American comedian scores greatest hit at Command Performance in London.'

Neither the *Times's* writer nor anyone else there that night was wrong. It was a triumph indeed at the hardest show any entertainer could ever have been asked to perform. The five girls who, during the evening, fainted from excitement proved that. They were just five among the 10,000 people who had started begging for tickets once Danny's name was announced and just five of the 2,800 who managed to get in to raise a then record of £14,000 for the Variety Artistes' Benevolent Fund.

No one doubted that it was more Danny's evening than it was the Royal Family's. The King and everyone else in the Royal Box joined in the choruses of *Minnie the Moocher* – by now to have done otherwise would have been roughly equivalent of Danny failing to stand for *God Save The King*. Prince Philip and Ambassador Lewis Douglas, whose role seemed to be to pay court to his country's most prestigious export, were there. Probably the most devoted fan in the whole theatre was Princess Margaret. She sang, she pointed, she called out. Her sister Princess Elizabeth was the only member of the family away. She was awaiting the birth of Prince Charles.

Everyone loved Danny, it seemed. When he sang *Underneath The Arches*, it was roughly the equivalent of his handing over his ration book and buying ten penn'orth of fish and chips.

The only person disappointed with what Danny did that night was Sylvia – and, even if inadvertently, she let the whole world know about it.

Instead of cheering him on from those wings as he hoped, Sylvia had been feeling less than pleased with the way it all went. Minute by minute she counted up the things he failed to do, mentally criticising his timing, his choice of material, his reaction to the audience, and all the time looking anxiously towards the royal box.

Finally, when he came off stage, she rushed with him to his dressing room. 'You loused up that one,' she said. Even if Danny didn't take particular note of that sage judgement, a reporter who had been sitting in an alcove of the dressing room, waiting for Danny to take off his make-up and give him an interview, did.

That was to far, in performing her duties as Danny's number-one critic. It was a time for resolutions, and the principal one she was making now was never to criticise her husband again – until she had made sure there were no reporters present to record the scene.

If Danny *had* 'loused up' that show, Sylvia appears to have been the only one to have noticed it. Again, it was his performance that was regarded as the sensation of the night. Not for nothing, most people seemed to think, had Mr Kaye been chosen to top the bill for the King and Queen.

Later the Kayes were presented to the royal guests. The Queen told Sylvia: 'Tell your husband how much we enjoyed seeing him again.' He didn't need to be told.

Just a few people pretended not to be impressed. London University students burned a Danny Kaye effigy on their Guy Fawkes bonfire, a tribute indeed, especially since Winston Churchill was set alight too.

The Variety Artistes' Federation complained. They didn't object to Churchill being consigned to the flames, but they thought it insulting to the man now accepted as the greatest member of their profession alive, especially one who 'at great cost to himself travelled 12,000 miles just to help our poor and distressed.' That was overdoing it some. A 'command' to appear at the show was just about the highest honour any artist could possibly get.

The students compromised – and burned the body of their effigy but left his head alone. The University's rag committee went one stage further. They sent Danny a rhyming telegram:

OUR LOVE FOR YOU IS BURNING TRUE
TONIGHT IT WILL CONSUME YOU
BUT HAVE NO FEAR THE IDEA HERE
IS NOTHING BUT TO BOOST YOU.

Danny was in Paris at the time of the burning, but sent a message of support, nevertheless, to those who thought of him. Meanwhile, he *had* managed to see another model of himself. He unveiled the one that had been made at Madame Tussauds since his last trip to town.

London over for the time being, he and Sylvia flew back to Hollywood and *The Inspector General*.

As John Green recalls it: '*The Inspector General* was not a happy time.' But he says 'I loved it'. Not least of all the music he wrote. The score Green produced for Danny's 'busy eater' routine in which he appeared to consume a thousand dishes placed before him was indeed monumental.

[102]

'This was the period in which, I think, the relationship between Danny and Sylvia was at its lowest ebb,' Green told me. 'There was frightening tension between them.'

Jerry Wald, 'a very strange man', produced the picture, but was 'not the greatest peacemaker'.

Green added: 'The tension that existed on our set spread out like a cumulus cloud over the whole Warner lot during the making of the picture.'

'It was not a happy time.'

Sometimes, he remembers, they shouted at each other. But that wasn't all. 'Better that they should have shouted at each other than gummed up. They didn't talk.'

But there were moments of levity, too. Not least of all at Warner's dining room, particularly with the studio's resident Hungarian, director Michael Curtiz – he of the 'bring on the empty horses' fame. Curtiz was a superb director, as *Casablanca* and a string of other pictures to his credit proved, but next to him Sam Goldwyn always sounded as though he had just won an elocution contest at Balliol College, Oxford. The English language had to take a breath to recover from the Curtiz treatment.

Once at the dining room when Kaye and Green were present, Curtiz was talking about houses. He said that he lived 'in the hills, Universal around.'

Said Green: 'Danny, Sylvia and I grabbed our napkins and stuffed them into our mouths and had to leave the table. We couldn't stop ourselves breaking down.'

Today, whenever he sees the Kayes, John Green only has to say 'Universal around' for everyone to fall down on the floor.

Between them, they adopted a Yiddish vernacular that Leo Rosten would have felt privileged to share. Particularly the stories of Mr Kaye's friend 'Caplan' who materialised at parties at the home of Dore Schary.

'Vot,' he would say to uninitiated guests. 'Vot you don't know Caplan? Caplan was a Jewish fellow what made comeback balls. You don't know what is comeback balls? Comeback balls is a yo-yo. You throw der ball and it come back to you. You don't know from that?'

After Mr Caplan, Danny Kaye would do a 15-minute spot at these parties, recalling the old Jewish man, straight out of a deep session studying the Talmud, who was a chain smoker. He would sit down on the floor with a cigarette dangling from his mouth, trying to get perhaps a quarter of a word between wheezing coughs.

'We were always together at these parties and Danny was always on. You didn't know from Caplan. Dr Caplan was a great

[103]

tycoon, who didn't only make comeback balls. But what de hell was it he did make? Everything he made, this Dr Caplan.'

Parties indeed seemed to be where Danny enjoyed being 'on' most. But because he was Danny Kaye, it wasn't the kind of entertaining most people did at show biz gatherings. There was always entertainment of some kind. Singers would get to the grand piano – try and stop them – and perform. Gagsters would find their way to the centre of the room and tell stories, sometimes pinching the bottom of a curvaceous blonde on the way or stealing a tray of canapés from a waiter as he tried, not usually successfully, to wend his way through the crowds.

Danny's approach was always a lot less conventional. His method frequently was simply to stand behind another guest's chair and discuss politics – it could, at that time, either have been a detailed treatise on why Harry Truman ought to run again for the Presidency or how the Soviets were consolidating their role in Eastern Europe. It all would sound terribly reasonable and intelligent – until, as the monologue went on, one realised that the sentences were becoming more and more a recital of pure gibberish. Before long, everyone else was convulsed in laughter. Which was precisely the aim of Warner Bros and everyone else connected with *The Inspector General*.

The idea of the story was basically an old and somewhat tired formula, and one that was as familiar to people who enjoyed comedy films as the very notion of going up to a cinema box office and buying a ticket. It was simply a case of mistaken identity. The man on screen is playing the part of a character who cannot possibly be the person he claims to be, any idiot can see that, but the people he meets can't.

In this case, the idiot played by Kaye is confused with the government inspector expected by the corrupt burghers of the town in this mythical country. Gogol wrote his story about Czarist Russia; for reasons that no one has been able to explain, Warners decided to make it somewhere else, even if it were in the general direction of the original location. Now, *you* and every sensible person seeing the film would know that Danny couldn't possibly have been the government inspector – unless the government had been taken over by the residents of the nearby mental asylum. But the burghers didn't know and somehow you had to laugh at it.

The Inspector General cannot be remembered as one of the great Kaye films, but it had its moments, moments that no one can take away from it or from the people responsible. He adapted the *Minnie the Moocher* routine by getting two sections of the characters in the village being visited by this government inspector to repeat nonsensical sentences – and then do it in counterpoint. The song was called *The Gypsy* and it was brilliant.

That sort of thing usually needs a live audience to work properly. But when Danny did it, people who had paid for movie tickets, joined in the chorus, and that, too, was very unusual. But with Danny Kaye, the old irresistible electric force made people feel they had to do it.

The Inspector General was no great sensation. Walter Kerr, the distinguished American critic, wrote that in the film, Danny 'seemed to be trying to take a leaf from Chaplin's book to replace verbal trickery with pantomimic devices and Kaye must be given credit for the intelligence with which he seeks to adapt himself to the medium, but it didn't work.'

Soon after work on *The Inspector General* finished, Danny went back to Brooklyn – to see his father and make his début on the professional stage in his old home town. Jacob Kaminsky, now 76, was there in the audience, seeing his son working live for the first time in ten years.

He was overwhelmed, brimming with glory, 'qvelling' once more.

He had heard of the enthusiasm with which Danny was greeted in a live theatre. Inwardly, he had wanted most of all to have been at the Palladium and see his boy David meeting the King and Queen. But this night was enough. Danny Kaye was king and he was there to see him receiving the allegiance of his subjects.

Danny was not a little glad to have the old man there, too. Halfway through the proceedings, he stopped the orchestra and told the audience: 'My dear father is in the house'.

Jacob was even more overwhelmed than before. Now he was not just father of a big star, but a star who remembered his father, and not just remembered his father, who told all the people in the theatre – and the friends and neighbours to whom he had been bragging for all those years – how much he was welcome there.

He couldn't contain himself any longer. As the audience clapped politely – they would have clapped *Anatole of Paris* a little louder – Jacob got up from his seat and started bowing . . . once . . . twice . . . three times.

What he didn't realise was that apart from those in the seats nearby, nobody really knew where he was. The bows were somewhat futile gestures.

'Wait,' shouted his son who somehow saw what the old man was doing, 'wait till I turn the lights on. They can't see you.'

The houselights went on. A spotlight picked up the beaming image of Jacob Kaminsky and he bowed all over again.

'Now you know where the ham comes from,' said his son. Jacob was glad to know that Danny, the nice kosher kid from Brooklyn, wasn't speaking gastronomically.

[105]

Jacob was enjoying all the trappings of being Danny's father. Not long before, he had flown from New York for a holiday in Miami, every elderly Brooklyn Jew's idea of the perfect vacation.

The other passengers were concerned about the possibilities of getting sick in the air. Jacob had no such fears. He told them, 'I'm Danny Kaye's father.' He was convinced that made all the difference. 'Does anyone think I'll get airsick?'

The only one who worried about the effect of flying on the old man was his youngest son. It was long before the jet age, aircraft cabins were not pressurised. Danny phoned his Miami hotel. Wouldn't Mr Kaminsky prefer to return home the old way – by train.

'Train?' asked his father. 'What's that?'

As always with stars of Danny's calibre, the big question for show business writers seemed to be the simple one of what his next project would be.

Yes, he was going to make another film. But this one would be totally different. For the first time, he was going to play a living character. Yes, he would be a funny man, but one with problems. A real live entertainer, the kind who a generation earlier had achieved the sort of response that Danny Kaye was now enjoying.

Now who would fit that description? Jolson? Hardly, he didn't look anything like Kaye and there had been that splendid film *The Jolson Story* just two years before, which had made Al as big a performer now as he had ever been in his life. Eddie Cantor perhaps? Not really. Danny was bigger now than Cantor had ever been. Both men were American and Jewish and in other respects, too, could have been seen to have similar backgrounds as Danny. This choice, though, was very different. The subject suggested for the new Kaye film wouldn't be Jewish, wouldn't even be American. Instead, Warners thought it would be great for him to play a Scotsman – Sir Harry Lauder.

Danny's Scottish accent was as good as his English, as good as his Russian, as good as his French. Audiences at the Palladium had discovered this. His Scots accent, in fact, was as good as his American. What was more, he was extraordinarily tempted by the idea.

He and Lauder had never met. But it was a matter put right in June 1949 when, yet again, Danny came to London and yet again wowed audiences at the Palladium as audiences at the Palladium had never been wowed before – at least, not since Danny's last appearance.

Lauder was ecstatic about the young American. 'I know it seems funny,' he told the *Daily Graphic*, 'but although I've met nearly every big variety artist of my day, the meeting with this young red-haired performer from the States is the greatest joy of all.' (You didn't have to believe *too* strongly that it was really Lauder talking and not some ghost of a *Graphic* reporter). 'He is a born trouper. I have no doubt about that. He is so great that I was thoroughly honoured to know that the "wonder man", now at the top of the ladder of fame, should come to see an old man like myself.'

What he didn't report in that piece was the advice he would give Danny: 'Be yourself and don't try to be somebody else.'

Did that mean he wouldn't now be making the film? Lauder liked the idea, was deeply flattered by it. But the picture, like so many other Hollywood schemes, was to be a dream in the old man's pipe.

The visit to the great Scots entertainer followed on Danny's baptism – if that isn't a wholly inappropriate term for the Jewish kid from Brooklyn – of a British audience outside of London. He was heading the bill at the theatre which English show people tended to think was only one step less deadly than a confrontation with the Gestapo – the Glasgow Empire. Hardened performers – Morecambe and Wise just prior to their television sensation among them – were known to cry into their handkerchiefs and call for their mothers when contemplating what that Glasgow audience could do on a Saturday night. Crowd behaviour at the Celtic-Rangers match was like that at a Royal Ballet première by comparison.

Danny rode it all out without, apparently, even noticing. The only hiccup was that local Lord's Day Observance Society zealots pleaded with him to make sure that no tickets were sold on Sundays. The Glaswegians gave no impression of being put out – although one clergyman in Liverpool hearing that people had been queuing all Sunday for tickets for his show there, before opening in Manchester and Birmingham, remarked 'I'm ashamed of my city. It's a disgrace.'

Danny replied: 'It's out of my hands.'

They loved him in the provinces as they had in Glasgow. They rallied to all the usual Kaye routines, with a goodly number of Scottish suggestions, including a couple of Will Fyffe and Lauder take-offs. When Sir Harry was helped into the theatre, Danny did the true entertainer thing and welcomed him from the stage. The Empire rattled its chandeliers and lifted its roof – the kind of reaction that could only normally be guaranteed if bottles of Haig or Bells were given out with the tickets.

Later in his dressing room, Danny asked him how he managed to maintain that popularity for so long.

Lauder gave the answer he was expected to give. 'You'll be like that yourself one day Danny. Just keep giving them the kind of entertainment you've given tonight and they'll love you till the end of your days.'

Via the pen of the newspaper writer, it comes out fairly syruppy, but there's no doubt that the old man told him something of the kind.

Lauder delighted in giving the impression that he went to bed with his crooked stick under his arm, his tam-o'-shanter on his head and a wee deoch and doris in his hand. That, too, was showmanship. The very idea that Danny Kaye could take over his kilt was, to some, little short of sacrilege. But 'wee bonny Harry' as this very astute knight of the realm liked to be known, would have loved it.

Or was that just good publicity? Old showmen never die, they merely dance away.

'Like Danny, I was once up there myself, and I know how he feels.'

Danny was plainly a welcome guest at Lauder Ha'. Sir Harry told him he knew all about his work, had seen all his films.

Naturally, they compared notes about show business in America – which Lauder himself had experienced since the early years of the century – and about entertainment in his heyday compared with this post-war time. They also got into the kind of detail that a couple of old timers could be relied on to get to. Danny was smoking a cigarette. 'Och,' said Lauder, as the *Graphic* would have liked us to believe – it appears he spoke as though reading a music-hall script – 'that's a lassie's smoke.'

At Lauder Ha', the veteran entertainer was enjoying his pipe. He said he wouldn't dream of putting anything else in his mouth.

What cannot be doubted is that Danny really did admire Sir Harry and all he stood for. He wasn't the only Briton whom he admired. Like many another self-made man, he had an innate respect for well-educated artists and musicians, to say nothing of men of letters.

In 1949, Britain's most distinguished living writer was the long-bearded Irish socialist who seemed at the time to be on the threshold of immortality. In his nineties, George Bernard Shaw was another object of a Danny Kaye pilgrimage. Shaw, the wit and cynic to end all other wits and all other cynics, was for reasons no one has ever been able to explain, willing to receive Danny at Shaw's Corner, the picturesque little house where he lived at Ayot St Lawrence in Hertfordshire. It was there that many of the Shaw masterpieces had been penned – in a shed at the back of the rose garden, heated by one small electric fire.

Why it is surprising he received Danny so willingly was simple – he had never heard of him. And he told him so.

[108]

A neighbour, Mr Stephen Winsten saw it all and reported it had, however, been a 'very merry occasion'.

It was Mr Winsten who issued the invitation to Danny, and arranged for GBS to join them during the afternoon they had together. 'I wanted him to spend some time in a real old English country home.'

They talked in the garden, shaded by Mr Winsten's apple trees and later they did an act together. Shaw doing an 'act'? Well, they called it charades and anyone at the Goldwyn studios or who had ever attended one of Dore Schary's parties knew that Danny was the best charade player within a few hundred miles of the Grand Canyon. This time by Mr Winsten's account, Mr Shaw gave him a run for his dollars.

'There was no conversation. The whole act was quite spontaneous and carried out in mime. Danny sat on the lawn looking whimsical and picking daisies and GBS strode up to him and slapped him heartily on the back and so on.'

Afterwards, Danny told him: 'I can quite see, GBS (didn't everyone call him GBS?) why you have a certain disrespect for actors. There is none of them as good as you. You should have been an actor yourself.'

Mr Shaw had been known to say much the same sort of thing himself.

Danny admitted he had been quite nervous meeting the grand old man. Finally, Shaw said: 'I don't know whether or not I approve of you.'

There was a different kind of 'entertainment' for Danny later that evening. Between shows at the Palladium, he saw how Britain's National Health Service operated at the Middlesex Hospital.

This was not, however, just another example of Kaye's fascination with medicine and surgery getting the better of him. He went on stage that night, convinced he had broken at least three or four ribs. On the way back to London from Ayot, his car collided with another. Danny only bruised those ribs in the crash apparently. It was, naturally enough, a chance for more gags. The Palladium audience heard all about the crash and reacted as every Palladium audience was known throughout the world to react to whatever he wanted to do. It was yet another example of how he could do no wrong to those ticket buyers.

As always, the Press had been watching Danny's triumphant progress.

'Tonight, they brought out the fatted calf, roasted it and served it to Danny Kaye on a red carpet,' recorded Leonard Mosley in the *Daily Express*.

'To those who complain that London nowadays gives an hysterical Kaye reception to ALL visiting American turns, he provided the answer. He got a welcome that was tumultuous – but was something extra, too.

'It was in the clapping, in the answers to his calls from the stage, and a quality in the silence with which everyone watched him. And I think it will be a long time before this special quality is created by anyone else from across the Atlantic. Danny Kaye came on the stage . . . with an expression on his face rather like a boxer, slightly doubtful of his chances of winning the championship of the world.'

As Mr Mosley noted, the championship was his – without having to fight for it.

Certainly everyone seemed to think so. People tried to find ways of thanking him for the pleasure he gave them. Sometimes, it was a bottle of Scotch left at the stage door. Occasionally, a packet of cigarettes. Taxi drivers expressed their admiration by refusing to allow him to pay his fare.

Sylvia was the first to notice that all this was having a chastening effect on her husband. He wasn't so uptight, so now the relationship that existed between them was able to ease, too. She realised that she would have to behave differently towards him. 'It doesn't mean I have to baby him,' she said at the time. 'Now I hold tight, but with open fingers.' It could have been a line from a new Sylvia Fine song.

But she had to hold tight somehow or other, or she would have lost him for good. She hadn't accompanied him on stage since Dena was born and this inevitably meant a loosening of the reins. With Sammy Prager sitting on her piano stool, it was clear that Danny was totally the boss of all he surveyed. For her to try to show otherwise at home would have made for the kind of difficulties both agreed they could do without.

Back home in the United States, *Life* magazine presented to their readers 'The Ambassador From Brooklyn' under a headline declaring 'Danny Conquers England'.

The Times in London was more reserved, but finally joined in the general welcome.

'Those who are not blinded by the dazzle of Mr Danny Kaye's reputation may see in him a music hall artist whose success consists largely in ignoring the conventional limitations of the music hall. What he does is not fresh, which implies the continuance of tradition but new, which does not. Since we live in an age which values the strangeness of sounds for its own sake, Mr Kaye will punctuate his songs with neighing and whinnying which his positive personality leads the audience to accept as excrutiatingly witty. This, is, however, the least of his effects. More notable is his daring in drawing on a number of gestures and intonations generally regarded as effeminate or at least exceedingly precious and not satirizing them, so that he more than doubles his means to underline and vary the more conventional of his songs. Yet what distinguishes Mr Kaye from other personages whom the public chooses to idolize is his sense of the value of words. The poor little usual vocabulary of the music hall is swept away and extinguished by a many-coloured host of words out of literature, shimmering evocative, mysterious words in whose jungles Mr Kaye's more fascinating songs take the oddest turnings. . . . We can think of no one else who would venture to entertain a music hall audiences with a comic song about Stanislavsky or point out to them that the difference between a Russian comedy and a Russian tragedy is that, though everybody dies, they all die happy.'

The *Daily Telegraph* had fewer inhibitions about him. W. A. Darlington, one of the most important critics in London, wrote: 'Only a few times in a lifetime of playgoing can anybody [have seen] the wonder which is brought to pass at the Palladium by Danny Kaye – to see, that is, a great entertainer playing on an entranced audience like a master musician on his instrument.'

Meanwhile, Danny's old chum Hannen Swaffer, once more telling the world that he had seen them all and knew them all, told his readers in the *People* newspaper that 'Danny Kaye got the biggest cheer since . . . Danny Kaye.' Which said a very great deal.

A. E. Wilson in the *Star* noted: 'For an hour the slim, shock-headed wonder boy had the audience in the hollow of his hand. He entertained with breathless and infectious high spirits. He danced and he pattered. He sang gipsy songs, demonstrated the flamenco, lapsed into a sudden mood of Slavic melancholy and with a flick of flexible and eloquent fingers and the encouragement of his engaging smile, urged the audience into a lusty, imitation of his lightning flow of gibberish. It was the triumph of magnetic personality. I have seen nothing to equal this extraordinary command over an audience. No matter what he did, he had the audience with him all the time.'

And it was not just the Press who were close to being ecstatic at having Danny Kaye in their midst once more. The Royal Family were paying him tribute, too – and extending the franchise to other royals, too. This time, the Duchess of Kent – she had been widowed in the war – brought her two oldest children, the young Duke and Princess Alexandra to see the show.

You didn't have to be either psychologist or theatre expert to know that something uncanny was evident here, more polished even than last time, more certain, he was less likely to admit that he was shaking – even though he probably was.

[111]

Some idea of how it was going to be was evident as early as the first rehearsals – although how someone so totally unpredictable as Danny Kaye could rehearse at all might have seemed a little puzzling.

He goes from one idea to another – through *Minnie the Moocher* with Wolfie Phillips and the band one moment, the next stopping them in mid note and saying – 'How's this?'

'This' could be either a totally different way of singing *Ballin' The Jack* or a new idea completely. 'Did you ever see,' he asks Val Parnell who is sitting in the third row of the stalls, knowing perfectly well he is about to be enchanted, 'the kind of feller come on the stage to sing a song and he's got everything it takes to sell it – lovely clothes, charming smile and loads of punchy gestures . . . Only he can't quite stay on pitch. . . .'

As he says it, Parnell realises he is on at the birth of what may seem a totally spontaneous new routine, but one which he and Sylvia have perfected a thousand times on their piano at home. He suggests that Mr Phillips might like to strike up *Begin The Beguine*.

Danny is exquisite in the mime and the preparation leading to the opening note which he says is straight out of the 'era when jazz was polite'. Before long you hear the first notes croke in his voice. The singer that Danny is imitating looks as though he doesn't notice. He sings a little more. Perfect. The voice matches the style. And then there it is again. . . . The people in the theatre break up. They haven't heard it before. They will hear it again – and not only from Danny Kaye.

It's cold in the theatre that day and Val Parnell is concerned that his stars might get ill. 'Would you like some warm woollen socks?' he asks him. 'I can get you some lovely, long hand-knitted ones. Would you wear them?'

Perhaps the socks come from Mrs Parnell. Britain is still racked by austerity and rationing has not come to an end.

This was a typical scene. The day was also as typical as any in the life of Danny Kaye in Britain. During the lunch break at the Palladium, Danny decided that it was more important not to waste the time than to just sit around, resting and eating.

So he took a trip to the Tower of London. It turned out to be a useful opportunity to study the effects of the blitz on London nine years earlier. He had previously flown over Hiroshima and was interested in comparing the results of the two sets of war damage. It was easy enough to do. The City of London and the East End were still badly scarred by the bombing. There were weeds growing between the cracked and shattered flagstones, but there were bomb sites all over and little or no rebuilding anywhere. St Paul's may have never looked more isolated and majestic, but it was

[112]

representative of a tragedy to the city and Danny decided this was an opportunity to pay his homage, a gesture of thanks perhaps to the audience who had been so warm and wonderful to him.

Going round the Tower was also a chance for him to show how much he knew about England. A Beefeater showed him around. It wasn't special treatment. American tourists were trickling into Britain now on holiday, and Danny didn't look very different from any of the others, even if his tie wasn't loud like those of his typical compatriots and there wasn't a camera slung quite so obviously around his shoulders.

He was interested in the Yeoman Warder's speech patterns. He told him he didn't think he came from London. 'Was it the West Country?'

'You're right,' said the man, throwing out his blue and red-robed chest emblazoned with the Royal monogram, 'GR'. 'Yes, I come from Bath.'

It was as if Professor Higgins had moved from Covent Garden to the East End. When two girls asked him for an autograph he replied in a quiet, subdued cockney. They disappeared fairly quickly, disappointed that the man they thought was the big American star was nothing of the kind. Danny felt pleased at his triumph, but he should have been nothing of the kind. The girls would have liked to have had Danny Kaye's autograph. In June 1949, it was worth a very great deal. He called them back. 'Say,' he said to one of them in a voice they more readily recognised. 'Aren't you from Wales?' She could have been from Mars, for all the intelligibility of the excited reply she gave him. She was a new victim of the incorrigible disease that had struck London show fans.

This strain of the Kaye epidemic was quite as strong as the ones that had gone before. It was so mainly because Danny *demanded* that audiences become infected. This was a two-way thing or it was nothing. Again, the comparisons with Jolson are highly relevant. Like Jolson, he asked for requests from the people who paid to see him. Like Jolson, too, he called for the houselights to go up – 'to see who's here'.

'I'm here,' a child in the audience yells out. 'You're smashing'. It was a phrase any one of the people out there could have used – and the amount of applause that it got seemed to show they wished they had. When they started screaming with delirious calls for different numbers, he at first ignored their declarations of love – for that is what they were – sometimes for up to two or three minutes.

He wore grey flannel trousers and a brown sports jacket.

He did what he had always done, got them to repeat his nonsense patter after him, but then he divided them into two sections and played one off against the other.

[113]

The Danny Kaye modesty was quite as infectious as his control over the audience. In the midst of a song, he suddenly held his hands up, cut the orchestra and said: 'It's nice to come back and hear this, and yet it somehow scares you. Because you wonder how long it will last.'

He sang a song about a sugar daddy 'who wanted to eat his cake while he still had teeth' and he wowed the audience into a strange kind of submission singing the oh-so-gentle *Candy Kisses* which was fast now becoming a Kaye standard.

Once, he asked the people out front, 'Who's the greatest actor in the world?' They replied 'Danny Kaye'. When he gave every impression of believing it, he really was acting very well indeed.

At the end of the show – or, a least, at what was made to look like the show's end – he walked off, the cries from the audience were audible pleas of panic. He responded as they hoped he would, but were afraid that he wouldn't. If a test of a trouper's real ability is his timing, Danny Kaye had to know when to exit. He had sensed that it was not yet and his public were grateful for it.

The house was in uproar as the audience clamoured for numbers. It seemed impossible for anyone to say anything that would be heard more than a seat away. Danny heard it. He simply stepped closer to the footlights, held up his hand and said: 'Hush.' Suddenly, as though a switch had been turned off, the place was totally silent. You could have heard a cynical critic drop.

Then he adopted his *Walter Mitty* RAF voice and declared, 'Now, shall we not lose control?' Losing control was what all Kaye audiences could be depended upon doing in the course of a show.

One evening, he brought Sid Field on to the stage, with an amount of praise that didn't seem to overbrim into insincerity. The British comedian appreciated that, and so did the audience.

Not that he had gone into it all certain he was going to be a big hit. Chevalier once told me that the reasons for an entertainer succeeding were part of what he called the 'mystery' of show business. To Danny, it was a mystery from the moment he signed his contracts to go on until the final curtain and the last clap of applause that he heard. He still tried to make it seem like they were all at a party.

And this was going to be one of those parties that scared the hell out of the host before it got going. 'I feel like a glass blower who sets out not knowing quite what he will do, and somehow blows the right shapes. Now I've got to blow again and try to produce the same pattern.'

And it was a pattern he had to recognise as carrying his own trade mark. Before signing for this Palladium trip, more than one enterprising impresario had come to him with suggestions that he try somewhere bigger – like the Royal Albert Hall for instance.

Danny was distinctly unimpressed, not to say too daunted by the prospect. The Palladium held roughly 3,000 people; the Albert Hall more than double that. 'But I won't play to more than 4,000 people at a time,' he said. 'I just wouldn't go over.'

And he added, more than convincingly, because on the altar of greed many a star had sacrificed his entire career and Danny knew it, 'I could have earned as much in three one-night stands as in a whole week at a variety theatre. But I'm not going to throw my reputation away for the sake of quick money.'

He had arrived in London on this trip with at least 25 minutes of new songs and new comedy ideas up his sleeve.

The crowds outside the Palladium were so thick that police had trouble making way for cars and taxis, said *The New York Times*. Needless to say, tickets couldn't be had for love or money. Every seat was booked long before the show opened.

Above all, the business loved their new prince – as did those associated with that business. *Picturegoer* magazine, which had not exactly been uncritical of Mr Kaye, and its publishers, Odhams Press, gave a luncheon in his honour. The Lord Mayor was there. So was War Minister Emanuel Shinwell and Danny's friend Lewis Douglas, the US Ambassador who again could be depended on to say that Mr Kaye was America's real diplomat.

The Lord Mayor suggested that this was worth taking up. Perhaps Mr Vyshinsky – who had spearheaded most of Stalin's party purges and had now taken over from Mr Molotov as Russia's principal expert in saying 'niet' – might bend a little if Danny got close to him. He didn't say it, but it might have been an amusing, not to say confusing confrontation. The Kaye touch would have turned to a wholesale recital of gibberish which no one would have understood – except Mr Vyshinksy who would have thought he *should* have known what it was all about.

People who met Danny for the first time said they were flattered by the kind way in which he received them. He asked names and remembered them through the length of a conversation.

It seemed to show that he had matured with success. It sat well on him. But others said that it wasn't good to get too close to him before a big show. He didn't drink, he didn't eat – apart, that is, from the heads of anyone incautious enough to ask how he was getting on.

And as Cecil Wilson reported in the *Daily Mail*, he was inclined to interview reporters who came to interview him. He told them he wouldn't be back to England until 1951 – because he didn't want to outstay his welcome. And then he turned to one pretty girl, 'How long have you been working in newspapers?' She told him and then, in a prescient display of women's lib countered, 'Say who's interviewing whom?'

There were still those who weren't totally sold on Danny Kaye, but they were difficult to find. Matthew Norgate wrote in *Tribune* that Danny was different from most other comedians who were simply playing parts. 'Danny Kaye . . . is playing himself. If he reprimands us, he does so as a joke, and quickly reverts to his projection across the footlights of his own self. And even this is almost more a concealment of ego than self revelation. When he takes us into his confidence, he is no Cheekie Chappie (a reference to the top English music hall comedian of the day, Max Miller), but a vaudeville performer talking about his job. He doesn't believe in climaxes, he says, squatting on the floor in order to chat more comfortably, and proves it by so contriving the end of his turn that he, alone of any immensely popular favourite I remember, is not still clamoured for after The King has been played. And in all this there is pandering to the bobby-soxers.'

Mr Norgate was plainly put out at first by Danny claiming the evening to be the happiest of his life. But he was overwhelmed before long. 'No doubt,' said the writer, 'he says it every night and in that . . . part of the act, but as he said it there was nothing fulsome about it, and certainly nothing self-congratulatory, which also was a change.' As the writer said, 'Unlike his compatriots, he somehow seemed to mean it.'

That was what most people seemed to think, particularly those who were in the business of giving Danny awards. They were coming so thick and fast now that people could have been given the impression that the award givers were hoping that something that Danny had would rub off on them.

In June 1949, while he was in London for the Palladium show, he received England's National Film Award, an honour that hitherto had gone exclusively to British films and stars. It was presented on behalf of the *Daily Mail* by Gracie Fields, which most people seemed to think was a fairly obvious meeting of equals. Gracie said some marvellous things about Danny and Danny said some flattering things about Gracie and the place she had in show-business history.

It was no more than what the whole of Britain seemed to feel. An American newspaperman told of getting into an Underground Tube train the morning that Danny's departure was being reported in the three London evening papers. Sitting next to him were a couple of bowler-hatted office workers who, apparently didn't know each other and were observing the traditional courtesies of leaving the other completely in peace. One, though, glanced at his paper and turned to his neighbour. 'It's a lot different with him gone, isn't it?'

'Aye,' said his travelling companion,' 'tis.'

The headline of the paper said simply: 'OUR DANNY'S GONE AWAY.'

Once again, he left Britain for home, basking in the warmth of a mutual love affair. On his last night at Glasgow, the tough audience had tears in their eyes – a state of affairs usually ascribable soley to a lack of whisky – and sang 'Will ye no come back again'. He promised that he would, and he meant it.

But there were other people who were saying anything but flattering things about Danny.

BALLIN' THE JACK

IF HE WERE SUPERSTITIOUS AND BELIEVED IN OMENS, THE FLIGHT home to Los Angeles should have convinced Danny that there was trouble in the wind – literally. They were over the Atlantic, past the Irish coast when one of his plane's engines packed up and the aircraft had to limp back to Dublin.

For a time, there were rumours that the plane had crashed and Danny, along with everyone else on board, had been killed. Indeed, newspaper headlines to that effect appeared everywhere.

Once it was established that Danny was alive and well another legend developed, that he had calmed everyone down and spent the entire flight down to Ireland entertaining the passengers. It wasn't like that at all – at least Danny himself said it wasn't.

On other occasions, he had been known to sit down to eat and put his food down his ear, or cover his eyes with a pair of ear muffs. But not now. As he said a couple of years afterwards: 'I talked to people, but don't let anybody tell you I made with a joke. I was too scared.'

It wasn't the only thing that had made him scared.

The political climate in the United States was getting very unpleasantly hot. It was to get hotter, too – and a lot more uncomfortable for studios – full of writers, directors and producers, to say nothing of stars who were not going out of their way to say that everything about America was wonderful and nothing about Russia was good. Before long, it would be almost enough to admit one had voted for Roosevelt to have the investigators knocking on the front door.

For the moment, the paranoia was creeping up and groups were being set up all over America, and particularly in Hollywood and New York, with, it seemed, the principal object of proving they were hunting more reds than anyone else.

It reached ridiculous proportions as early as June of 1949. Most dangerous of all, the allegations were given the stamp of approval by the FBI. J. Edgar Hoover had not yet established himself as the arch reactionary, union persecutor and megalomaniac that he would later be exposed to be.

Now, apparently with Hoover's approval, Danny was named as a member of the Communist Party. He was in good company. Fredric March, Edward G. Robinson and a host of other well-known names were included – and this was long before Senator McCarthy had begun his hearings involving people in the motion-picture industry.

The FBI said the details had come to them via a 'confidential informant'. Fredric March in particular had been 'active in the Communist infiltration of the industry'. Frank Sinatra, still in his heyday as a pop singer, was at the top of the list along with Danny Kaye, whose name was singled out by the Press as the most interesting of all.

It was not only unsubstantiated but a dangerous defamatory lie.

The Government of Harry Truman came out loud and clear condemning the report, but the smoke it produced was deduced – as Hoover knew it would – as having emanated from a fire that had to be put out.

Paul Muni, Melvyn Douglas, John Garfield, Sylvia Sidney, and the President of Boston University, Daniel L. Marsh were listed too, when – again against the expressed wish of the Government – the report was read at the trial of Judith Coplon, an employee of the Department of Justice who was accused of stealing Government secrets with the intent of passing them to Russia.

But the list of names multiplied. Katharine Hepburn, Gregory Peck, Orson Welles, Lena Horne, Pearl Buck, Clifford Odets and a former Vice-President of the United States, Henry Wallace.

'These and others,' said the report, 'are typical of a group which has appeased the Communist line. [They] have persistently viciously and dishonestly attacked the [UnAmerican Activities] Committee. All have attacked us without having once directly challenged a single finding of the Committee. They are typical of individuals within the various Stalinist orbits about whose activities in Stalinist programmes and causes your Committee has presented factual reports or has taken sworn evidence.'

It was vicious and nasty. Frank Sinatra, showing a little of the pugnaciousness for which he would later become famous, said: 'This . . . unjustified attack gives every American good reason to be critical of the Committee. If they do put it out, I'll show them how much an American can fight – even against the State, if an American happens to be right.'

An American Society for Russian Relief was mentioned. Danny said he had never heard of it. 'I am not going to make any comment on anything this guy mentions. But it seems to me like a lot of hooey.' If that 'lot of hooey' had come up before the McCarthy hearings three or four years later, it would have been a lot more dangerous. For the moment, however, there was his career to think of.

Warner Brothers had to decide what they would do for a follow-up to *The Inspector General*. They had a five-picture contract with Danny. But before long, it was mutually announced that the deal was being terminated.

The Palladium and the Glasgow Empire and the other places in between had convinced him that really he was most interested in doing more work on stage, making more live audiences eat out of the palm of whichever hand he was offering to his public at a particular moment.

The Inspector General, although it had its moments of pure Kaye, still wasn't a *Wonder Man* or a *Walter Mitty* and that was clearly the kind of star audiences not fortunate enough to see him in the flesh wanted. It nevertheless produced for Sylvia and himself at least $310,000, the sum they had been promised as associate producers on the film together with 35 per cent of any profits. There were to be some, but how much at this stage, no one could tell.

In May 1950, the *Saturday Evening Post* consummated the belief that most people had about Danny Kaye now being at the top of his profession – despite all the anti-Communist smears and the relative failure of his last two movies.

It published a piece entitled 'The World's Highest-Paid Buffoon', which was really something of an accolade in itself, particularly to someone as inherently insecure as Danny Kaye.

In one opening sentence, Joe Alex Morris summed him up: 'Danny Kaye is a slim, thin-faced redhead who can burlesque a dozen fantastic characters with the greatest of ease and who would be happiest if he could put them all in the spotlight at the same time before a big audience. Since nobody has yet figured out a way for one man to be a crowd, Kaye does the best he can by amalgamating a little of everything into his own stage personality and by instinctively seeking the centre of any stage with aggressive charm and no little persistence.'

Mr Morris, like most people, wondered how seriously Danny took his art. He told him he had no ambition to play Hamlet. 'I like to be funny.'

And he was continuing to be so. American theatres were hoping to repeat the Palladium success and he was being booked all over the country. Wherever he played, Americans found that their sense of humour was little different from the British. In fact, they loved the way he guyed his RAF pilots as much in Miami or Montreal as in Manchester.

The greatest compliment of all to Danny as to any other entertainer was the respect in which he was held by his peers. Jack

Benny, who knew not a little about the art of comedy, not least of all about what made people like *him* so much, confessed that apart from his bosom pal George Burns, Kaye made him laugh longer and louder than anyone else. In fact, in the midst of one of Danny's routines at a private party, Benny could be seen literally lying on the floor, pounding the carpet in a state of near delirium. The fathers of both men would have appreciated that and over the years they did.

It was certainly easier seeing Danny actually performing than it was watching him getting ready to perform. In a way, it was as if the success he had achieved was in inverse proportion to the difficulty he found in adjusting to the fact that there was an audience out there waiting for him.

He called it his 'manic-depressive' stage, a terminology not at all hindered by the opening lines of *The Lobby Number* from *Up In Arms*. Not only was he not an easy person to talk to while he waited for the orchestra to strike up his opening music, he was not a nice person to be in the vicinity of. On a good evening, he could be found in the wings dancing an Irish jig – to help him limber up. Sometimes, he would sing snatches of his songs, and if the songs always sounded like gibberish, they were more nonsensical at these times than usual. On a bad night, he would stir up trouble – passing on the word that something was wrong with the lighting, or the scenery or the sound systems, while he stood in the corner watching the mayhem about to break out. On a really bad night, he snapped at people who were basically his friends or there simply to help him. Worse still, he would be morose and generally unpleasant. The cloud of depression that settled over his head seemed ready to escape on to the stage and into the auditorium. The fact that it never did was a compliment in itself to the kind of appeal he had and the way he used that appeal.

On stage, on a film set or just playing charades at a party, the thing that struck those around him was Danny's boundless energy. It was exhausting simply to be in the same room as he was. It must have been harder still to live with him as Sylvia was discovering more and more. Yet still the marriage continued.

His world seemed to be his comedy and his comedy his world. Just occasionally, fans would write to Danny asking him to be 'more Jewish' in his act. It was a time when Jewish comedians wore their Judaism on their shirt fronts like spilled chicken soup or gefilte fish stains. The State of Israel had newly been established and Jewish entertainers talked about the psychological symbolism of the event, told Jewish stories or sang Jewish songs.

Danny wouldn't do that. He still said that the theatre was not a place to be Jewish or Irish or black or white. But, as John Green,

Dore Schary and everyone else who went to parties with Danny and Sylvia some of the things he did would have sounded very strange indeed from a non-Jewish comedian. Sometimes, his Jewishness would come out at the most unexpected times. Once he made a flying visit to London just before the festival of Shavuot, or Pentecost, when it was customary to eat dairy foods. 'I've only come to find a nice piece of cheese cake for my father for yomtov (Hebrew for the festival),' he said.

In Paris, couturière Ginette Spanier found that he struck up an immediate, strong relationship with her because he discovered her own background.

She was walking through the salon of Maison Balmain of which she was *directrice* when she noticed a couple, sitting on a pair of gilt chairs seemingly being studiously ignored by everyone else around them. They were Americans, she discovered. They had asked for M. Balmain himself and he was being found.

Mme Spanier asked if they were being attended to. She was told that they were. Were the manequins primed? They were. Yet the Americans looked not only as if they were being ignored, but that they didn't like being ignored either.

'Who's the man?' she asked.

'*Il s'appelle* Danny Kaye,' she was told.

Now Mme Spanier, an attractive, extremely cultured lady born in Britain but who spent most of her adult life living and working in France married to a fashionable doctor, will gladly describe herself as the original stage-struck awe-struck girl.

But unlike other stage-struck women who never appear on stage themselves, she has had the advantage of knowing some of the great stage personalities of her age – and knowing them very well indeed. Laurence Olivier, Noel Coward and Maurice Chevalier are just three names who through the years have been very very close to her.

Finding herself in close proximity to Danny Kaye was a moment for her diary and roughly the equivalent of being able to record the sale of a sable coat in the salon's log.

She walked over to him with that air of sophisticated charm that Frenchwomen seem to have in abundance. A word from Ginette Spanier had been known to soothe many an angry millionairess into more than mere compliance, even into a degree of submission. Women who had walked into Maison Balmain to complain left convinced that the house had paid them the great compliment of agreeing to sell anything in the first place.

'I'm so sorry,' she said. 'I'll see that M. Balmain will attend to you straight away.'

The voice charged a battery in the Kaye brain. 'Ah,' he said, 'a British broad.'

[122]

'British?' asked the attractive Frenchwoman who had been through the war running from the Nazis – and who now had every reason to be extremely proud how French she looked and how French everyone thought she was.

How did Monsieur Danny Kaye – pronounced, it seemed, with a distinctly French intonation – know?

'Because,' he said, Ginette had used the phrase 'straight away'. 'If you had been American,' he told her, 'you would have said, right away.'

Such things did seem to separate Danny Kaye from other people in the world of show business. He asked her name, and then added a seemingly obvious question. 'What's a British broad doing in a French joint?'

She told him she was married to a Frenchman. What did he do? Danny asked. 'He's a doctor,' she replied.

It wouldn't have sounded any better to Danny if she had told him she was his long lost younger sister. To Danny, a doctor was still one of the gods inhabiting Mount Olympus. But there was more excitement still to come. The 'broad's' name was Ginette Spanier. But what was the doctor's name?

She told him it was Seidman. 'That makes sense,' he said. 'Come on let's leave this joint and meet that doctor husband of yours.'

So the British broad was also a Jewish broad. As Ginette told me: 'It was the first time being Jewish seemed important to someone else since the war. Then, we were lepers. Now someone wanted to be with us *because* we were Jewish. I hadn't been accustomed to that.'

Danny didn't become an intimate friend, although they did meet socially several times after that. 'He became quite strange and disappeared from our lives, but I'll always be grateful for that original meeting. He made it nice for us to be thought of as Jewish and it's a feeling that has remained with me ever since.'

Most Danny Kaye fans still believed that their idol could do no wrong. The disappointed ones were generally those who couldn't get into one of his shows – or who had got used to the idea of an annual season of Danny Kaye radio programmes. These, however, were now part of the Kaye of the past. The 'O'Brien – no Ohio' routine had worn thin and both Danny and Sylvia found the pressure of a weekly show just too much. Besides, they no longer needed the money.

One week at New York's Roxy Theatre brought him $37,000 – more than anyone else had ever earned there. His recording work, some of it now devoted to discs for children, gave him an annual income in the region of about $50,000.

It was estimated that he netted something like $650,000 in 1949, which was little short of phenomenal. The agency handling his show's account extracted a promise that Danny wouldn't appear

[123]

on any other radio programme for another year at least. He didn't find that at all difficult to agree to.

Neither would he ever agree that he changed his act wherever he did it simply because a new audience was sitting in their seats beckoning him. 'Audiences are composed of people and deep, deep down underneath', he told one writer, 'people are the same the world over. They come into the theatre covered in a few veneers of their own personalities and prejudices. American audiences like to think they are tough and hard to get. A myth has developed that English audiences are cold, unemotional and unenthusiastic. They are not, but they like to think they are.'

He was trying hard to prove that he really was as nice as all the writers said – only those who knew him well knew about the flaws in his character. Now, the member of the class of 1926 at Public School 149, Sutton Avenue and Wyona Street, Brooklyn, was expressing his gratitude for what little education he had received.

He established a permanent fund for awards of excellence in music and dramatics at the school, a fund that was officially launched with a presentation to the President of the school's alumni association, Municipal Judge Daniel Gutman.

Meanwhile, other stars were invited to comment on the phenomenon that was Danny Kaye. In a feature in *Look* magazine screen beauty Hedy Lamar declared: 'Danny Kaye's romantic appeal is that polished continental flavour one associates with pre-war Paris or Vienna.'

It could have come direct from a Press agent's blurb, but the puffery went on, much to the delight of Danny's Press agent, no doubt. Bob Hope told the magazine: 'I take my hat off to Danny Kaye's complete mastery of ultra-smart comedy.' Anyone would agree this was praise indeed, and the kind that Danny, as any other professional comic would agree was the most important of all.

Dinah Shore, who worked with him five years earlier – although by now, judging by the lightning success of recent years that must have seemed a great deal earlier – declared: 'When Danny sings a popular ballad, he has the ability to make people forget – why they came to hear him sing!' It was a studied joke, but it did tend to make the other comments seem that little bit more artificial.

And then there was Fred Allen, best known as the comedian who had a running feud on radio with Jack Benny: 'Kaye's instinct,' he said, 'for the right material is amazing, for he is invariably correct in his choice of what to say – and then says it.' Well perhaps the Press agent wouldn't have written that. All in all, however, it wasn't doing Danny's image any harm at all. If you're going to be insulted, then it is as well to have the insults come from a top comedian rather than a disgruntled, jealous failure.

Praise and flattery came in many forms. American *Vogue* magazine made him the centre of a still-life collage in which he was surrounded by objects that the artist regarded as typifying the many moods of Danny Kaye. There was a wig, an umbrella, a turkey and a violin – the last probably symbolising the pizzicato of his git-gat-gittle routine. Also, a yo-yo – doubtless the best visual demonstration of his sense of timing. Oh yes, and a sand pail that showed Danny was best known as an exponent of fun, and a milk bottle. What could *that* have meant? His continuing adolescence probably.

Sylvia would have recognised that quality in her old man, and Dena would have done so, too. When he got on the floor to play with his daughter, it was less as a father romping with his infant child, more an equal playing on equal terms. In years to come, other children would find a similar relationship building up between them.

Sylvia told a writer about her working relationship with her husband. 'He sits quietly listening. But if what he hears excites him, he'll get up, start looking over my shoulder and begin to create.

'These are thrilling moments. I love watching something I have written come alive in him, in his face, in every gesture. I know what I have had in my head, but what he does is something better. Wonderful as a performance of his is in its final version on the screen, for me it is second to the first moments.'

For years, Danny had been telling people that his career came first, and certainly it appeared that way. But now he was saying that the folks at home were number one. This even meant that the BBC had to do without a transatlantic phone-call interview with him – at a time when such things took a very great deal of organising. No, he said, he couldn't possibly do the interview, he had promised to take Dena for a picnic. Every Sunday, he took her to a local playground where she rode a pony.

Now, he had a more ambitious plan for their recreation periods together. He bought a set of miniature golf clubs and they were going to play the game as though it were the most important thing in either of their lives. Actually, golf was becoming as important as just that to Danny.

He took to it like the little white duck he was now singing about on his latest hit record, to the lake near the Hillcrest Country Club.

The Hillcrest was the principal Jewish social club in Los Angeles, frequented mostly by very monied Jewish entertainers. Al Jolson held court at the club's round table every lunch time while Jack Benny, George Burns, Milton Berle, Eddie Cantor, George Jessel and anyone else who was anyone else listened intently. The other members were generally in some branch of show business – if they weren't performers, they were producers, agents, lawyers and accountants. On Sundays, they brought their wives and children along, the younger children to play outside, the older ones to play inside in what was California's most sought-after marriage market.

Membership was very definitely restricted (not in the sense of some of the other California clubs who wouldn't allow a Jew near their premises; Hillcrest had been known to take in the occasional 'token goy' and then got its revenge on all the others – by striking oil on its links) to those who not only had a very great deal of money, but who also gave away a great deal of money to charity. Charitable contributions have to be proved before anyone is allowed in to membership.

Danny went there for the golf, a game he proceeded to treat with the deference he had previously reserved for his profession or his family and which in years to come, in various degrees of permanence, he would give to other pursuits that suddenly took over his life.

'It was quite amazing,' Milton Sperling, a top Hollywood producer and former Warner Bros executive – he was at one time Harry Warner's son-in-law – told me.

'Danny came to the club one day and I'm sure he had never played a game of golf in his life before. In a matter of a couple of hours, he not only knew enough about the game to get by, he actually beat one of our best players. Soon he was the best damned golfer in the place. And that's typical of the man. He has the same sense of coordination playing ball games as he has working on a film set.'

What Milton Sperling did not say, although he later agreed, was that what Danny Kaye also had was an intensity of purpose that makes the task in hand all consuming, and one that won't be finished until he is the best damned participant in the activity anyone knows.

He wasn't yet internationally known for it, but in the early 1950s, he was treating the family kitchen in a similar way to the manner in which he treated the Hillcrest golf course. Danny had discovered that cookery represented a challenge that was possibly second only to getting the King of England to laugh at his antics and join in his songs.

It wasn't that he was trying to find a way of making the family food taste better because he didn't like the way it was made already. He never ate what he cooked himself, but manipulating the various ingredients (to the point of making his own sausages; the kind you bought in a supermarket or even in a high-class private butcher shop wasn't good enough for what he had in mind) was perhaps the nearest thing he knew to standing poised over a patient lying on an operating table. No one has yet come forward

[126]

with proof that he heard his sausage machine, or the spit in his oven or even the dish washer making noises that sounded like 'ta-pocket, ta-pocket, ta-pocket', but Walter Mitty never found a dream come true the way Danny Kaye was discovering his reaching fruition over a hot stove. In years to come, this would take on almost fanatical proportions, cheered by admiring reactions from recipients of his bounty, but for the moment it was just a great hobby.

Possessions brought out a similar kind of intensity in him – like the new electric blanket which he bought at the time few other people even knew that there were such things. He had decided that he wouldn't go to bed at night without his blanket – even though there was no way he or anyone else could get the cover's switch to stay on.

Sylvia was to report: 'When I came back from cleaning my teeth one night, I was confronted with this scene – next to Danny's bed on a table was the blanket's thermostat switch, propped "on" by a golf tee held by the mouthpiece of the phone.'

As Sylvia said: 'Danny, who a few moments before had been brilliantly improvising as the baritone of *La Traviata* was now sound asleep. His feet were sticking out at the bottom of the long bed.'

She added: 'I didn't know whether he would sleep through the night, or suddenly wake up craving potato pancakes or a trip to Florida.' None of that was unusual. It was simply one of Danny Kaye's less predictable phases – which was the most predictable thing of all about him.

Once more, Danny announced plans for a new project that would excite audiences as much as it excited him. This time, it was going to be a whiz . . . a film filled with magic ingredients. Danny would star in the production, which would normally be enough to have audiences ringing theatres begging for a chance to book seats. But this time, it was not going to be enough. In a blockbusting musical called *Huckleberry Finn*, based on the lovable Mark Twain character, this real-life Huckleberry Finn was going to co-star with the second greatest dancer in screen history, Gene Kelly (Fred Astaire would come into Danny's life at a later stage).

The film would be produced by Arthur Freed, the man who in a few months would have the greatest success in his life making the greatest film musical success of all time (starring, again, Gene Kelly) *Singin' In The Rain*. And to top it all, it would be directed by another giant of that kind of business, Vincente Minnelli. 'Unfortunately, it just never happened,' Minnelli was to tell me. The reason was undoubtedly that bringing so many talents together – each talent represented a very great deal of money – was more difficult than any of them could have individually predicted.

There were still hopes that Danny could be persuaded back to Warner Brothers, but apart from a brief scene in *It's A Great Feeling*, starring Dennis Morgan and Doris Day, written by *Wonder Man* writer Melville Shavelson and his current partner Jack Rose, there was nothing. *It's A Great Feeling* was one of those films practically every studio turned out at this time – for no better reason than there were so many stars on the books, they needed to find ways of using them. This picture used the Warner Brothers back lot for a set and every star who wasn't actually working on something else to fill in the space between the opening credits and the card that said 'The End'. Danny did a 'turn' set at a railway station.

It would be surprising if he thought very much of that movie. He was filling in time and pleasing Jack Warner between live appearances in various other parts of the country. He was much more interested, in truth, in finding out new secrets in medicine. Psychoanalysis was his latest kick in 1950, a subject he constantly discussed with psychiatrists whom he seemed to meet as easily as movie producers.

One of them was Princess George of Greece, who had been trained by Freud himself. 'I despise the word "normal",' he was saying at this time. And the Princess agreed. She told him, 'The normal man has yet to be found – and when found, cured.'

It sounds a little pretentious, but Danny was serious. To him, it was no less sincere than when he told a Palladium audience that he loved them.

Now, he was telling the studio gang at Twentieth Century Fox that *they* were the ones he loved most of all. He had reason to do so probably. *On The Riviera*, the first film he was to make for the studio, had a tried and trusted pedigree. It had been made twice before. That should have been reason to stay clear of this particular project, except that the new script did appear to have some saving graces, not least of whom were Corinne Calvet and Gene Tierney.

As usual, the people who really could experience Danny at his best were those working on the film while it was being shot – like Nellie the hairdresser. Early in the morning, loud screams could be heard from the room where Nellie operated with her dryer and lotions. Danny was chasing her around the room and then through the corridors. 'Nellie,' he was calling, 'Nellie. Come back to me. You're starving me for love!' Meanwhile, like the conga line in *Up In Arms*, everyone else within earshot – and everyone appeared to be in earshot – followed on to see the fun. Sylvia was to swear that people who hadn't been on time for years would deliberately get to the studio early so as not to be left out of this distinctly Kaye performance.

It turned out to be yet another of the more pedestrian Kaye

movies, even though it was nominated for an Oscar for art direction. (It didn't win.)

Danny's own Oscar was called *Popo The Puppet*. He introduced the number in the film and it became one of the most popular of his career. The picture was a lot less memorable, and wasn't exactly helped by yet again – and not for the last time – giving Danny a double role to play. What had previously served as vehicles for Maurice Chevalier and Merle Oberon – when it was called *Folies Bergère* – and for Don Ameche and Alice Faye – as *That Night In Rio* – was now available for Danny as an American entertainer hired to impersonate a former French aviator and now business tycoon. It is fair to say that audiences would have been a lot happier had he tried to find a better way of impersonating Danny Kaye.

Not that he – and various studios – didn't try. Sam Goldwyn thought he could lure him back with a new *Walter Mitty* picture. It was an idea that appealed to Danny as much as to the mogul and a script and various routines were worked out for a picture that even had a title, *The Adventures of Walter Mitty*. That could have been seen as a true acceptance of undoubted fact – the role had been the best Danny had ever played. But this, too, was just a daydream that wouldn't happen. Neither did plans for yet another stab (if that isn't an unfortunate term) at *Macbeth* and at *The Pied Piper*, a role that would probably have suited Danny down to his upturned slipper.

There were those who had come to the conclusion that he was very much happier on the golf course – wearing the cheapest sweater the pro shop could sell him (he saw no point in buying clothes or anything else just to impress people) – than he ever was on a movie set.

He might have said that he got his fun entertaining his own friends, who were always as enthusiastic and as adoring an audience as any in a large auditorium. At about the time Ginette Spanier was discovering something about herself thanks to Danny Kaye, Danny was driving the famous Dr Charles Mayo in search of the nearest psychiatrist's couch.

Dr Mayo was, of course, known for the clinic he had established in Rochester, Minnesota. On this occasion, he was in France for his daughter's wedding and he and Danny were at the same party, Kaye as usual soaking up every single detail he could obtain from the internationally renowned physician about the latest discoveries in medicine. It was a mutually flattering experience – Danny immensely gratified that a man of such international standing in the medical world would not talk down to him, the doctor because the top showman of the day was spending so much time with him.

The doctor was in a very mellow mood and didn't notice his

fellow American slide out of the room, having first noted the number of the telephone by the doctor's side. In a room nearby, Danny picked up another phone and dialled the main number in the house. He asked to be put straight through to Dr Mayo.

The physician came on the line and was almost instantly embroiled in a discussion with a man whose voice owed not a little to Maurice Chevalier. He was, he said, *un docteur*, who admired Monsieur le docteur Mayo very greatly and proceeded to discuss in that highly convincing French accent, but using words in English that seemed to have been fractured by a sledge hammer, some of the theories that Mayo had been discussing himself just minutes before. The doctor was not upset. He was in his element. That his own ideas were being so respectfully received all those miles away from his own clinic was gratifying indeed.

Ultimately, he made the Frenchman an offer. 'You must come to America to visit with me,' he said. 'Come via Chicago. But get the plane, not a train. The train goes to Minneapolis.'

'But I have no weesh to go to Minneapolis,' said the phoney French voice.

'Yes, I know you don't want you to go there, that's the point,' said Mayo.

'Why do you tell me I have to go to Minneapolis. Eet is not necessary,' responded Kaye enjoying every moment.

'Well,' said Mayo, still playing the patient foreigner but developing by now a distinct red tinge to his complexion. 'I'm trying to tell you not to go to Minneapolis.'

For 20 minutes or so the conversation proceeded. Danny offering the required number of 'mon Dieux' to keep the momentum going and the doctor all but pulling his grey hair from his scalp. He was in full flow when Danny gently rested the telephone on the desk next to where he was standing and glided equally quietly back to where Sylvia, Mrs Mayo, their daughter, son-in-law and host and hostess were staring perplexed while the good doctor, uninterrupted for once, was getting over his message of directions to the Mayo Clinic from Chicago's airport.

'Now,' said Danny standing by the doctor's side, and still using that French accent, 'let me explain to you why I weesh not to go to Minneapolis.' For some reason not readily explainable, the doctor seemed to think it was very funny indeed. That, too, was part of Danny's art. He has always been adept at making the people he plays to feel as though they are an audience of one. When he *had* an audience of one, that person would feel as though he were sitting in a theatre.

For the moment now, there was a show he was going to have to get into. It was called Korea.

ME AND THE COLONEL

KOREA WAS TO BE AS IMPORTANT A MILESTONE IN THE STORY OF twentieth-century entertainment as it was in international politics.

The futile war fought when the totalitarian Communist North Korean armies invaded the corruptly administered South Korea was seen by a host of show people as providing them with a completely new made-to-measure audience.

It was, after all, just five years since the end of World War II – the conflict that had established the two Korean states in the first place – and many leading performers looked back on that war as being their own shining hour. To many of them it was a chance to relive it. To others like Danny, it was an opportunity to experience at first hand what the veterans had told him about their work with the USO which had operated the show tours.

And indeed they had been exciting times – to say nothing of the undoubted boost to morale which the tours had been.

Danny himself saw it as a great opportunity for a new audience – and a relief from some of the problems that had not been exposed with all the publicity he had received in London.

These didn't just centre around his relationship with Sylvia, although this was as unconventional as ever. Worse, he knew that his father was seriously ill. Jacob Kaminsky had had a good part of his stomach removed in a cancer operation and had gone to his two older sons to recuperate. Danny needed a trip like the journey to Korea, if only to see new troubles which would help him forget old ones.

A minor matter had also been raised, although he didn't take it very seriously. The Danish Government had asked him to forget plans to make a new film for Sam Goldwyn. Why the government in Copenhagen of all people were entering Danny's life at this stage will soon become apparent. (He said he couldn't even consider it. He had a contract with the producer.)

For the moment, he was thinking about Korea. And indeed it wasn't only memories that confirmed the sheer excitement of troop entertaining – even if the show people during World War II sang in mud that was knee deep, roasted and sweated in the tropics and fairly froze in the Arctic zones where American troops were stationed.

Men came home and told wives and mothers of what they had seen. Fred Astaire, Bing Crosby, Bob Hope, Jack Benny, Jolson . . . they had all done it. Newsreel footage showed the beams on the faces of both the entertainers and the entertained.

Within days of the war breaking out and the United Nations – which meant mostly Americans – going to the aid of the South, there were queues of performers waiting to join them. Al Jolson had been the first, an exploit that was to kill him within weeks of getting back. But from the battlefront on his arrival at Pusan, Jolson had given a radio interview to Louella Parsons in which he begged other entertainers to follow his lead. He said they would hate to have missed the opportunity of seeing the pleasure their visit would bring to these 'kids'. And he added, 'they *are* kids'. Danny Kaye was the first on the list of people he named who ought to get out there quick.

Whether that call had anything to do with it or not, Danny Kaye went to Korea and was never to be sorry. It made an enormous impact on him and introduced him to a whole new kind of entertaining.

'There is only one word to describe the Danny Kaye show (in Korea),' reported *Variety*'s special corresondent Capt. Robert E. Burns. 'Everything went according to schedule and Kaye sang and danced his way into the hearts of these wonderful troops, most of whom had to return to their foxholes after the show.'

Now, that was precisely the sort of thing that anyone writing anything about the Korean war had to say. The troops had to be described as marvellous or wonderful or terrific or brave because otherwise people might start asking why they were there in the first place, a state of affairs not to be encouraged by the War Department and certainly not by the people who were encouraging other show folk to go out there.

This trip to Korea provided Danny with a number of surprises, not the least of which was the fact that entertaining troops in battle conditions was a whole new activity in every sense of the word. Then there was the size of the audience. In one performance, he had 15,000 troops filling a huge amphitheatre, ready and willing to eat out of those expressive hands of his.

All his previous inhibitions of playing places like the Royal Albert Hall seem to have been as nought now. The man who didn't think he could get over to a crowd that was more than 4,000 strong at a time, was now enthralling 15,000 of them, the biggest show audience he had ever seen, let alone played to.

The theatre had been built, as part of the USO's efforts, on the side of a mountain. Other performers had spoken of bullets pinging and shells exploding while they were playing. The military authorities were taking no chances while Danny was on. Anti-aircraft guns were stationed at strategic points around the open-air auditorium. Helicopters, being used to this extent for the first time in warfare, flew overhead.

Sammy Prager, who had got more used to the London Palladium, accompanied Danny on a specially made portable piano that could be folded up like a large suitcase. They took it from the amphitheatre and places like it to other spots where there were men who wouldn't be able to get along to the big shows. In tiny gun emplacements right in the front line and in apparently more secure staff–operation centres further away, Danny saw the men at work and did some work himself – as if he were an advance man for his own show and giving away samples on the journey.

He sang *Candy Kisses* for one group of homesick soldiers and gave a perfect rendition of *Tchaikovsky* for another. The fact that most of these young soldiers wouldn't know a Mazursky from a Molotov didn't stop them enjoying every tongue-twisting stanza.

Not all of his audience was American either. There were the British and Australian contingents of the UN forces, too, as well as Greeks, Belgians and the recently-arrived group from Thailand. What Danny was offering was suitably international to appeal to them all.

What is beyond doubt is that by entertaining the troops he was giving youngsters very unwillingly taken away from home and family a chance not merely to uplift their spirits but to see an entertainer they would never forget.

As *Variety*'s correspondent noted: 'In the coming weeks and months, as the men spend the cold and damp Korean nights lying in their pup-tents and foxholes, they will talk about today, rehashing the show over and over again, thanking Danny and the rest for what they did to bring a ray of sunshine into their hearts in a foreign land far away from home.' 'Danny and his troupe are gone now,' said Capt. Burns, 'headed for another unit in their whirlwind tour of the front lines. They will long be remembered here, remembered for their gracious manner and unselfish determination to bring a little touch of home to these men who are giving up so much.

'Kaye wanted to remind them they were not forgotten men and he proved it with a great show – a clean show, without smutty jokes, that the chaplains and all the troops enjoyed.'

There was so much to do when he got home – more records to make, more films to consider, more shows to present. But first there was that personal matter.

He returned to the United States, to find that his father was much worse, and immediately made arrangements to fly to New York. But he arrived at Idlewild Airport at the precise moment that Jacob Kaminsky was dying in Brooklyn.

It was the kind of blow that comes to every devoted son – and not unlike millions of others, a time for reflection. Danny knew what he had owed the old man. Friends said that he should have the comfort of realising the pleasure he had given his father, but it *had* been very much a two-way street and at this moment he was the one feeling grateful.

When the going was tough, Danny had one outlet that always made him feel better – he could go to London. In May 1951, he was back at the Palladium. Not because it was an escape from the pressures at home, not least of which was his see-saw relationship with Sylvia, but because he had a previously signed arrangement to go there again, and the Palladium and Danny Kaye were like a very good dish prepared by an ace chef. Kaye, who was no novice in the kitchen himself, could always be relied upon to serve up what the British audiences would want.

On the surface nothing could go wrong, although he didn't see it that way. The fact that he appeared to have a life-time lease on the theatre was not enough. Even Bob Hope's crack that he was going to play the Palladium 'with Danny Kaye's permission' wasn't totally sufficient to assuage his doubts. It was probably good that he had them. It made the fulfilment of everyone else's expectations even more important.

He was told he was going to see a different Britain from the one he had known before. This was Festival of Britain year and the country was about to put on its brightest face to show that it had finally recovered from World War II. His welcome was as warm as ever.

The anonymous critic of *The Times* seemed to say it all: 'Mr Danny Kaye's performance at the Palladium last night settled one point: he is not the dazzling flash in the pan which pessimists have sometimes feared he might be. His act is better now than it was.

'Mr Kaye has been weeding out such of his countless eccentricities as were merely odd, and it is now possible to have a good view of a lively and original talent. He is an excellent mimic. He can take off the cockney and the Scot and the French cabaret entertainer who M. Chevalier has passed off to us as typical; he is an excellent mime, witness his man on the telephone who cannot get a word in edgeways. He still has an evident feeling for the witty word. But this time he pays more attention to the witty deed.'

The *Daily Mail* noted that he was on stage for an hour and ten minutes 'and it didn't seem a minute too much. In other words, the

[134]

36-year-old entertainer [he was actually 38, but nobody was really counting] was greater than ever.' And the *Daily Mirror*: 'Danny Kaye strode on the Palladium stage last night on his third visit to Britain [the critic had forgotten Danny's Royal Command Performance], flicked an eyebrow and put an audience of 2,000 [what happened to the other 1,000? I wonder] in his pocket in ten seconds flat.'

He had tried to disarm London's show biz writers – all of whose names he remembered and he showed that he had remembered them – at a tea party (no one wanted a mere Press conference for Danny Kaye) at the Prince of Wales Theatre. 'Let's face it fellers, I've *been* discovered – and the thrill can't be the same twice.'

There was more than a little truth in that. As he said on his first night: 'Do you realise what it's like to be in town for a whole week and wait for today? And when it comes, you'd give anything in the world to be some place else?'

So could that thrill be the same twice – for anyone?

In fact, most people seemed to think that, yes, it could be. The Palladium management certainly did. They were guaranteeing him £56,000 for his eight-weeks run (remember, this was 1951!) and every penny they expected to take at the box office was there – as everyone concerned thought it would be. A lot more besides was returned to unfortunate hopefuls among those who lined up every day for tickets or sent cheques and postal orders in by letter.

Once more, there were new songs, new routines, a cockney song, an Irish song – and his *Symphony for Unstrung Tongue*, in which he imitated every instrument in the orchestra. It would all prove to make Val Parnell's investment more than pay off.

Actually, Parnell wanted Danny for 12 weeks – he said he would be America's contribution to the Festival – and offered him £85,000 for the privilege, but even Kaye felt he couldn't stay in England that long. He had only just got back from Toronto where he had made about $100,000 for 14 performances at the exposition there.

Festival organisers had hoped he would appear at the Festival proper on London's South Bank and a figure of a quarter of a million pounds was bandied about. If he had accepted that kind of sum, it would have probably have brought down the Labour Government at least six months before it finally did fall to the then Mr Churchill's Tories.

And yet for the first time, there were now people who were casting doubt on Danny's brilliance. His friends had long known about the other side of Danny Kaye – his secret life, as Mr Thurber might have put it. No one would have suggested that he was anything but exciting, undoubtedly one of the most intelligent, brightest entertainers in the contemporary theatre. But he could be

[135]

extraordinarily difficult to deal with on a personal basis. And now there were writers saying much the same thing about his public persona.

In London, Kenneth Tynan, at the time best known as an actor – he had just played in Alec Guinness's version of *Hamlet*; one critic described his performance as 'quite dreadful' – turned to the writing that would before long make him one of the best-known critics in history, and attacked Kaye.

'Is he great?' he asked in the *Evening Standard*. And then proceeded to answer himself. 'I say No!'

'How is it,' he asked again, 'though we shake our heads in wonder, we do not surrender?'

Tynan said he had seen Danny perform six times and was willing to admit he had his strong points – 'though a good parodist, he is principally a vocal virtuoso, whose maddest moments are his sweetest. He gimlets his voice into a snakepit of supple gibberish and we feel as astronomers must feel when a new planet rolls into focus – amazed and incredulous in the face of absolute novelty.' Yet, he said, he had never seen anyone helpless with laughter. It seems fair to comment that he was not nearly as observant as he liked people to think – and what about all those other people who had been writing those kind things about him? Somehow, to Mr Tynan none of that really mattered.

'They had come to see a streamlined freak,' he said. 'If he had done anything so simple and direct as to squeeze tears of joy from their hearts, they would have felt cheated. They were content that he should be odd; they could puzzle over him and tell their grand-children they had seen him.'

The under-stressed tirade went on, ever more bitterly. 'He has, in excess, that disarming unselfconsciousness in which the best Jewish entertainers have always been rich.' (What *was* he *not* trying to say?) 'And when he uses its strength to twang the Jew's harp of his voice, he is an artist. But during those off-duty periods he ceases to be an artist and becomes, with dangerous ease, a charmer.'

Tynan bowed to the fact that girls thought him lovely and nice and that he showed his reverence of Harry Lauder and Will Fyffe by imitating them. 'He likes London and sings a cockney song – a frankly banal one as it turns out. As Dr Johnson said in a similar connection, it is like watching a dog walking on hind legs; the single point of interest being, not that it is particularly well done, but that it is done at all.'

Danny Kaye had brought the house down with *Maybe*, *It's Because I'm A Londoner*, and *I've Got A Lovely Bunch of Coconuts*. But that didn't impress Mr Tynan at all.

If that was tough, it was nothing like as hard as what was being said back home. Walter Kerr, taking time off from his usual territory on *The New York Times*, paid due recognition to Danny's conquest of London, but said that as far as the folks back home were concerned, it wasn't enough.

Kerr knew a thing about the theatre – less about London. He said Danny was carried 'nightly through Trafalgar Square on the shoulders of the Home Guard.' What Danny was doing in Trafalgar Square after an evening at the Palladium at least a couple of miles away he wouldn't explain. As for the Home Guard . . . what has since popularly become known as 'Dad's Army', the volunteer force mostly made up of men too old to be soldiers, had been disbanded about seven years earlier.

But that is nit-picking about a nit-picker, or, rather about someone who was much worse and saying worse things about Danny. This was more dangerous because, on the whole, what he said was true.

Danny, he pointed out, was a London legend. But . . . 'the tragedy of Danny Kaye is that he is not an American legend and apparently is never going to be one. He has the makings, as past performances here and the more recent London triumphs clearly indicate. He has that peculiar personal magnetism, that capacity for electrifying an audience on contact, which sometimes turns musical-comedy performers into national heroes. Good actors don't always have it. Reliable musical-comedy men are frequently without it. In fact, the moment you call a musical-comedy man "reliable" you mean that he *hasn't* got it. The "it" in question is a kinetic and projective personal quality which binds an audience emotionally to a performer, which breeds love rather than respect, which engenders a fierce and underlying loyalty rather than a judicious admiration. Danny Kaye could, for the asking, or at least for the working of it, belong to the happy company of Bert Williams, Montgomery and Stone, Al Jolson and George Cohan. Danny Kaye, however, prefers Technicolor. His is perhaps the most conspicuous waste of talent in the contemporary theatre.'

Mr Kerr in that one sentence was not merely commenting on the contemporary Danny Kaye, he was providing a sad preview on the figure of the future. Already in 1951, at a time when it seemed his abilities knew no bounds, Kerr had come to the very assessment which would become so apparent in years to come.

Kerr compared him with Gregory Peck – not the first time the comparison had been made with the actor who would probably have never made it very big on the stage but who had chosen just the right medium for his work in movies; a medium that gave him the chance to use his good looks and his control over just the right

[137]

gestures. Danny had not chosen the right medium for himself. Kerr decided that he took the wrong step – for his own good.

'The problem here, then, is not the theatre's need for Danny Kaye. It is Danny Kaye's need for the theatre, if he is ever to be as big as his talents permit. The size of these talents is beyond question; whether they are being given, or ever can be given, adequate scope in films is questionable indeed.'

Mr Kerr allowed Danny a certain benefit of the doubt he was creating in people's minds. 'Danny Kaye is not precisely a failure in pictures. In fact, he is just enough of a Hollywood success to keep him working at films until his real career passes him by. His pictures make reasonable amounts of money. He has a certain established, although not pre-eminent, position among film critics. He can, no doubt, have a fairly longish screen career and earn himself a decent, though not a fanatical, popularity with the international film audience.

'The trouble with Danny Kaye in pictures is that he has chosen a medium which is inhospitable to his most striking . . . talents. . . .

'He is still expected in each film to throw in a few sops to his older admirers, to those who know his reputation as a maniacal satirist and who have followed him devotedly from his earlier days in the theatre. While a new audience is being built, this audience is not to be lost. Result: two or three times per epic the nice, naïve and gentle young man breaks out into the most extraordinary displays of sophisticated mayhem.'

Again Mr Kerr was right.

The advantage Danny Kaye had was that he was very sophisticated indeed. The disadvantage was that he was so sophisticated he thought he could afford to ignore warnings like these.

Not that he didn't know he had his limitations. On his last night in Scotland on this trip, there were tears running down his cheek as fellow artists performed the now traditional ritual of singing *Will ye no come back again* to him.

A woman standing nearby was brave enough to ask him why. 'Because this wouldn't happen in America,' he said. But moments like that, as far as his own confidence in himself was concerned, were rare.

He knew where he was going and there wasn't a thing that was going to divert him from that path. Life was good for Danny Kaye – providing he didn't have to spend too much time with Sylvia conducting the metaphorical orchestra. He was delighted to have Dena to play with, and to look forward to having as a future soul mate, someone to take the advice he was planning to give.

'Dena my darling,' he told her, 'you must love what you do. When I was growing up in Brooklyn, I loved being the boy in the

[138]

neighbourhood who sang and cut up. Later, when I became a professional entertainer and times were hard, my love for my work made life easier to bear.'

He was thrilled with his golf and his cookery and the success he was having playing table tennis with friends in the business.

He knew he was the best darn party guest in the Beverly Hills circuit and he was convinced, rightly, that London – Mr Tynan apart – loved him. The career he had planned for himself was developing just the way he wanted it to.

The trouble was that articles like those would appear more and more in the papers of the world. Some written out of spite like the Tynan piece. Others, like Kerr's, seemingly written from the heart much more out of sorrow than anger – though it was easy enough to be very angry indeed about the way Danny was allowing his career to be managed. Eddie Dukoff was officially managing that, still apparently allowing Danny no more than £100 a week pocket money. But there can be no doubt that Danny himself was the man in charge.

And there were still occasions when even in Britain the name Danny Kaye wouldn't open all doors. In Scotland in July 1952, the Royal and Ancient Golf Club at St Andrews refused to allow him through its doors – because he was neither a member nor had been introduced by one.

It was embarrassing because in a blaze of publicity Danny had driven up to the club in a Rolls-Royce and waved to a crowd of spectators, who were in the process of blowing him kisses when the doorman shook his head and put up the palm of his hand to prevent Kaye going any further. He was later allowed to play at the St Andrews New Golf Club, which belonged to the town.

Others would shake their heads at some of Danny's doings in another part of Europe. But when he and Sam Goldwyn announced they were getting together again, all seemed very rosy indeed. Danny was going off to Denmark soon. He was, announced the avuncular Mr Goldwyn, going to make the life of Hans Andersen – or Hans Christian Andersen as the storyteller would for ever afterwards be known.

HANS CHRISTIAN ANDERSEN

IT WASN'T A FILM THAT WAS GOING TO SATISFY THE PURISTS – EITHER the purists who still worshipped at the shrine called Danny Kaye or those who had been used to a dose of Hans Andersen in their mother's milk – to listen to the outcry it would seem that some of them heard the Andersen tales before they began suckling at their mothers' breasts.

The Kaye purists were upset because the picture avoided precisely what had upset Walter Kerr so much in his piece the year before – there wasn't a single opportunity for anything that even vaguely resembled 'sophisticated mayhem'. The Andersen devotees took it as a near sacrilegious insult that their idol should be played on film at all – and then by an American. . . . To the Danes in general and the experts on the works of the man who was their national storyteller in particular, making the film at all with a foreigner in the lead was a gratuitous insult.

Those doubts aside – and they worried people less as time went on – *Hans Christian Andersen* was to be probably the most important film in Danny Kaye's entire career.

Out of a Danish pastry of a movie, Goldwyn and Kaye had created a concoction which most people who had had anything to do with it – or had even just seen it – would be unlikely to forget.

It was a no-holds-barred production at a time when Hollywood was deciding to pull in its haunches. Later that same year of 1952, the big studios were going to try to meet the challenge of television with screens that vied with each other for being wider and higher. Goldwyn, the only one of his breed who decided that since he saw no way of beating television he should join it by recognising it was here to stay, believed that the size of a screen was not the answer. Quality and size of effort was.

His film was to cost $4 million – all, as usual in a Goldwyn production, from his own pocket.

From the beginning, and probably to ease the minds of its detractors above all else, it was emphasised that this was not intended to be a biography of the man everyone in the world had previously called simply Hans Andersen. It was a story about a

[140]

storyteller, the kind of tale a storyteller himself might have woven about himself. Or, as the opening titles of the film emphasised:

'Once upon a time, there lived in Denmark a great storyteller named Hans Christian Andersen. This is not the story of his life, but a fairy tale about this great spinner of fairy tales.'

In the hope that the Danes' ruffled feathers would be satisfactorily smoothed, he invited the Danish Government to come over to watch the filming and then to give – he hoped – their stamp of approval on the finished product. And as if that were not enough, he made it clear that there would be a very evident Danish presence on the screen, in the form of Paul Bruhn of the Royal Danish Ballet.

It was going to be colourful, very cheerful and full of the kind of tunes the Samuel Goldwyn studios and the music publishers knew would be hummed and sung all over – so they not only made money via record sales for Mr Kaye and everyone else concerned, but also provided a mighty advertisement for the movie.

No one would suggest that Hans Christian Andersen ever sang a song even vaguely resembling *Wonderful, Wonderful Copenhagen* (which he and everyone else in the film persisted in calling Copen-ha*r*gen, to go with his own name of H*ar*ns) but it was played on turntables and on radio programmes all over the world for years afterwards. (That song, incidentally, was included to placate the sensitive Danes. It was a very good move for all concerned. The song jumped to the top of the hit parade. Danny Kaye made a lot of money and the Danish Tourist Board could record the greatest number of visitors streaming into their country that they had ever known. *Wonderful, Wonderful Copenhagen* was the best public relations gimmick they could possibly have dreamed up.)

It was, however, as one might already have guessed, a picture beset with difficulties – not least of which were the angry comments from the Danes. When Danny, at the suggestion of an over zealous PR man, not only went walking in Copenhagen in an outfit not unlike the one worn by Andersen himself, but posed lying down in the great man's actual bed, it seemed as though everyone in the country wanted to pummel Mr Kaye into something that was not at all most people's idea of a Hollywood film star.

But there were other worries, too. Sam Goldwyn picked Frank Loesser to write the score. Mr Loesser produced some marvellous songs, and not just the *Copenhagen* number. *Inch Worm* and *The Ugly Duckling* became hits in their own right. But Goldwyn wanted something more exciting than just songs.

Since so much of the film was centred around Andersen's love for a ballerina – they meet when the cobbler is brought to her theatre to make her a pair of dancing shoes; an offer he is unlikely to refuse since he has been brought from jail to perform this function – Goldwyn saw it as an opportunity to make it the most spectacular ballet of all time.

Loesser couldn't write that sort of music. So he told Walter Scharf, who was the musical director, to do it instead. Goldwyn proceeded to issue his instructions to the man who at the time had worked on dozens of films ranging from the Bing Crosby-Fred Astaire picture *Holiday Inn* – the one that introduced *White Christmas* – to the early Alice Faye musicals – to produce a score. It sounded rather like an estate developer ordering '20 yards of books' for his new houses.

Goldwyn, as has already been established, was not the legendary Hollywood mogul with abysmal taste and appalling manners who was only interested in making money not works of art. He may have fractured the English language in the course of eating his breakfast, but he had enough taste to please the pallets of everyone who ever saw a movie and thought it could be a rewarding experience.

Planning the music for the *Andersen* ballet, however, brought out a totally different kind of man. 'How long,' he asked Scharf, 'was the longest ballet ever used in a picture?'

Scharf thought he knew the answer but took his time to consult the books. It was the one Gene Kelly choreographed in *An American in Paris*. 'How long was that?' asked Goldwyn. 'Fourteen minutes,' said the musician who wasn't used to assessing artistic success with a stop watch or a tape measure.

'This one has got to be eighteen minutes,' said the mogul. No mention of quality, of what sort of music would have to be written, how it was going to match the rest of the action and fit into the picture; just how long it was going to have to be. It also would involve delicate changes of reels in inconvenient places – the dot in the top right hand corner indicating the time a reel had to be changed always came in a natural break between scenes; now Goldwyn wanted one in the middle of a ballet sequence?

But since Sam Goldwyn was who he was, Sam Goldwyn after all, the ballet Scharf presented for the picture was precisely 18 minutes long.

Scharf's ballet score was a highly complicated arrangement of several pieces of music by Liszt. That it was made to sound like an original piece of work is itself a tribute to the work of one of the people generally regarded as a backroom boy of films, as indispensable as the cameraman, but apart from the occasional recognition of an Oscar nomination, is generally not one of the names on everyone's tongue.

[142]

The *Mermaid Ballet* that resulted wasn't just longer than any other in a film before. It was also very much more expensive. It cost all of $400,000 – the budget for many a full-length movie of the time.

As the ballerina, Moira Shearer looked as if she were going to be stupendous.

It was planned to take two weeks shooting the ballet, a time that, predictably enough, was exceeded, with a 28-member *corps-de-ballet* who were only partly responsible for the 100,000 man hours of work that went into it – that was the kind of statistic film studios love dishing out at the time like a menu in the executive dining room. The dancers earned $55,000 for their trouble.

It was, however, symptomatic of what Goldwyn himself was determined would be unsurpassed for his definition of quality. One was almost tempted to imagine at the time that even if the story and the performances weren't up to much, people would stay to watch and to wonder at all he had put into it. And that was not an unreasonable assumption.

For the statistics lovers, take in, too, more than 5,000 square feet of sets all designed by Antoni Ciave, who came over from Paris to plan them. They cost $160,000, a figure that would make a producer today dance with joy but which in January 1952 made even Sam Goldwyn's heart flutter just a little bit uncomfortably. Costumes accounted for a further $55,000.

And if you fancy contemplating money a little more, think of the rhinestones that were used as the mermaid's tears (shed the moment she realises the handsome prince will never be hers). These 15,000 little sparklers amounted to a total of $472.

It all fitted in with Goldwyn's determination to make it the most important film he had shot since *The Best Years of Our Lives* and one he hoped would possibly go down in history as the best to date. He could ask no more of the fulfilment of a dream he had first had in 1936.

Sam's earliest problems were mere minor difficulties compared with the one that came about after filming had actually begun. As Walter Scharf tells it, this was a problem in which Danny Kaye did not want to become involved and Scharf himself was turned into a Danish uncle if not a Dutch one.

The problem concerned Miss Shearer, who, before starting work on *Andersen*, had been a fairy godmother to every little girl who ever dreamed of being a ballet dancer. In *The Red Shoes* she produced more oohs and aahs from her audience per inch of film than in any other movie in history. Now, though, she had a problem. She was pregnant.

'We were on the stage when I first heard about this.' Walter told me. 'I had noticed she was bulging slightly, but I didn't think very much of it. She was standing up against the bar, you know by the big mirror at which ballerinas practised.'

As he said, the problem was not so much the little bulge that was evident in November 1951. It was much more the big bulge of the middle of 1952. There were six more months of work to do and it was plain that even if Moira had the stamina to complete it, what she didn't have was an answer for completing a normal and successful pregnancy without anyone finding out about it.

Goldwyn had to be told. A special 'audience' – for that was the sort of level on which people operated as far as the studio head was concerned – had to be arranged.

'We planned the audience – but only after Frances, Sam's wife, heard about it first.' Neither of them knew how to tell him without making the German invasion of Denmark a dozen years before seem like an outing for tourists.

'I think we ought to let Danny tell him,' said Scharf.

He was at first less than willing to be brought in. 'I want to be in China when you tell him about this,' Kaye told him. He expected the floor of the Goldwyn lot to open up and consume all within its reach when Sam heard the news.

But Danny did go to Goldwyn. He didn't tell Sam Goldwyn the news, he soothed him, he joked him. 'I was so impressed,' Scharf told me. '*I* was scared to death.'

But it was Danny's company that eased things along, with Moira in tears.

'By the time Sam heard about it he was quite calm and simply asked his casting people to try to find someone else.'

They picked Zizi Jeanmaire, like the choreographer of the film, Roland Petit, a major figure in the Paris Ballet, who happened to be in Los Angeles at the time in the company's production of *Carmen*.

No one seemed to have discovered at that stage that Mlle Jeanmaire couldn't speak English. But even though she would have to do quite as much speaking as dancing in the movie, it wasn't yet considered important. It was just another problem.

But there were times when it seemed very much more than that. There were voice tests that made what little hair Sam had stand up on end.

'He went blue, black and purple,' Scharf remembered for me. 'What are we gonna do?' he asked. It was Danny who helped return the mogul to his normal complexion.

He started working with Zizi to help get her round the problem. From the moment he realised there were difficulties, he decided to give her Mr Kaye's personal attention. There were typical Danny Kaye elocution lessons for the French beauty.

'Where you going?' he asked her.

'To the block,' she answered.

'How can you go to the block?' he responded. 'To the block! You mean round the block, you dope.'

There had been others, and there would be more to come, who took that sort of talk as a personal insult. Not Zizi. She laughed.

He mimicked her, and in so doing dragged out of her enough English to complete her dialogue scenes – to say nothing of being able to sing the more than convoluted lines of songs like *No Two People*, which had words in them that suited perfectly the cultured English of Miss Shearer and the verbal gymnastics of a Danny Kaye, but were not exactly made to measure for a woman who recited verse sounding as though she were ordering one of M. Balmain's gowns.

It was Danny's charm that carried him through. And not just with Mlle Jeanmaire. Walter Scharf's mother Bessie Zwerling was a leading actress in the Yiddish theatre. When Danny found that out, he demanded to be led to the telephone. From then on and for the remainder of the picture he phoned Mrs Zwerling every night speaking all the time only in Yiddish, reminiscing about the Yiddish theatre of the old days, telling jokes and exchanging recipes.

'It got so,' Scharf recalls, 'that my mother would talk about "My friend Danny". She said that they talked all the time.'

But he wasn't all sunshine and light on the picture.

One thing was very different about this film – Sylvia wasn't there. Sam Goldwyn made it very clear that he didn't want the complication of having to deal with her before telling Danny that he had a special idea on a certain subject. That was a very unusual situation for Kaye.

Even though Sylvia wasn't in her usual position of seeing her husband through words she had specially written for his own form of acrobatics, there were still tensions. Things had to be done Danny's way.

'I guess it had something to do with where he came from,' said Walter Scharf, whose roots were precisely the same as Danny's. 'New York, if you're not careful, can teach you to demand a sense of power. It is why he would have liked to have been a surgeon – the power over a patient with a knife; or to conduct an orchestra or even to play chef.'

Sometimes at the studio, he would sit alone, not wanting to be interrupted. Playing golf with Scharf at this time, the musician would be lucky to get as many as 20 words out of him in four hours.

But they were friends and had been so from the moment they first met.

[145]

A few minutes after that first meeting, Kaye put his arm around Scharf's shoulders and said, 'This is for life.' That was unusual, to say the least.

On *Andersen* as well as on the other films, Danny's highs and lows were more than obvious. One morning, he could be clowning around with the make-up girls, in the afternoon, he was sitting morosely in a corner by himself.

'Mostly, he was quite delightful,' recalls Scharf.

As for Sam Goldwyn, it represented, he believed, one of the most significant ventures in the history of the cinema.

The cliché is that it represented a challenge to Danny. It was that. But it was also a great opportunity for him to develop an approach to his work that he realised he had barely skimmed before – communicating with children. He knew he could do that well enough with Dena, but she after all was his own daughter. Yet, he had heard that kids on two continents loved the records he had made with children in mind.

He could not possibly have known how important this part of his life was going to when he first sat down on a set to tell a gang of child extras a story.

At first, it wasn't to be assumed that Kaye was even going to make the film.

But he saw it as a perfect opportunity to prove he could be as big a star in America as he was in Britain, that his talents could be extended beyond the git-gat-gettle variety. And he had that hunch about working with children. . . .

The rapport was something that even he hadn't experienced before. He was helped in no small way, however, by the script – provided by a master at the game, Moss Hart.

Danny appears to have had more trouble with his make-up and the tailoring he was offered than with either the script or the musical score. On his first day on the set at the Goldwyn studios at Santa Monica Blvd he was given a haircut. He looked at himself in the mirror and decided he didn't like it. Sylvia didn't like it when he got home. None of the other people who had appended themselves on to him to form an entourage liked it either. Neither did Danny like his socks. He was persuaded by the designer that they blended perfectly into the rest of his outfit. And then there were his trousers. . . . Danny thought they were too thick and heavy. The Goldwyns were consulted. Yes, they agreed, the trousers were too thick and too heavy. The coarse-looking woollen material was changed to doe skin, but made to look on screen as though they were neither of the quality nor as well made as the studio had really created.

Danny decided he liked the jacket he was given well enough to start clowning in the dressing room – the usual signal that all would be, if not well, then at least reasonably acceptable. 'Wee!' he shouted, 'and I've got pretty red socks!' They had been changed, to order.

The shoes would be more difficult. 'Whatever you do,' he ordered, 'make 'em good and comfortable'. So good and comfortable they had to be.

If the studio and wardrobe people had been worried about Danny's fussiness over his costumes, compared with the dance led them by Mlle Jeanmaire (not the kind of dance she was being paid to lead) he was a boy scout who had just been seen across the road by an old lady.

Most people remember him being entirely professional once shooting began. He had found a part that seemed to suit what he was looking for. And he got on with those children so beautifully. At the same time, he exhibited talents no one had yet imagined he had.

The fairytale about the spinner of fairytales took as a starting assumption that Hans Andersen was a simple cobbler who was much happier gathering a group of kids around him than collecting a batch of nails in his mouth. It is equally assumed, however, that the man who is the despair of the local schoolmaster in the village of Odense – for taking the children away from their lessons – was a craftsman, hence the enthusiasm with which he is released from jail to mend the ballerina's slippers.

Moss Hart's skill was in making the germ of an idea take on huge proportions in the film, without anyone realising that the episodes so ingeniously knitted into the picture were not constructed as a whole, in a single breath of inspiration. There was, for instance, that ballet, the one that Sam Goldwyn wanted to be four minutes longer than *An American In Paris*. Hart shaped it so that the ballerina would believe that the loveletter penned by the poor cobbler was, in fact, the outline script for the ballet itself.

More important for Danny himself was that it gave him the chance to sing many more ballads than he ever had before, the kind of songs that were all the rage in those pre-rock'n'roll days of the early '50s. His duet with Jeanmaire (the 'Zizi' turned out to be more of a nickname than anything else; she didn't use it in her credits), *No Two People*, was a big hit.

Most significant of all was that Danny had to dance in the film – and even when he wasn't dancing, he moved as though he were, doing steps of his own, and teaching others how to move at the same time.

Walter Scharf summed it up: 'I think this was the only picture I've ever worked on where the choreographer was the actual star

[147]

himself. Roland Petit only understood about ballet and was concentrating on the ballet movements.'

It was Danny himself who told director Charles Vidor and Harry Stradling, the cameraman, where he was going to perform. He'd say: 'Right, now put the camera here because I am going to move across like this.' Actors who were really comedians who also sang songs with a very pleasant light voice didn't usually do that.

'I remember vividly,' recalls Walter Scharf, 'when we were doing the *Ugly Duckling* number, how he schooled the little boy with the shaven head. He took him under his wing and put him at ease. He told Harry Stradling how he was going to use his hands. He was calling out all the shots.'

Danny planned the *Inchworm* number and arranged, much to his musical director's amazement, how the children reciting their tables would work in counterpoint to the main melody.

'He designed the entry into Copenhagen – where there were 20 barkers, working against each other. I don't remember any film, including *Funny Girl* with Barbara Streisand, where the stars worked out everything. It wasn't because he was laying down the law for the sake of doing it. That was a perfect example of just how far his talent stretched. He took direction perfectly and he would generally do what the experts on the set suggested, but he knew the camera and he understood the theatrical possibilities of everything. Needless to say, he knew everything about make-up, too – and would tell the department – who, of course, gave him the very best people in the business – what they should use. He was the most informed man I've ever met.

'That was one side of him that most people never knew. Why Danny has never directed a film on his own, I don't know.'

The film took 53 weeks to make, and it was not an easy 53 weeks for anyone, even when Danny was being very, very good and was entertaining staff with his patter or turning from English to Yiddish to gibberish in the space of a few minutes.

One of Danny's problems was that he liked to be heard, hated to listen. 'There were so many occasions when we were making *Hans Christian Andersen*,' recalls Walter Scharf, 'that Danny would just turn off. I'd talk to him and realise that he was somewhere else. At first, I'd take a leaf from his own book and talk gibberish to him. Then, I'd simply say to him, "You weren't listening to me, were you?"'

But there was an innate kindness in him, too, says the man who was involved in so much of the musical side of this picture, as well as its other aspects.

If Danny's Professor Higgins act had not revealed where the person to whom he was talking came from, he would ask. That was

[148]

the signal for an entire conversation to begin, based on how much he knew of the person's home town and the kind of work he did.

Says Scharf: 'It was amazing how this put people at ease – but also how much it turned the conversation the way he wanted it to go. He totally disarmed you. If he wanted a conversation with anyone, he would find out all about him first. It was a question of doing his homework. it was Danny's way – and it worked.'

Scharf maintains that sometimes it was hard to be tolerant of him. He told me that his own wife resented the fact that when Danny came to their house for dinner, he would never say how much he liked the meal. He would then always leave without saying goodbye to his hostess.

Hans Christian Andersen was very different from anything Danny had ever done before. He liked it because it was just that. But there were still those who saw it all as a retrogressive step. They were the ones who liked their Danny the way he was in *Walter Mitty* and *Wonder Man* – if only the stories and Danny's other half hadn't been allowed to get in the way.

Bosley Crowther, writing in *The New York Times*, was not over impressed by it all. Goldwyn's team, he said, had 'constructed a large fable out of a lot of smaller fables – and little more. And the mediums through which they have done this are mostly decoration, music and dance, with accuracy or even plausible definition of the central character incidental to the whole.

'The consequence is a handsome movie – in colour, of course – in which the French dancer, Jeanmaire, races and twirls in graceful beauty through a couple of lovely ballets, the best of which is from Andersen's tale of *The Little Mermaid*, written by Roland Petit and performed to music by Franz Liszt in which Danny Kaye sings and acts out some saucy Frank Loesser songs in the role of the story-telling cobbler who falls in love with the ballerina and – well, that's all.'

Mr Crowther did not share my view that the story was put together fairly craftily.

In one review in the paper he stated: 'Quite simply, Mr Hart has not created a character for Mr Kaye to play, let alone a credible reflection of the famous Danish teller of tales. His Hans Christian Andersen is lumpish, humourless and wan. No wonder Mr Kaye is unable to stoke up magnetism in the role.'

But he added: 'However, he does bravely manage to make merry with Mr Loesser's songs and convey something of the jovial spirit of a musical fairy tale. His singing of *Wonderful Copenhagen* with a variety of choruses is full of bounce.' And he said Danny 'puts ingenuousness and flavour' into the other numbers.

'Even so, all of these items seem strung together like trinkets on a chain.'

[149]

His general conclusion was no happier. Writing in the Sunday edition of the paper, he went on:

'The inevitable means to the end of trying to be entertaining in this day and age is obviously to fill them with "production", let history, legend or fable be what they may.'

The *New York Times*'s view was not unique. In fact, it was difficult to find a single critic who liked it as much as the audience would.

'Without any clowning to do,' commented the *Saturday Review*, 'Danny Kaye is simply not very interesting, and it's hard to get worked up over his encounter with a ballet dancer in Copenhagen and his rather foolish mooning about her.'

That, actually did hit the nail into one of Andersen's boots, if not into Danny's head. The story was that even Dena complained about the film – because she didn't like her daddy being locked in jail. It may or may not have been true. The fact is, however, that while audiences who loved colour, spectacle and children's stories thought the movie had tremendous charm, they were basically the people who lined up every time a new Walt Disney film was released. The people who would have been willing to sell their collective birth rights for a seat in the front stalls at the Palladium or who loved every convoluting moment of *Tchaikovsky* were grievously disappointed. And it was difficult to forgive anyone who was responsible for that – no matter how skilfully it was put together, and, despite what anyone else might have said, skilfully put together it was.

The *New Yorker* complained that Moss Hart's script 'credits Hans Christian Andersen with a simplicity bordering on active idiocy.

'As Mr Hart has it, Hans Christian Andersen was a shoemaker in a sort of community that the Shuberts used to construct when Romberg was lining out his songs. With the Shuberts of course, it was Alt Wien, but what the hell, Denmark's on the same continent.'

The Danes were equally unresponsive. Their top critic Arne Sorensen wrote in *Information*:

'It will cost America's reputation so much that it will take the United States Information Service in Denmark 50 years to make up the loss.' He agreed with that bit about the Shuberts and Sigmund Romberg. The atmosphere of the film wasn't Denmark at all – but 'a German principality'.

The paper *Berlingske Aftenavia*, said that the film 'has nothing in common with Hans Andersen except his name and the titles of some of his stories.'

Every stop was brought out of the Goldwyn publicity factory to make the picture a hit, and not just the little idea of persuading Mr Kaye to take a nap in the great man's bed, which took a lot longer to

[150]

die down than anyone could have imagined. It was as though sleeping on Andersen's pillow was just a short distance away from jumping into his shoes. They didn't know that the Odense museum did, in fact, have a pair of Andersen boots on display – and, yes, Danny did try those on. If the local Hans Andersen Society had heard about that, their protests to the US Embassy at Copenhagen would have been tougher still. As it was, their angry note demanded that their complaints be forwarded to the Government in Washington.

The Press in Andersen country took every step as a further personal affront – and an opportunity for themselves to show what great patriots they were. Nothing was better in that first decade after the end of the Nazi Occupation than to fly the flag by knocking a foreigner.

Danny's excursion into the bed was taken as a good enough reason to attack Goldwyn's audacity – they didn't use the word 'chutzpah' in Denmark, but it amounted to the same thing – in making the film in the first place.

It all plainly upset Danny – as though he were himself responsible for a nation's honour, when all he had really done was take on a role which he personally considered challenging and believed others would enjoy just as much.

He nevertheless thought it was incumbent on him to explain if not apologise. 'I am playing the role as straight as I possibly can. After reading the script, I couldn't see any of my particular brand of comedy. I have as much respect for Hans Christian Andersen as the Danes, and as much warmth in my heart for his writing as the millions of kids who have enjoyed his stories.'

The lines may have sounded a bit like a Press agent's pitch, but it did seem to encompass most of the things he would have wanted to say at the time.

'Of course,' his statement went on, 'there are a few delightful moments in the film where I sing and dance with a group of children. If it becomes funny, it is naturally that way. There are also many fantasy sequences in the film in which I either sing or dance or both. I think they have been handled entertainingly and with a great amount of visual appeal. If the audiences find these routines delightful, and chuckle, I can't see where this is an 'insult'.

The complaints, however, continued. Some of them were more serious than others. There was, for instance, the tongue-in-Danish-cheek note from an organisation called The Copenhagen Committee. They said that they were threatening to dismiss the head of national tourism – presumably for making Danny's visit so easy for him; without realising at the time just what the movie was going to do for the country's hotel and restaurant industry. Few Danes had yet contemplated how many people were going to sing about Wonderful Copenhagen – even if they didn't know how to pronounce it properly.

But most damning of all was this choice comment: 'Your own reputation with the Copenhagen girls, which has been mighty good since they found you have red hair, is in serious danger.'

The letter pointed out a serious linguistic fault in the Copenhagen lyric. 'A Danish girl doesn't say "nein",' the letter pointed out with mock seriousness. 'She says "nej", pronounced "nigh!" – if, that is, she doesn't prefer to say "yes" – which is "ja".'

To underline the point, the writer, one Trier Pedersen – who plainly had more of a sense of humour than his fellow members who authorised the complaining letter in the first place – sent Danny a copy of a guide to Copenhagen – which he admitted had one serious deficiency. 'Unfortunately, there isn't much in it about Copenhagen girls. But they're certainly worth getting to know.'

Sylvia might not have been surprised if he contemplated taking Mr Pedersen's advice.

Despite all this, Danny *was* treated fairly royally while in Denmark. When he met the Prime Minister Erik Eriksen, he handed him a copy of the script. At the Parliament building, other members of the Government greeted him. Later on, so did his own opposite numbers in the Danish theatre. Now, what Danny had previously done in London with Sid Field and Ted Ray, he did with the luminaries of the Danish musical stage. In July 1952, it was revealed that most of the country turned on their radios to hear Kaye and the Danes joining each other on the air while – yes, you guessed it – Danny tried his tongue at Danish. No one understood him very well, but his accent sounded so good the listeners were left feeling rather ashamed that a foreigner knew their language better than they did themselves.

When he gave a Press conference, he confessed that some of his usual bravado was missing. 'I came here to see if you would murder me,' he told his audience.

The New York Times reported that the conference was attended by as many people as the then still General Eisenhower and General Matthew B. Ridgeway had had when they met Danish newsmen. The journalists called Danny the 'five-star actor'.

The film may not have been as much a milestone in film history as Goldwyn dearly wanted it to be, but it was an important sea change for Danny – who had managed to prevent himself being washed up along with the mermaid's statue on the rocks of Copenhagen. The trouble was that he thought that was the sort of film he ought to make again. Other people would spend a lot of time trying to convince him that what audiences wanted to see most of all was the real Danny Kaye.

THE PALACE

THE PALACE THEATRE ON BROADWAY WAS ALWAYS SOMETHING OF AN oddity. It stood within a pigeon's flight of the George M. Cohan statute and you could reach it with a paper aeroplane made from a folded up programme for a tragedy playing at a theatre down the road.

Surrounded by legitimate theatres, some playing serious plays, some large-scale musicals that were part of the fabric of what was once called The Great White Way and which over the last 40 years has become the sleaziest thoroughfare on earth, the Palace was a memorial to something quite different.

The Palace was the last of the temples of vaudeville, one of the few theatres still surviving in the 1950s honouring the tradition of the 'two-a-day', the acrobats, the dancers, the singers and the comics who twice a night had audiences perched on the edge of their seats.

Every week, a top act, usually from the world of films or radio – and just occasionally from the up-and-coming medium of television – would headline the bill at the Palace. It represented the pinnacle of success. All the greats had done it – all, that is, except Al Jolson who had said he would only go there if he could be sure that Jack Benny, Eddie Cantor and his other contemporaries would be in the audience and he could order these 'slaves', as he delicately called them, to applaud. Judy Garland made a record in which she declared, not without reason, 'Until You've Played The Palace You Haven't Lived.'

To Danny Kaye, the Palace represented what he hoped would amount to the Palladium on Broadway, his chance of seeing American audiences paying him the sort of attention those in London had paid, extending in effect his love affair.

Danny knew it was not a thing he could take lightly – particularly after what the critics had been writing. But he had to have the right occasion. That came in January 1953 – his 40th birthday.

Really, the news must have been something of a surprise to the audiences who had been following him over the years. All that achieved so far, and still not 40? Well, the Palace was the place for him to prove that an old man into his fifth decade was still capable of doing reasonably well.

And just as he had said all those lovely things about London, he was ready to declare himself for his home city.

It certainly was a time to tell the people who were about to line up for tickets that he was *their* Danny. He showed friends the souvenirs from past triumphs – including a programme autographed by the Royal Family – but said that what he wanted most was a demonstration of love from his own people.

As he said: 'California is only a place to hang my hat and work from. '(It had to be hoped that the people back home in Beverly Hills didn't read this). But even though it was a 'great place for kids' it had certain limitations.

'Brooklyn's different. It's not a city. It's a state. A glorious state of mind.' That should have been guaranteed to bring them in. And they did. They brought their popcorn and they sat and watched their favourite Kid From Brooklyn making with all de 'dems' and 'dose' which de fellers in de joint could be relied upon to identify wid.

He was coming to Broadway with the finest of recommendations – the folks in San Francisco loved him almost as much as those in London. The editor of *Daily Variety* Joe Schoenfeld saw the show at the city's world-famous Curran Theatre and invoked the now anticipated comparison. 'He's the nearest thing to Jolson as a full dimension and marathon entertainer. He has the remarkable ability as did Jolson of holding his audiences spellbound for interminable periods and then take them up and down the full scale of human enjoyment.'

It was also an opportunity for him to get back to his git-gat-gattle routines which would be mixed more smoothly than most people would have expected with the ballads and soft songs from *Hans Christian Andersen*.

He also did his *Molly Malone* for the Irish in the audience, and Harry Lauder's *Wee Deoch and Doris* for the expatriot Scots. The Walter Mitty pilot came out to tell the people from Brooklyn – and those from Queens, the Bronx, Manhattan, Staten Island and even the ones who had come by bus from further afield – that he had a great affection for England, where he would make a film after completing his Palace run.

'No one has been exaggerating Danny Kaye's genius for entertaining,' reported Brooks Atkinson in *The New York Times*, saying for the live show everything that his colleague couldn't say for his most recent film.

'He sang, talked and grimaced for an hour and three quarters at the Palace last evening, and everyone came away beaming and

[154]

refreshed. Even the crowds massed in Seventh Avenue seemed to have been having a good time, being in the neighbourhood.'

Mr Atkinson didn't say so, but it was plainly encouraging, not to say gratifying, to know that Danny was offering the folks back home the kind of fare he had apparently been limiting to the foreigners.

'Apart from being very skilful, Danny is a good egg; and perhaps the sightseers outside the theatre felt cheered up by the happy look on the faces of the theatregoers who were coming out and heading home.'

The critic was pleased to know that Mr Kaye had 'acquired a lot of scope' since his *Let's Face It* days – as if his movies hadn't proved precisely that. 'But he is essentially the same Danny – with the triangular face, the sharp nose, the curly blond hair (Mr Atkinson had forgotten what Sam Goldwyn had done to the colour, or hadn't noticed that in recent weeks, he was allowing it to go a little closer to its original red colour) and the smile. He can race through a scat song like a greased-lightning and sing a romantic song with all the sweetness and sincerity it deserves.

'If there is any change, it is in the direction of the mellowness. As a performer, he is cleverer than he used to be, but there is no suggestion of cleverness in his style, particularly after he has got the audience warmed up. He is all amiability – neither patronizing nor unctuous in manner. For he probably likes entertaining.'

That he did.

The theatre itself had something to do with it. He probably thought how marvellous it would have been to have his father in the audience. He knew the old man would have 'qvelled' all over again. It was doubtless in the mind of his two brothers, too, who came along to see their famous younger sibling receiving applause like a king being presented with tribute from visiting dignitaries.

Danny was aided, too, by having Sammy Prager at the piano, doing all the things for him he had done in London; each depending on the other for a kind of telepathy that indicated what was going to come next, for Danny no more had a script at the Palace than he had done at the Palladium.

Prager, Walter Scharf remembers, was more important to Danny at this time than any wife could possibly be – and it certainly seemed that he was spending more time with him than he was with Sylvia. There was also the little matter that he was more willing to go along with what Danny was doing and thinking than ever Sylvia had been.

Brooks Atkinson liked everything about this new show.

'He has put this entertainment on many other stages, and probably everything has been tried and calculated. But in the theatre, it seems like pure improvisation, some of it wild, some of it mocking, but all of it fresh and spontaneous. You discover in it none of the hokum of the vaudeville personality . . .

'He mimicked the fierce Spanish male dancers who stamp as if they hated the stage. He burlesqued formal singing and he delivered one of those sentimental homilies with which vaudeville performers love to drench an audience.'

There were the usual ingredients, including the words of *Tchaikovsky* to stun those who hadn't heard them before – and who would go out to buy the Columbia record the next day – and to impress the intellectuals in the audience who made their first forays into the Palace for the Kaye show.

Mr Atkinson concluded: 'He is a crisp performer with a quick, satirical mind. But there is not a mean bone in his body. He holds no one up to ridicule. Nor is there anything in bad taste throughout the whole evening, for he does not have to stoop for his laughs.'

It was obvious, said the critic, that the orchestra liked it as much as did the paying customers. 'That is the perfect tribute in any show with music. For no one can fool the musicians. Danny is a good entertainer in the royal line. Once he had established contact with the audience last evening, it was down hill and shady all the way. Everyone, including Danny was having a wonderful time.'

And once more he was going to have it in London. Never a difficult task for Danny Kaye. Britain was now on the crest of a prosperity wave. But it hadn't forgotten Danny Kaye – although it wasn't going to be the fellow the British audiences had got to know. In fact, for the first time since 1938, he wasn't in England to appear on the stage of the Palladium. He didn't need that kind of 'fix' for the moment – the Palace had helped exorcise the need to feel an audience clammering for his attentions.

Now he was in the British capital to make a film – the first he had ever made away from a Hollywood studio. *Knock on Wood* had a number of scenes in London streets, although it seems to have taken an astonishingly short time to get from the West End to the City.

Most of the action was, however, in the studio – and not all of it the kind that was to be seen on the screen. Danny and Sylvia had now formed their own company, Dena Productions, with Columbia distributing the movie, and had gone into partnership with the two whiz kids of Hollywood, writer-producers, Norman Panama and Mel Frank. They didn't always get on – to say the least. But it was to be a picture they are both pleased they made. So is Michael Kidd, one of the best dancers in Hollywood, whose choreography in *Seven Brides for Seven Brothers* was to go down in film history as probably the finest example of male dancing just about anyone ever saw.

It was again a bespoke Danny Kaye story – much more up his neck

[156]

of San Ysidro Drive than *Hans Christian Andersen*, although not fated to be nearly as well remembered – which most Kaye devotees would agree is a disappointment.

In this story, Danny played a neurotic ventriloquist with two dummies – which may have sounded a bit like *Wonder Man* and a bit like *On The Riviera*, which was precisely what people wanted them to be.

Of course, it wasn't a straightforward story about a ventriloquist. Nine years after the end of World War II, America seemed to be in the midst of spy fever – McCarthy helped the craze along – so it was not at all unreasonable for Danny's dummy to be used as a receptacle for stolen plans.

It also provided a good enough opportunity to bring a psychiatrist into the story, always an interesting ploy. Making the psychiatrist an attractive woman gave another opening to Paramount's casting department. They selected Mai Zetterling for the part at a time of her life when she was a very sexy lady indeed.

She wasn't an obvious choice, however. In fact, there were very great difficulties in finding a leading lady at all. The part, as written was for an English woman psychiatrist. But, as Norman Panama told me, that was easier said, or written into a script, than done.

'We went through a whole list of English actresses without finding one whom we thought suitable. Finally, we came to the conclusion, "why does she have to be English?" We decided that she didn't have to be and chose Mai Zetterling who was Swedish.'

Mai had made her international début in a film called *Frieda*, ten years before in which she played the German bride of a British Army of Occupation soldier. That didn't go at all well with a nation who had been told not to fraternize with the Army. *Knock on Wood* was a lot less controversial. Danny was extremely charming to her. 'He was very good at being charming to people whom he had to be charming to,' Panama recalled. 'There were times when his neurotic personality brought out the depressions in him and he didn't mask them when they came. But when he wanted to be the life of the party and charming, there was nobody in the world who was more charming than Danny.'

Altogether, it was a highly successful film; not least for the partnering of a group of men who were to play an increasingly important part in Danny's life, in one case in deep friendship, in the other two in what was to become a highly charged relationship that was somewhat less happy. Whatever else, it was all a meeting of extremely vital talents.

Michael Kidd's dancing was on the verge of becoming legendary in Hollywood – to come in the next few months was not only *Seven Brides for Seven Brothers*, but also his acting (and dancing) role with

Gene Kelly and Dan Dailey in *It's Always Fair Weather*. That was soon followed by his masterly choreography in *Guys and Dolls*.

It was also a meeting of writing talents. Mel Frank and Norman Panama were at the time two of the most highly valuable properties among Hollywood writers. *Knock On Wood* was their baptism working with Danny – *and with Sylvia*.

For them both, it was to be a salutary experience.

'I find it very hard to say something positive about Danny,' says Mel Frank today with the benefit of 30 years of hindsight. But then he adds: 'I do have good feelings about him. Obviously, it was a highly ambivalent relationship.'

It was the highly ambivalent relationship born out of a ten-year period as partners.

He had more personal brush-ups with Danny than probably anyone else who had worked with him. In this film, as in the movie which followed, Panama and Frank also shared the credits for being producer and director.

Said Frank: 'I think Danny knows that he is not a nice guy – deep down, but I think he would like awfully to be a nice human being. This has got nothing to do with the fact that I am in love with his talent and devoted a great deal of time to it – with very little to show, apart from a few credits and very little money.'

Just why Mr Frank is less in love with Danny Kaye, human being, will become more obvious as the account of their relationship together proceeds. *Knock On Wood* was to be their least troublesome and tedious venture in their ten years together.

And he learned a great deal about being a director from Danny's performance as a film star, even if not as the character he played.

'Danny will find a way of finding out what it is about you that is away from normalcy. And he will make it so funny that other people will die laughing. But it will be at your expense.'

There is a great deal of the sadist in a number of comics, Frank believes – part of the knowledge he says he picked up from his sessions on a psychiatrist's couch a little before Kaye himself went into analysis, which was quickly becoming *the* Hollywood thing to do.

Frank introduced his psychiatrist to Danny about this time and the doctor brought his wife along – 'a sweet, lovely, darling little woman. She is a scientist with the faintest Hungarian accent.

'Danny heard this. He knew who her husband was. He adopted the most exquisite accent to mimic her. Now that was very funny. But she was most uncomfortable. After 30 years in this country, the last thing she wanted to be thought of was as a Hungarian. Her husband was a leading figure in his field, she was established herself . . .'

[158]

Other actors on the set loved Danny. But there were problems. One scene had to be shot 27 times – for some reason, Torin Thatcher the British small-part actor, felt inhibited by Danny's presence and kept fluffing his lines. On the 26th take he was perfect – but another actor then decided that was *his* cue to blow them.

'Well, Danny just collapsed at that. After 25 takes of one actor getting it wrong, another one comes along and destroys the 26th. Was Danny funny!'

Danny was thought very funny by practically everyone who saw the film. Everyone, that is, except the Italians. Danny believed he was the only one who could put the right intonation into whatever came out of his mouth – even in other languages.

Now, everyone knows that Danny's mastery of other people's accents was brilliant, second to none. He was convinced – and so was everyone else connected with the picture, for that matter – that he could do the dubbing of his voice better than anyone else. 'Just give me the words and I'll do them,' said Danny.

Panama and Frank, in their capacity of producers, agreed and jumped at the opportunity. Kaye sounded brilliant – to Panama and Frank and doubtless to Danny and Sylvia, too. The Italians weren't so sure. One Italian critic wrote: 'The film was very, very funny. But who dubbed Danny Kaye's voice? It sounded like a German.'

It was like Danny's trip to Japan again. Then, he recited gibberish so well that even the Japanese thought he was speaking their language. The Italian critics were a little more sophisticated. They knew that he wasn't.

He was a lot more convincing as a ballet dancer. Near the end of the movie, Danny escaping a couple of killers, finds himself backstage in a ballet. He puts on ballet costume and gets pulled on stage. There's nothing to it but to try to convince the heavies he was just another member of a *corps-de-ballet*. It was very much like the closing scenes of *Wonder Man*. Except that this was harder.

In the earlier film, he had to sing and act, two abilities he was known to have in abundance. This time, although he was making a pantomimic mess of the thing, he had to appear, even if only at first, to be a professional dancer in a company of highly professional dancers. The dancers used by Panama and Frank were, in fact, the best they could find anywhere in America.

Michael Kidd had the responsibility for making sure this somewhat difficult *tour-de-force* came off.

As he told me: 'I seldom enjoy anything I've done. But when I sat and watched this I burst out in laughter. I couldn't control myself. It was so funny and so spontaneous. I'm usually sitting there,

[159]

holding my head, wondering how to make the changes to get things right. But not this time.'

Danny, he says now, 'was unquestionably the quickest person I've ever encountered in all my years working in Hollywood. He has a remarkable knack of absorbing what you are going for; he would get it at once.

'I worked out something for some length of time – because I like to get it straight for myself. Then I'd show it to Danny. And he'd take a look and boom! He would get it straight away – just as he, without any musical training and unable to read music, could sing the most complicated musical arrangements. I don't think he has the inhibitions that the rest of us have. He doesn't have those blocks. He just goes straight into it.'

It all worked perfectly – as much because of the attention to pure balletic detail as to what was accepted as the more conventional Kaye comedy approach.

Mel Frank was equally impressed.

'For eight weeks, Danny did nothing but work on his ballet routines,' he now remembers. 'He got so good that one of the dancers in the company told him that had he wanted to, Danny could have been one of the greatest dancers of all time. Imagine that!' Eight weeks after the first time he put his foot in a ballet shoe, one of the greatest dancers in America said he could have been an equal. That was not just a prodigious talent, it was virtually saying that Danny Kaye is a genius.

Michael Kidd is the first to confirm that. 'Not just in the actual dancing, but in the suggestions he made while preparing it all. They were hilarious – and extremely creative.

'Every moment, every beat had to be very carefully set. We all knew that he could sing well as he did in *Wonder Man*, but this had to be very carefully staged. Every step – every movement – was arranged. Nothing about it was ad-libbed. It had to look spontaneous – and hopefully it looked that way.'

'He knew everything he was doing.'

But it was in the full, detailed complicated rehearsals that Danny's suggestions were aired and put to the test, a test that he invariably passed with flying colours.

It came home to Kidd, with the perfect eye of the choreographer of distinction that he is, in a *pas-de-deux* routine Danny had to perform with Van Adams, the exquisitely beautiful ballerina whose work he had to appear to be so carelessly ruining.

'You come to this part of the stage,' directed Kidd. 'You're carefully avoiding people and your about to make an exit into the wings when you see one of the killers lurking. So you have to turn around and go the other way.'

'How about,' suggested Danny, 'if I do it this way . . ?'

Danny suggested doing a funny walk after clinging to a pillar.

'And that's what he did. It was absolutely hilarious. We set it to music and it was wonderful; far, far funnier than anything I could have thought of.'

Perhaps in that one scene we had the recipe for Kaye's brilliance as a performer. Everything he did, looked spontaneous. Nothing on which he worked resembled a hard thought-out routine.

Fred Astaire mesmerised audiences with the precision of his dancing. Few question Astaire's position as the greatest dancer the screen has ever had. People across the oceans and across the generations have marvelled at what he achieved – in long, single takes that were always the epitome of perfection. Nobody knew that he had sometimes 64 attempts at the same dance before he had satisfied himself. It was years after the event that Ginger Rogers herself told me for the first time that they danced so much and with such effort that her satin slippers were stained red from the blood oozing from her soles. But it didn't take an expert on either dancing or the cinema to realise that every step had been mapped out previously like a military operation.

Danny, on the other hand, was in the business of making everyone think that what he did was always an instant reaction to circumstances he would have given every inch of his red hair not to have happen.

'He plays everything with the utmost conviction,' says Michael Kidd. 'If he's meant to look befuddled, he looks befuddled. If he's supposed to be merely doubtful, that's how he looks. I think he has the quickness to absorb, to feel that character and act that character and how that character feels without going into the complex Stanislavskian in-depth search for that character.'

Michael Kidd remembers something else about *Knock On Wood* – the recurring relationship between Danny and Sylvia.

'Scenes between them were, shall we say . . . interesting,' he recalls.

'She would write a song and sit down and play it for him. And he would do it one way, while she would suggest a change. He would be furious, get angry and shout and storm – and complain bitterly that she didn't know what she was talking about; that it was no good that way. She would wait, while he continued to shout and to fume.

'Then he calmed down.'

But it was only a Danny Kaye calming down. He continued to fume, to rant, to shout. Finally, he said to Sylvia, 'What is it you want me to do?'

She told him.

Danny looked at her and finally, with an obvious sense of reluctance permeating its way through the conversation, said: 'OK. Let's try it.'

As anyone who knew anything about Danny Kaye and his relationship with Sylvia could have predicted, he ended up doing the song the way she had planned all along. The wife's head on his shoulders was making itself felt.

Michael Kidd wasn't surprised either. 'There was this duality going on – knowing that she was bright, she was creative and that she knew what was going on. But there was the determination not to blindly accept what she was saying – for the sake of doing it. There was the anger of having to submit to a better judgment – which he would finally accept and when he accepted it, he would do it superbly.'

He remembers the film, on the whole, however, as a happy experience. 'Danny was extremely generous to everyone while working on *Knock On Wood*. I never felt he was trying to score off anyone else.'

Nevertheless, even a devoted Kaye admirer like Michael Kidd recognises that there are times when Danny can be extremely intolerant.

'If he doesn't like someone, or if somebody is nasty to him, he will be very cutting.'

That was not something Michael Kidd experienced at first hand. They hit it off the moment they met each other. And because it was Danny Kaye, there were good reasons why they should. In the first instance, Danny wanted to know where the dancer came from. When he found out that not only did they both come from New York, but that they were both Jewish and that their parents had come over from Russia in possibly the same steerage compartment of the same immigrant ship at the same time, he and Kidd were friends for life.

The fact that they had a similar sense of humour helped too. They laughed at the same sort of jokes, they told the same sort of jokes and Kidd shared Kaye's love of Yiddish and the accent that went with it.

It was very unlike the choreographer's first meeting with Fred Astaire on the set of *The Band Wagon*, of which he was dance director, and experienced the phenomenon of seeing eyes which had been directed at the gorgeous form of Cyd Charisse gradually move to and stay transfixed on the already middle-aged super star.

'Astaire was at first suspicious of me, even though he requested me, because I represented an entirely different kind of work. But Danny didn't have those suspicions at all. He was very, very friendly, which is his warmth.'

[162]

It was the time of Danny's earliest golf kick. Michael Kidd remembers going on the set for the first time, talking to Panama and Frank about their plans when the sound of a series of 'whacks' could be heard coming from outside the building. Every sentence the three men spoke to each other was punctuated by another 'whack' outside.

When the directors were ready to shoot, a message was conveyed to the source of the noise. 'Tell Danny to lay off until we've finished the shot.' When the bell rang to signal the end of the take, there was another 'whack' echoing through the cavernous sound stage. Danny had discovered golf and was using the moments when he wasn't personally required before the camera to practise his technique.

He had a canvas 'green' next to a small cubicle off the set with a row of tees. 'He was spending all his time going over the game and improving his technique.

'He wouldn't be going over his lines. He knew his lines. He only had to look at the page once and he knew everything.'

He didn't need to concentrate on his work. He had eliminated the blocks to natural concentration that most other people had.

It was an obsession that lasted until the next one came along.

At one time, he called up four or five of the top professional golfers in America and invited them down to the sound stage. Very cleverly, he would find a way of bringing the pros into the film, even if no one else realised they were there.

Norman Panama was less enthusiastic about Danny Kaye at this time than either the golfers or Michael Kidd. But he is less upset about Danny than Mel.

'My deep affection for what he was and what we were is still strong.'

Like the others, however, he experienced some of the traumas that came from working with Sylvia. 'She has always been immensely talented, but the problem was getting hold of her to discuss some work. We could never get to her or the music and lyrics she had written until the day before they were wanted. It seems that she just didn't want to be exposed.'

With Danny the problems were completely different.

'The hardest thing we had to do whenever we worked with him, both writing and directing him, was creating a 'sweet-guy' rapport between him and the audience. We were afraid to let the coldness that was exhibited in some of the other pictures come through at that stage.'

That was why *Knock On Wood* was tailored for him.

Sylvia's role in the picture was the one she adopted whenever she worked on her husband's musical numbers.

She was a very good editor. 'She has a very acute innate good taste. I don't mean that Danny is untasteful, but she just gave the impression of being more sophisticated.'

There were few of the expected problems of integrating one writer's work into that of another – or, as in this case, into two writers' work. Panama and Frank wrote a script with space for songs – Sylvia fitted the music into the plot, although most of his numbers were scat songs he could have sung in any of his movies.

'It wasn't genius time, as far as the songs were concerned,' recalls Norman Panama. 'But they were highly competent and Sylvia is a very talented person.'

From Danny, there was something extra. 'There is a particular joy, particularly in comedy, when you realise that what you write is going to be well performed.' He also had the art of improvising at the right time when that was considered necessary.

None of this made writing for Danny any easier. It was quite a task preparing a film about a man who is essentially an idiot to be played by someone who was super-intelligent as well as talented. The difficulty was solved by making Danny not so much the *schlemeil* of the early Goldwyn pictures, as a man so involved with the neuroses surrounding his work with his dummies (a frequently revisited theme, this) that he is virtually schizophrenic.

The problems didn't show and the script of *Knock On Wood* won an Oscar nomination.

'Danny was always on top of his material,' says Panama.

'What we did was to overlay what we hoped were enormously complicated plots over his expertise. It wasn't in his character to be a real *schlemeil* or a dope. You could push him around, but not in the classic sense.'

One complicated scene in which he knelt under the table at which the two heavies were sitting – one of them with a nervous twitch, the other kept pounding the leg that was alongside Danny himself – was shot in one take. 'It could have taken three days or more with someone else.'

At the end of the film, Danny and the two writers-directors-producers exchanged gifts and prepared for their next picture together.

It looked as if Sam Goldwyn had the right idea. He had bought the rights to the biggest Broadway smash in years, the Damon Runyon musical *Guys and Dolls*, and thought he could bring Danny Kaye back to the studio on Formosa Avenue and Santa Monica Boulevard with an offer to play Nathan Detroit, he of the 'oldest established permanent floating crap game in New York'.

Danny flew to New York with Panama and Frank to 'look over the property'. But, as Runyan would not have said, after casing the joint decided it was not for him. 'He thought the part was much too Jewish and therefore tasteless for him,' said Panama. Abe Lastfogel of the William Morris office didn't like it either.

'He was very self-conscious of Danny being Jewish and playing Jewish.' At that time, Danny never had, and – in conformity with the usual Hollywood pattern of the times, when a rabbi in a story somehow or other became an Episcopalian bishop or even a Catholic priest to satisfy the studios' sensitivities about their own bosses' origins – the giant agency was determined to keep things that way.

Panama and Frank, meanwhile, holed up in the posh Sherry Netherlands Hotel in New York for the couple of days in which it took them to observe the project, and decided that a suitable treatment was, indeed, possible. Sam Levine was brilliant on stage in the role. The writers thought that Kaye could be even more so – particularly with a version specially tailored for his own talents. But it was left to Frank Sinatra to play the role – with more songs and a lot less like the original conception of the Jewish Nathan Detroit.

Meanwhile the Jewish Danny Kaye was going to have to make a film about Christmas.

WHITE CHRISTMAS

EVERYTHING DANNY KAYE HAD DONE BEFORE HAD BEEN MADE TO measure for him, like any of the suits he wore in his films.

White Christmas was a different story, or perhaps it might be called a different carol, altogether. It's a picture in which he was to star with Bing Crosby – and they didn't come much bigger than Bing in 1954. Also on hand was the biggest woman singing star of the age, Rosemary Clooney, who had been entreating a delirious record-buying public for months to 'Come-along-a-my-house', and the attractive dancer Vera-Ellen, who in a younger incarnation had partnered Danny at the start of *Wonder Man*.

But Danny was not the first choice for the co-starring male role. In fact, he wasn't even the second choice.

The idea for the picture quite obviously stemmed from the most successful song hit of Bing's life – in fact, the most successful song hit of anyone's life. *White Christmas* had first been heard in the movie *Holiday Inn* 13 years before, the movie in which he co-starred with Fred Astaire.

Like a whole succession of musicals of the '40s and '50s, that picture had been little more than an excuse to bring to the screen a minute fraction of the catalogue of music by Irving Berlin, a man who in the course of more than 70 years in the business was to produce at least 3,000 songs – which was enough to keep any film maker busy for quite a long time.

Since *Holiday Inn* first thudded on to the consciences of audiences practically everywhere in the world, the *White Christmas* song – written to complete what Berlin liked to consider his sewing up of the American holiday market, to go with *Easter Parade* and *God Bless America* – had become the most popular yuletide ballad of them all; second only, the Irving Berlin music firm liked to say, to *Silent Night*. Which wasn't bad for the son of a synagogue cantor who had been born Israel Baline in Siberia in 1888.

Since 1942, the song has been heard from the middle of November until the New Year on every radio station serving audiences where either English or Christmas is known. By the late 1960s, *White Christmas* had sold a minimum of 50 million singles – half of them by Crosby – and has gone on increasing year after year since then.

In 1954, it made a great deal of sense to build a new film around the tune. It made even more sense to use it as another vehicle for combining the talents of Bing and Fred Astaire, who hadn't appeared together since *Blue Skies*, another Irving Berlin compilation made in 1948. All was set – until Fred became ill and had to bow out. At least, that was the story the Hollywood 'trades', *Daily Variety* and the *Hollywood Reporter* – which every day inform the film colony what is in the melting pot – gave its readers. In fact, what happened was that Fred decided he was too old for that kind of thing and didn't want to do it. Paramount then asked itself who could dance, do a decent comedy routine and act reasonably efficiently, too.

The studio, who were making the picture their first in the new VistaVision wide-screen, high-definition process, thought – no, they were convinced – they had the answer in the shape of Donald O'Connor, who had been so marvellous in *Singin' In The Rain*. It seemed a good idea. O'Connor was a popular favourite, extremely talented, able to dance and joke as well as act. In addition to the stars, there was Michael Curtiz to direct, providing he didn't get too confused about living 'in the hills, Universal around', and a fairly imaginative script by Norman Krasna, who was regarded by pretty well everyone in Hollywood as the scriptwriter's scriptwriter.

But then Donald O'Connor presented a problem. He sent the studio's contracts department a letter from his doctor saying that he had developed a bad back and wouldn't be able to even attempt a dance for eight weeks.

That was when Curtiz had the bright idea of bringing in Danny Kaye as a substitute. Since Panama and Frank had done so well by him in *Knock On Wood* and their joint company Dena Productions was still in business, it seemed a good idea to the 'Empty Horses' director to get them to handle the script, too.

That, too, was the story line being fed to the readers of the 'trades'. 'What happened,' recalled Mel Frank for me, 'was that Danny read the script and said that he would only do it if Norman and Mel could be brought in to punch it up a bit.'

Don Hartman, the producer who was a great friend of both the writers and Danny – he had written *Up In Arms* and *Wonder Man* – virtually pleaded with them to agree to do the punching up operation.

Ever since then, they have wished they hadn't – even though *White Christmas* turned into a highly popular picture that comes around every December along with trees and carols.

[167]

At no time was it really a Danny Kaye film.

He wasn't doing any of his usual *schtick*, the comedy routines that everyone had come to expect of him. Neither had he a script that offered the simple dramatic character he played in *Hans Christian Andersen*. For another, he was playing second fiddle, or second banana as American vaudeville parlance would have it.

In the story, Danny is a private who entertained at a Christmas show alongside the famous Broadway star who is also a captain of his division. The very day at which they are paying tribute to their retiring general – a delightful performance, this, from Dean Jagger whose own only regret was that he had to wear a 'rug', the toupee which he had been allowed to leave off the last time he had played a general in Gregory Peck's *Twelve O'Clock High* – the private saves the captain's life as a wall hit by a shell is about to fall on him. In gratitude, the captain agrees to look at the private's song, reluctantly agrees to team up with him in a double act, which then becomes a fantastic success. The remainder of the story is how the pair meet a couple of sisters, the Misses Clooney and Ellen, and with them put on a Christmas show in Vermont for the owner of a hotel who just happens to be the boys' old general. In the course of this not terribly inspiring scenario, Danny and Vera-Ellen spend most of their time trying to get Bing and Rosemary engaged to each other.

It wasn't a good role for Danny. It put him into a secondary position to which he was entirely unused and, on the whole, it showed. But it wasn't as bad a picture as either Mr Panama or Mr Frank now think that it was.

'We came in and made it a Kaye sort of vehicle, a kind of schizophrenic thing because it had to be rewritten from Astaire to O'Connor to Kaye,' said Panama.

But he remembers that Kaye and Crosby worked very well together. 'They had respect for each other. Crosby was another cold fish, but he was a meat-and-potatoes guy who like Danny came prepared. He was on the set at 9 o'clock but at a quarter to six he wanted to go home.'

'You didn't expect anything brilliant to happen intellectually, unless you were talking about horseracing or golf, but he did his job and he was an American institution.'

The two men didn't really have a great deal in common, but it was a reasonably satisfactory job of teamwork. 'Because we didn't come on the scene until the last minute, we seemed to have little to do with the workings of the picture,' Norman Panama now recalls. 'We'd go down on the set each day with a new part of the script and explain the jokes to Curtiz who didn't quite understand what they were about.'

As for the two male stars' relationship with each other, it was 'nothing' off the set, he says. 'They were both private guys.'

That wasn't, of course, the relationship between Danny and Panama and Frank. 'He became almost a third member of our team. We were constantly with him, constantly observing him.'

The early scenes in White Christmas not only set the tone for the story, but they also performed the function the writers had set themselves in the previous movie – finding ways of getting the audience's sympathy. It was as necessary now as it had been before to 'warm up' the public to what Danny was going to offer them. The one thing nobody could allow was for Danny Kaye to be anything but liked by his audiences. One of the biggest problems writing for Kaye was spending the first reel 'building up an empathy for him'.

'But,' he added, 'Crosby and Kaye were one hell of a team potentially – and had we written the script from scratch, it could have been one hell of a movie, too.

'But it turned out to be a carpentery job. It was a patchwork job. It was a terrible plot which we inherited. It now galls me that it's so popular because it really is a terrible picture.'

Mel Frank is even more scathing about White Christmas than his former partner. 'It's a piece of . . . .' he told me. 'On the other hand, it was one of the greatest jobs of writing technique that I've ever seen.'

The writers were brought in after the stars had been placed under contract, after the sets had been built on some of the biggest sound stages used in a musical.

Now, thirty years after it was made, Norman Panama is content to reveal that it 'follows very closely' on a film made at Warner Bros a few years earlier called I'll See You In My Dreams, the story of the songwriter Gus Khan.

Said Panama, 'It was a dreadful plot. I hadn't seen the Gus Khan story, but several years ago it came up on television. As I watched it, I realised there was something familiar about it. Every scene was virtually the same as one in White Christmas. Curtiz had directed them both.'

The constrictions were severe for any writers who value their craft and their ability to carry it out. The shooting schedules had been arranged in advance and couldn't be changed. There was a set formula in which Panama and Frank had to operate without the slightest opportunity for flexibility. They knew that it was to begin in a studio setting of the battle front, went on to Miami and then to Vermont. Curtiz and what military people liked to call the exigencies of the service dictated that.

'The movie I think was dreadful – although a lot of people liked it,' said Panama.

[169]

Unlike practically every other picture made in Hollywood, *White Christmas* was notable for being a film in which the director didn't merely brief his writers on the kind of story he wanted written, he told them the story blow-by-blow, scene-by-scene.

As Mel Frank remembers:

'Mike Curtiz, in trying to persuade us to do the film, told us the story. "He's crying," Mike said, "then she's going through the door".'

Curtiz's accent has become meat as much for the imitators who have outlived him as had Goldwyn's. Danny, of course, had a great time with it; the 'Universal around' bit was but a start.

As Curtiz outlined the story, Panama and Frank were getting less and less enthusiastic.

'I couldn't understand what it was all about,' Frank told me.

'There was Curtiz telling us his idea of the story in his thick Hungarian accent – "Danny Kaye doesn't realise that this girl really loves him and Bing Crosby doesn't realise that that girl loves him . . ." I said to him, "Is that the story?" and he replied, "Yes, that's the story." "Well," I said, "that's the lousiest f---ing story I've heard".'

Curtiz was totally bowled over by this. It was not the reaction he expected. 'This is the lousiest story you've ever heard?' he asked – and turned to Hartman to ask, 'Then what the hell am I doing with this picture?'

Hartman tried to persuade Curtiz that writers didn't always know everything, and eventually the two men had a meeting of their own. They decided they had to go ahead – if only for the $5,000 a week they would make on the project.

'We got $40,000 out of it because it took us eight weeks, eight terrible weeks of shouting and screaming at each other.'

The picture was owned three ways – by Crosby, Berlin and Paramount. Each of the three business machines, for that is what they were, agreed to give up three and a third per cent of their share of the profits to give Danny Kaye a ten per cent holding in the movie. Every Christmas, the picture earns Danny another fat cheque.

All of that from a film that is so popular with everyone but the writers.

The whole thing about it was that although there was no valid reason for Danny being in it, it did provide him with opportunities that he had no reason to despise. For one thing he did rather more dancing in the picture than he did in most of his movies. With Vera-Ellen he did a slow foxtrot which showed him to be as nimble on the dance floor as he was on stage. And then there was the *Choreography* number in which, in a black leotard, he aped the then

[170]

current fad of doing for dancing what the Method was achieving for the stage. 'Cats who do taps . . . are doing choreography.'

It was a movie that possibly would have benefited by at least one Sylvia Fine routine. But Irving Berlin wouldn't have been Irving Berlin if he had agreed to that. Not only did he insist that, as if handed down by holy writ, no one was ever allowed to parody any of his work, he would never allow anyone else's material to be interpolated into a Berlin score. (It became a piece of Hollywood folklore that when it was suggested that a note be inserted into a number in *Holiday Inn*, he insisted, it would have to be 'one of *my* notes'.)

Danny didn't get the best of the tunes in the film. *The Best Things Happen When You're Dancing* was clearly a legacy from the original script for Astaire. He sang it pleasantly enough in the soft, lyrical voice people had seemed to have enjoyed in *Hans Christian Andersen* and he mimed with Crosby – in what was undoubtedly the worst production number of its kind – *Sisters,* supposedly sung on a gramophone record by Clooney and Ellen. *Choreography* was the nearest to a production number and in *White Christmas* itself his voice was lost in the choir made up of his other three co-stars. *Snow* and *Gee I Wish I Was Back In The Army* met much of a similar fate.

To make things worse for Danny, the one song that was nominated for an Oscar from the film, *Count Your Blessings Instead of Sheep* was Crosby's, although it was reprised as a duet with Rosemary Clooney.

For the original version, Irving Berlin did the thing he was most famous for, provided a song literally bespoke for his stars, *A Singer – A Dancer* was going to be a second go at *We're A Couple of Song And Dance Men,* which had gone so well in *Blue Skies.* By the time Danny came to the scene, Berlin was prevailed upon to change it to *A Crooner – A Comic.* Danny learned it. Bing learned it, but after all that, it was finally decided to drop it from the movie itself.

Most of the picture, one is left with the impression that absolutely any song-and-dance man or any song-and-funny man could have played Kaye's part, something that had, *A Song Is Born* apart, never happened before. In fact, it takes the occasional funny face pulled by Kaye as only Kaye could have pulled it, to bring audiences face to face with the fact that it really is he up there on the screen.

Seeing it year after year on television, however, nobody would have any idea that the movie's two creators wished they had never had anything to do with it.

Danny himself now was ready for other things long before *White Christmas* opened in time for the holiday. He was off in search of the most unusual audience of his career.

ASSIGNMENT CHILDREN

DANNY LIKED MEETING IMPORTANT PEOPLE DOING IMPORTANT JOBS in totally different fields from his own because they enabled the real Walter Mitty in him to take another flight of fancy. He had a particular fascination with those who were consciously doing a job that helped other people. That, partly, was why he liked being around doctors and surgeons. It was almost as though he felt that by being near these people doing satisfying jobs, something of what they had achieved would rub off on him.

There has always been another factor in this: like a lot of major stars, it was difficult for Danny to become firm and fast friends with others who were performing in the same sort of show business as he was himself. Music men were one thing. Dancers were OK, too. But comedians? That would seem like trying to compete – which was another reason why he didn't in those early days like going to traditional show-business parties. When he was 'on', it was, like his conversation, on his own terms. He liked being the centre of attraction, but his practical jokes came when he was ready to play them. He sang his songs at the moment he wanted to sing them. He did his gibberish act when he was fine-tuned to do it. If the host asked him to perform, it had to be a very good evening indeed when he would agree.

It was talking to an offical of the United Nations Children's Emergency Fund that sparked an idea in his mind – to entertain children. He would give them all his *Hans Christian Andersen* routines and the other songs that children in America who were privileged enough to enjoy birthdays and Christmas had for long enjoyed on records. But the children he was going to sing to weren't those at all. Few of them would ever have seen a record player, let alone ever placed a disc on a turntable of their own.

The idea came from Maurice Pate, head of what was formerly called the United Nations International Children's Emergency Fund – hence UNICEF, which in true United Nations style, it remained. The scheme would also have the backing of another UN agency, the World Health Organization.

Danny wanted to go where the children had problems, to sing to kids whose language he didn't understand, but with whom he knew he could communicate in the only tongue that mattered. It was at first a pipe dream. But he was going to make it come true.

It was in the spring of 1954 that the idea was first put to Danny.

The UNICEF official had come to a conclusion that others would subsequently share – that Danny had a particular way with children. It was an extraordinarily intuitive decision, based on no more than a hunch.

As Danny himself told it in a *Reader's Digest* piece, the official said: 'We're trying to help some children grow up instead of dying at the age of eight to ten, and we'd like you to give us a hand.'

What he anticipated was that Danny would not only please the children, but having done so, would affect the adult population of the world to such an extent that they would help raise funds for the work that the organisation did. It was a time before children starved in Ethiopia and the Sudan but when in similar areas and in other countries all over the under-developed world, they were suffering from killer diseases like leprosy, yaws and the most appalling ulcers. For something like a cent, a life could be saved with a single innoculation of penicillin of anti-tuberculosis vaccine.

It was Danny's idea to take the idea still further. If people were to react to what he was doing, there was only one way in which he could achieve this – his way; which at the time meant making a film.

He convinced Hollywood to provide him with cans of Technicolor film and with a couple of technicians, and his own idea of *Assignment Children* was born. It was to be the most unusual Danny Kaye film ever.

For the next few months, whatever Danny did and wherever he went was recorded by the portable cameras that were in their baggage.

The hardest part of it all was telling Dena. Danny's relationship with his daughter was closer than ever. Sometimes it was difficult for her to understand her father's work. There was the time she was seen crying, standing in the wings while Danny was performing. 'What is it, honey?' asked a kindly stage hand. 'I don't like to hear people laughing at my daddy,' she replied.

That time apart, she seemed to understand *him*. Like many an adoring daughter she was able to read her father's mind almost before a thought had entered it. It was one bed-time that the secret inevitably had to come out. 'You're going away,' she said, and all he could reply was, yes, he was going away.

The places to which he was sent were very different from the kind of environment in which Dena was growing up. Not the beautiful nursery in which she was surrounded by her toys and other comforts of home.

Before he went, he offered to make life as pleasant for Dena as possible – a beach party every day. She reacted, he said, 'without enthusiasm.' Her daddy had already gone away from home.

It was to undoubtedly prove the most challenging experience of his life. Even if there were a movie in it at the end, it was to be his first professional task away from show business.

The United Nations gave him credentials. They made him an ambassador – an ambassador not in a formal cut-away suit as most of them were dressed in those days, but in a pair of fatigue trousers, a loose shirt and the kind of hat Sylvia was ashamed to see him wearing on a golf course.

But the piece of paper he was handed seemed impressive enough:

'The United Nations Children's Fund has the honour to appoint you its Ambassador-At-Large, charged with making known the needs of children throughout the world.'

Soon afterwards, Danny said that his first reaction was to say, 'Who me?' But, in fact, he knew it was a great idea. He saw it from two entirely different angles. It was both an opportunity to do a fascinating job of work and at the same time a means of helping a cause in which he was to believe passionately. It was also to begin what was in effect a royal progress. The man who had had royalty clinking glasses with him at the Palladium was now to be a prince in his own right.

The people to whom he presented his credentials weren't heads of state, but the kind who would have scratched their heads and laughed at the king's new clothes in *Hans Christian Andersen*. (The clothes didn't exist; they were part of a gigantic confidence trick. One thing Danny was determined on; he wouldn't allow this trip to ever be thought of as a confidence trick of any kind. And he was going out of his way to prove it.)

Certainly, it was not an adventure to be taken lightly. Danny knew that this could be the hardest audience in the world to win over, the kind who made a first night at the Palladium seem like a group of ladies in big hats taking tea at the parsonage.

But the challenge of it all was tremendous – right from the moment Danny's plane landed on the first leg of a journey that just seemed to go on and on.

They went to India, where Danny tried to put at ease a crowd of children waiting apprehensively for vaccinations. They didn't know what they were in for, what the pricking with the needles held by the men and women in white coats was all about – and what other youngsters had told them sounded very unpleasant indeed.

Danny saw that his job was to try to make things a bit easier for

[174]

them. But how? As he said, 'For me to be introduced to them as a movie star was obviously ridiculous. These children didn't know what a movie was. If I exploded upon them with a big fanfare, they'd only see a big-mouthed red-head who made a lot of noise in a foreign language and interrupted something much more important, such as drawing a picture in the dust or thinking secret thoughts. All children have a great sense of privacy and you violate it at your peril.'

It was that business of knowing when that privacy was ready to be violated and when it was sacrosanct that was to make his Assignment Children so successful.

His method was to find himself a lonely spot, under a shady tree or if there were no shady trees handy, somewhere he could be seen. Pure psychology told him that the best way of dealing with this situation was to hope that the youngsters would come to find him. Their curiosity to see him would be quite as strong as his to see them.

A good entertainer knows his audience and Danny summed up the people he was about to play to quite as well as any he had ever come across. 'When a kid finds out you're trying to amuse him', he said, 'he's willing to meet you at least half way.'

Later, he noted: 'When I was dancing and mugging, invariably some of the kids were trying to imitate me.'

This was one show where he didn't offer *Ballin' The Jack* or certainly not *Tchaikovsky*. But occasionally there would be reason to make the tongue twisters and if he didn't actually do all of *Minnie the Moocher*, there would be time for a great deal of audience response as the gibberish took hold. Sometimes, he had to do little more than make a funny face.

A former UN volunteer who was with Danny on one of these early expeditions told me: 'It was an astonishing kind of communication. Children who suspected all adults, let alone strange, white-faced adults, melted for Danny Kaye. I don't know what he was like as a person away from his own world of the theatre up till then, but I had the feeling that they melted him, too.'

It was easy to see why. The children were covered in sores, just as he thought they would be. Some had the swollen bellies that ironically come from never having enough food to put in them and which in girls ten years older would make them appear almost nine months pregnant. He had been warned to expect that. What he had not been prepared for, what no one could be prepared for, was the effect it all had on himself.

In a hospital ward, his accompanist Sammy Prager suggested that the children needed bringing out of themselves with a loud, sock-it-to-'em number. Danny suggested, instead, *Blue Skies* 'real easy'.

Before long, the children who could walk were hanging on to the legs of the portable piano that Prager had used in Korea as well as on to his own. Those who were stuck in bed had the look on their faces of religious fanatics who had suddenly found their god.

For 40,000 miles Kaye and his Assignment Children entourage trekked through India. In Delhi, they met Premier Jawaharlal Nehru, and his sister Mme Vijaya Lakshmi Pandit, who was the current President of the United Nations Assembly. It was one of those meetings when no one could be sure who was receiving whom. Ambassador Kaye was given the official treatment and the courtesies these highly urbane dignitaries were used to extending to more conventional envoys extraordinary.

But they, too, were conscious of being with someone who was distinctly extraordinary.

He gave the impression that he enjoyed being with the children much more than he did being with the legendary figures of the world scene – and that is not to say he didn't enjoy being feted by the mighty; he certainly did, if only because it seemed like poetic justice for the kid from Brooklyn to be treated so well.

He worked in a climate that hit a shade temperature of 109 degrees Fahrenheit in the village of Bij Vasan. He called his work there the BCG Campaign – a name that is now familiar to schoolchildren all over the western world, but the BCG anti-tuberculosis injections were as much a mystery at the time to Danny Kaye as they were to the children. What didn't remain a mystery for long was Danny's performance. He wasn't just in his element, he was in a world he had created for himself and he enjoyed being its leading citizen more than anything he had done since first mounting the stage in *Lady In the Dark*.

Not that everything was quite as easy as it looked. At times, Kaye the ambassador had to take over until it was convenient for Kaye the entertainer to start work.

The elders of one of the villages where the camera team alighted weren't sure they wanted their children to be assaulted in that way. So they smoked their hubble-bubble pipes and held a meeting. Danny decided that it was a matter for his kind of diplomacy. So he sat down with the elders, smoked a hubble-bubble with them and gave them another personal performance. The face screwed up, the hands went to his lips, the eyes feigned tears and the distinguished gentlemen of the village didn't know what had hit them. They laughed and laughed – until all they could say was yes.

While the boys and girls lined up for their injections, Danny performed for them. He danced and he sang. And he laughed himself, and he pretended to cry – and the children thought that even going through the worry and indignity of the innoculations

[176]

was worth it if in exchange they could get a command performance such as the one Danny Kaye was giving them now.

Two injections were necessary and it was much easier to do the second than it was to administer the first. There were plenty of cases when children queued twice – simply because they thought there would be more shows for them.

The whole of June 1954 was devoted to UNICEF and the making of *Assignment Children*. As a demonstration of how seriously everyone was taking it all, the Press of the world camped alongside Danny's own tent, went with him both to the medical stations and to the banquets that followed.

Rene Cutforth, one of the most eminent of British foreign correspondents, put it like this: 'Danny Kaye never put a foot wrong. Only in the very late evening did we ever see him relax. As Danny loafed about in his dressing gown we would discuss the next day's programme. At those conferences, sometimes we'd get a brief glimpse of the Danny Kaye everybody knew once more, concerned only with the next day's work.'

It was all proving to be the first demonstration of the great need Danny Kaye has to diversify. His golf may have been a hobby taken very seriously indeed. UNICEF was giving him an opportunity to open a whole new career for himself. And good work for others this certainly was, it was very definitely a brand new career experience.

There were times, however, when it wasn't all fun, even for Danny Kaye. Not even he would claim that all the children he saw languishing in hospital beds were going to get better. There were some famine victims for whom food of any kind was going to be too late. He shared the tears of hard-bitten medical and nursing personnel when hovering over the death bed of a little boy or girl for whom the hospital could do nothing.

'Anytime you have sick or hungry kids,' said Danny, 'you'll find drama.'

Sometimes, it was difficult not to avoid platitudes. He had a number of those and, occasionally, they tended to take the edge off what was undoubtedly a very useful and important exercise.

'No one can be happy – happy being himself or happy striving for something better – unless he has what I think is the "inalienable right". And by that I mean the inalienable right of every human being to function in the way best suited to himself for 24 hours a day. I believe that probably more passionately than anything else in the world. Without it, I don't think there can be any happiness or any hope for the fulfilment of one's own life.'

But there were always the cynical questions. Like the ones asked at a Press conference in the Indian capital. Was Danny arranging to have his films shown in all the cities he was visiting? It sounded a reasonable question to the reporters who asked it – but not to Danny who was deeply offended at any suggestion that he was using the trip as something of a publicity stunt. No, he said, he definitely was not allowing any of his movies to be shown while he was working for UNICEF.

What was more, he refused to pull funny faces for the Press. That was not why he was there at all.

And then they went to Burma, where the highspot of the trip was a visit to a crowded maternity and child welfare unit in Rangoon. From Burma it was Thailand. There, on the steps of a magnificent pagoda, Danny and his party watched children being treated for yaws. In Hong Kong, the next stop, Danny sat fascinated hearing how the infant mortality rate had dropped from 600 in the thousand to 60.

From Hong Kong to Africa. Always the same sort of response from the same sort of kids – for, he discovered, kids *were* the same everywhere he went, even if they looked different in photographs or on the big screen. Danny by now could barely notice the variety of their appearances.

Of course, there was propaganda in it all. The whole purpose of the trip was to make more propaganda. And perhaps, like all visitors being shown charitable work, the story was being overdone a little and perhaps Danny himself was taking it in a little more than he should have done – UNICEF's work was essential and magnificent, but the results were not quite all that the organisation would have liked them to be. Yet there were remarkable achievements, nevertheless.

Wherever he went, there were the visits to the heads of state and government that his UN credentials entitled him, in practice if not strictly according to protocol. Danny Kaye was important enough in his own right for these bigwigs to want to be with him.

In Turkey he was received by President Bayar. In Israel, Danny met David Ben Gurion, the founder Prime Minister of the state whose shock of white hair seemed wholly appropriate for a legendary figure who had grown used to being lionised. It was an unusual experience for Danny. The man whose Judaism in practical terms had been strictly emotional was suddenly confronted with a Jewish state that got all his juices going.

He entertained adults as well as children – and for the first time since his 'toomling' days in the Catskills found a language of communication which he had long consigned to his drawing room jokes and his tales of Caplian, the tycoon. To the Israeli-born sabras – who couldn't understand a word – and the survivors of the Nazi holocaust, alike, he joked in Yiddish, and sometimes in half-

Yiddish. 'You looking for something dorten (over there)?' For anybody else, the use of the familiar lingua-franca could be seen as a convenient cop out, an instant ice-breaker even in the heat of the Negev desert. Danny never needed anything of the kind. His Israeli audiences, like all the others everywhere, were his from the moment he first walked up to the microphone.

Ben Gurion appreciated the jokes, but the best of the lot were all on Danny. He first met the Prime Minister in his Jerusalem office. Kaye dressed the part, deciding that for the occasion, he had to look a bit more like most people's idea of an ambassador. He wore a neatly pressed suit, a shirt and a tie. Ben Gurion was in shorts and with an open collar. When the time came to meet the Prime Minister a second time, he decided not to be caught out. Danny was in shorts, an open shirt and his mangled golf hat. Ben Gurion, who was about to attend a highly formal function – rare indeed in Israel, but this was to be one of them – was in a suit. It raised one of the best laughs of the tour.

There was another dimension to the trip, the significance of which in Danny's life would only become obvious in the years to come. To help defray costs of the tour – not a penny went on UNICEF's own bill – Danny conducted the Israel Philharmonic. Yes, Danny Kaye, comedian, dancer, and 'toomler' of wide experience, who couldn't read a note of music, conducted the Israel Phil – universally accepted as one of the great orchestras of the world.

Before long, it would become one of the great passions of his life, but the audiences who paid to see him emoting from the podium every bit as enthusiastically as on any other stage were not disappointed. The orchestra played *The Star Spangled Banner* while Danny girated in a way no other conductor had ever done. When it came to the piccolo part, Danny didn't just use his baton, he gave a perfect impression of a piccolo in a way that even the high-brows appreciated.

What no one could be sure of was just how the *orchestra* would appreciate it. After all, here were graduates not just of Israel's own music schools, but of some of the greatest conservatories in the world, men who, had it not been for Adolf Hitler and the holocaust for which he was responsible, would have been soloists and leaders with the finest ensembles in Germany, Austria and in practically every other country in Europe.

Danny knew it was going to be a tall order, but not only was this an ambition fulfilled, it would also raise money for the cause – neither fact having much bearing on the way the musicians saw things. 'Some of the expressions on the faces of the musicians have never been seen before,' he said afterwards. 'They ranged

[179]

from bewilderment to shock, to resentment and sheer anger. But they played magnificently.'

Some were even reported to have enjoyed the experience. It was a story that would be repeated again and again over the years.

The journey was just the start of a series of expeditions that Danny constantly repeated. It became an all-consuming activity, like his golf. As far as his adult Anglo-Saxon audiences were concerned, it was to be somewhat more serious. It would mean they would before long be seeing rather less of their idol. For the moment, however, Danny was content.

He not only felt he had gained something from the young people he met on his trips – and the writer who a generation later coined the phrase 'Children are people, too' might have taken a lesson from Danny Kaye – but he also thoroughly enjoyed what was a totally new experience for him.

In Africa, he did an unheard of thing – performed tribal dances with black women, sang and clowned with the children in mud hut villages, and was still received by the whites of South Africa.

It was in Nigeria that he met Sam. Sam was a little boy covered with the effects of yaws that were so bad, he resembled a relief map of the continent where he had had the misfortune to be born. Danny never knew the boy's real name, but he called him Sam – and Sam he became. In a way, Danny adopted him. Sam was the boy whose progress he watched. Sam was the boy Danny had the cameras trained on as he played and fooled with him. And Sam was the boy with whom he made sure he was photographed two weeks after he had his penicillin treatment – and was practically cured.

It was difficult for him not to try to get a message across wherever he went. He tried hard to show that he was meaning everything he said from the bottom of what appeared to be a big, big heart. There was no reason to disbelieve him – particularly when he said he wasn't going to pull the wool over anyone's eyes.

'I could say that I was an underprivileged child, that I, too, didn't have enough food to eat. But it wouldn't be true. One of the reasons I'm interested in UNICEF is because it's as non-political as you can get. I wouldn't sit here to tell you what the United Nations can learn from children, but we adults *can* learn something from children. In fact,' he said with all the insouciance at his command, 'adults make the best children.'

It was true, and a ready-made audience to whom he had a ready-made show. Except that Danny Kaye was no more willing to give the same audience the same show than he had ever been before. But there *was* now a song that every audience wherever he went wanted to hear. It was the one Danny Kaye record that seemingly was being played on every radio station everywhere that his name meant something – *Tubby The Tuba*. It was a piece that started as a children's song, but turned into a perfect means of crossing the age barrier. It was another one of the Kaye standards that would become identified with him not because it was such a brilliant song but because he made it sound that way. Another example of his reciting a nursery rhyme and having people worshipping him for doing so – except that this story of the musical instrument was Danny Kaye's before it was anyone else's; in fact, it never was anyone else's.

'Adults get more of a kick out of children's records than kids do themselves,' said Kaye at the time. 'It's like electric trains.'

The children in Africa didn't know much about electric trains, but they did like *Tubby*.

He also went to Europe.

He was to confess to one failure – in Greece, where a three-year-old girl had made up her mind not to smile. For 15 minutes, Danny tried, and tried and tried – and for the first time in his life gave up. All the faces were there, all the antics, but nothing could make the pretty little child smile.

He had better luck in other parts of that country, however. In Athens, he was received by King Paul and Queen Fredericka. In Belgrade, President Tito gave him equally royal treatment, probably more so – the communist leader constantly out-royaled the royals.

Kaye in concert or among children, it was the same Kaye – in a milk-distribution centre in Yugoslavia or in the august surroundings of the Royal Albert Hall in London where he stopped over briefly for the première of *Knock On Wood* and made his only commercial of the whole journey. He said it was his favourite film – a judgement he has never since rescinded.

When he went to Turkey, he played at an opera house – once more, as in London, proceeds going to UNICEF.

In Italy, it was a polio ward in Rome that brought home to him the torment of children that was international and not confined to the slums of India or the jungles of Africa. It was before the days of Salk vaccine and polio was a scourge that no one thought would ever be eradicated. He saw children crippled from the disease and thanked his luck that Dena was not one of them.

He saw a nurse taking a group of little boys through the pains of their abdominal exercises. Danny saw it as an opportunity to perform. He took his cue at the counts of *uno, due*. On the first command, the children were expected to arch their backs. When the second one came, they went back to a lying-flat position. Danny counted, Danny made faces. Danny appeared to be suffer-

[181]

ing along with them. The kids hadn't laughed so much since before they were taken ill. And everywhere he went, he met the leaders of the countries and told them what he had found.

It was as important a part of his work as actually making friends with children who didn't appear to have much influence in the world.

Pope Pius XII, a cold, severe man who plainly had never heard of Danny Kaye – and if he had would have disapproved tremendously of his religion – nevertheless accepted the advice of the American Ambassador and various UN dignitaries and agreed to grant him an audience. Old Jacob Kaminsky would have enjoyed the irony of that one.

He was rarely a great one for protocol. In Vienna, he was received by the President at the end of a particularly tough day. 'Do you mind if I sit down?' he asked the Head of State of Austria. 'Well, I'm supposed to ask you first.' said the President.

'Do you mind asking me then?' said Danny.

At Bonn, UNICEF gave Danny a banquet, very stiff, very formal. Danny Kaye decided he didn't like things that way. He stood up, clinked his glass and demanded a new toast. 'To the gentleman,' he declared as the other guests looked approvingly at what appeared to be a new diplomatic comment. 'To the gentlemen who serve UNICEF . . .' The faces of the UNICEF officials, big and small, glowed, but Danny hadn't yet finished. 'To the gentlemen who serve UNICEF,' he repeated 'The waiters'. At which everyone present stood up and drank a toast to the waiters.

Assignment Children was every bit the huge hit everyone thought it would be. Nine million people saw the movie all over the world – some in plush movie theatres in America or Britain; some on the occasional communal televisions sets that were very slowly and gradually becoming a feature of life; some in makeshift cinemas in a jungle clearing.

Danny was to say that he saw it as a means of helping in some way to provide 40 million bottles of milk and as many samples of medical aid to children who might otherwise have died. That was some achievement, even though there have been – and increasingly so over the years – those who have cast doubt on his motives for accepting this unconventional ambassadorial role. Whatever else, the results, the end and the means to that end, were able to speak for themselves, even if not always as eloquently as Danny himself was able to do.

Much of what he said hit home – and hit the headlines. Had there been an International Union of Children, they would immediately have made him their Life President if not their patron saint. He was saying all the right things, all the things the kids

[182]

would have liked to hear – had they had an opportunity of doing more than sitting in his ready-made audience, or playing at being extras for his cameras.

As he himself put it: 'Climate, language and environment in each country may be different, but all children behave in the same way. It's very simple. The minute a child feels that there's affection, the minute he sees someone trying to reach him, he tries to understand. And the minute a child realises that an adult is trying to make a fool of himself, then he laughs. Then I can communicate.'

But he came unstuck a few times, too. The trips were not always what he anticipated they would be. Sometimes, he had to make speeches he didn't plan. Once in Paris, he began a speech in what he thought was impeccable French – only to be told that he had, in fact, said, 'I can't help the train, although the rattle snake is limping.'

He tried not to limp himself. But it was hard not to. The journey was exhausting. Danny had done the narration to a film which in its raw state ran to 9,000 feet. It was originally planned that Danny would narrate the picture in its French, Spanish, Portuguese and Italian versions. But he then decided that might be expecting too much of a star who didn't speak any of those languages.

So they settled for a brief Danny Kaye introduction, while a star of the country to which the film was aimed would do the rest. Maurice Chevalier did the French version – and then announced to the world that Danny was going to play him in a film biography. That was even more remarkable than Kaye wearing Sir Harry Lauder's kilt and this latest idea didn't get any further than the previous one.

Certainly, the idea appealed to Danny. But for the moment the UNICEF bug was biting as deeply as the mosquitoes he was hoping would be banished by the organisation's treatment.

By and large, everywhere he went, Danny was receiving the plaudits of his audiences and enjoying receiving them. That didn't mean that the snipers who from the start imagined some sort of personal gratification – or worse – had stopped their activities. Others complained that his 1950s version of the Great American Showman was allowing himself to be used as a political tool. Danny riled at this. 'Children are highly non-political. I would not have taken on this tour if there had been any political implications.'

There was worse to come. Some people could see no point in it all. One had the audacity to say to him – and it's an argument that has been used in many more recent famine situations – that surely malaria, tuberculosis and various kinds of starvation were 'nature's way of taking care of over population'.

The man who put just that to Danny, added: 'I don't mean to sound cruel, but. . . .'

Danny replied that he thought he was as cruel as he did, in fact, sound. But then he wondered. As he said afterwards: 'I saw he wasn't a cruel man and I told him I thought that was a very logical argument.'

But then Kaye added: 'Why don't you try it out on yourself the next time your child gets sick?'

In fact, his blood had a low boiling point when he heard things like that. He was dealing, he said, with children only half of whom would survive their fifth birthdays.

What he seemed to achieve, and what all those people who lined up to see *Assignment Children* watched him achieve, was getting on equal terms with the youngsters who were his newest devoted fans. It could have been very patronising – and would undoubtedly have looked patronising. But when Danny got down on a chair, and put his hands together in a prayer sign near his forehead and a little black boy did the same thing, they were blood brothers, as much as two children who cut their fingers and put them close to each other, as a sign of unity.

Occasionally, he got so close to a child that he felt he wanted to adopt her and cart her back to California.

But he realised he had to be on a relationship that was strictly that of entertainer and audience. 'You have to go along with other people's ideas of you – and I accepted the invitation. Believe me, it has been worth it.

'There are children all over the world who need help. All I have been able to do has been to use what better off people have given me by the way of name and fame to help *them* to grow up.'

The 40,000-mile trip took seven weeks and covered 11 different countries. He satisfied himself he had been of some help.

'Without help, those children may never grow to be mature people who can think and fend for themselves. All *I* had to do was to be cheerful.'

It was enough for the important people of the world. All of a sudden, Danny found himself receiving awards – not Oscars or the other Hollywood tokens of a performer's standing in the eyes of his contemporaries, but like the one the National Conference of Christians and Jews gave him for promoting goodwill. Before long, his study shelves in the house in San Ysidro Drive was filled with statues, citations, and various pieces of imaginative sculpture.

The United Nations, in particular, were very grateful. Danny Kaye was the best thing to have happened to the world body since it first drew up its charter. Dag Hammarskjöld, the Secretary-General, praised Danny's contribution and said that its work

[184]

would never have succeeded in the way it had without him.

What the United Nations could do, the United States Congress could at least equal. Danny was feted as a hero by Congress soon after *Assignment Children* opened in Washington.

Danny gave the Congressman a tip: 'Anyone can communicate with a child. Particularly if he makes an idiot of himself.' That was what he always aimed to do. His duties, he told Representative Frances P. Bolton, were simply to create chaos for his audiences. She and everyone else who heard that could understand exactly what he meant.

Once he and *Assignment Children* had become part of the every-day story of America, it was time for a new departure for Danny Kaye – his début on television. He had always been scared of what was still a new, under-developed medium. Like a lot of leading entertainers, he was frightened of a form of entertainment that ate up in the space of a few minutes, routines which a great performer could otherwise spread around for years.

But this wasn't going to be a Danny Kaye show as such. *The Secret Life of Danny Kaye* was about the UNICEF trip. CBS took a whole page in *The New York Times* and other papers to publicise the project: 'You will follow the joyful trail of Danny Kaye at his best as he entertains the children'. Since it starred Danny Kaye, and was presented by Edward R. Murrow, the first great commentator of American broadcasting, it promised to be something rather special. It was.

Murrow himself said of Danny's début on the show: 'Unless we ruin it in the editing, it will be the finest thing ever done on TV.' This from a man of Murrow's standing, was a compliment indeed.

The show was part of CBS's *See It Now* series which is still remembered as one of the programmes that showed how it all should be done. But Danny wasn't sure he wanted to do it again in a hurry. 'I know what a powerful medium it is,' he said, 'but I don't want to leap haphazardly into it. I enjoy making pictures, working in the theatre and making trips like this one. But I couldn't do all that and do commercial television satisfactorily at the same time.'

As he said then: 'I think the children in it will speak far more eloquently than anything I can say.' It was to be his cri-de-coeur for long afterwards.

'Some day, when's she's older,' Danny wrote in that *Reader's Digest* piece, I'll tell my daughter why her father changed.'

MAYBE IT'S BECAUSE
I'M A LONDONER

IT WOULD NOT BE FAIR TO SAY THAT DANNY WENT ON HIS UNICEF trip for any reason other than that he thought it would do some good. But no one would deny that it did a tremendous job of work for his own image.

Everyone in Hollywood knew he was popular and that his films took money. What very few people were saying was that a Danny Kaye film was an artistic success. His brilliant personality numbers apart, there wasn't a single Kaye movie that made critics drool with delight. And yet in the early spring of 1955, the Academy of Motion Picture Arts and Sciences awarded Danny an Oscar. But it wasn't for any particular film. Instead, it was a special award, plainly owing a great deal more to *Assignment Children* and the work he did on his 40,000-mile journey than for *White Christmas* or any of the other movies.

The citation was clear. The Oscar was presented for 'his unique talents, his service to the Academy, the motion picture industry and the American people.' The American people showed their usual enthusiasm and seemed glad enough that he had the little statuette to take back with him to San Ysidro Drive.

They didn't necessarily say so at the time, but the British people were pretty glad, too. The year of the Oscar was also the year of his return to the Palladium. Bob Hope wasn't wrong in saying that he had to ask Danny's permission before agreeing to appear at the theatre. Seven years after his original performance at Argyle Street, the place was still his, every other American star who had featured there in the interim merely keeping the stage warm for him.

The 1955 Palladium season was my own personal introduction to the live Danny Kaye. Others who saw him this time, singing his new hit song *Life Could Not Better Be*, would declare that some of the magic had gone. What had disappeared was that sense of serendipity. It wasn't a delightful surprise discovering that Danny Kaye was great on stage. Everyone knew he was the best living entertainer anywhere.

Even some of the notices this time were lukewarm. They disturbed him. Sitting in his Palladium dressing room, he admitted that was so. 'I would be less than human if I didn't like good notices. But this I welcome. I hope I *have* changed. I don't believe talent is something you take out of a box just for the show. You have to grow and develop all the time, as an entertainer and as a human being.'

In fact, Danny was better when I saw him than he had been on opening night, an occasion when there were audible sighs of disappointment from members of the audience. It wasn't a vintage Kaye night. If he had been like that in 1948, chances are Danny would never have been the adopted son of London that he had become.

He knew it himself. He had a cold that night. He was still desperately tired after the UNICEF trip. It unnerved him that he wasn't as good as he himself was used to being. He felt uncomfortable.

It was as new an experience for him as it was for his audiences – although in truth, only those who had seen him before were aware of it. The idea of Danny Kaye being nervous was plainly preposterous. So was the notion that maybe he had already had his greatest moments. It was, however, true. The visit marked the beginning of a new Danny Kaye, a different Danny Kaye and, some would say, a Danny Kaye who had lost his touch.

What it did not mean, however, was that Danny no longer commanded attention. His achievements of the previous years were enough to create for him a pedestal of his own, the kind that Greta Garbo still had years and years after saying that she wanted to be left alone.

That certainly was not Danny's stand. He wanted attention every bit as much as people wanted to give it to him. But he was concerned. Where was the hysteria?

'The response,' he declared, feeling more than somewhat bewildered by it all, 'is warm, solid, adult.' In fact, he said it was 'even more exciting than it was the other times.'

One would imagine that this was a kind way of kidding himself. For me, sitting in the back stalls of the Palladium, it certainly was exciting. But was this the excitement of a youth who went into the theatre knowing he was going to see the most vital performer alive. I doubt if I should have admitted it to myself, even if it was.

Worst of all for Danny was, however, the problem that Johnny Ray had been at the Palladium recently and the teenage girls who shouted, called and swooned for this skinny singer with hearing aids who cried on stage, formed bigger crowds than any Danny was now getting. That of itself was no threat, since the Kaye crowds had the reputation for being more sophisticated than the bobby-soxers who craved this pop idol. But where were the ones who queued at the box office for the show next night?

Not all the Press was critical, by any means. *The Sunday Times* thought it necessary to ask: 'Has Mr Danny Kaye at the Palladium this year been praised as highly as he ought?'

The critic came twice to see Danny's show and he noted 'with special delight a quality he is sometimes said to lack. I mean, pathos.

'Mr Kaye is no sob-stuff mountebank, no Dickensian sentimentalist. His pathos has no signpost pointed at it, labelled, "This is where you cry".

'But I cannot believe that any sensitive person can hear him sing *Madame, I like your crepes suzettes* without feeling the pricking of tears in his eyes. Yet there is nothing obviously sad about this poem; indeed I am horrified to think what a player of less fine mind than Mr Kaye could make of it.'

Back home, *The New York Times* was equally impressed with what Danny Kaye dished up at the London Palladium.

Brooks Atkinson reported: 'After an absence of four years, Danny Kaye has brought himself and his crazy quilt of songs and drolleries back to the Palladium. . . . To judge by the pandemonium inside and outside the huge music hall, everything is likely to be jubilant for the next six weeks. . . . He is in top form. His eyes are bright, his grin is cheerful and intimate, his hands perform idiotic ballets and he is still master of the informal style of entertainment.'

But there *were* those who said otherwise, and it was these who may now have been seen to have provided the writing on the wall. For the moment most people were happy to turn a blind eye to it. For himself, he still wanted, still demanded the attention of a real live audience. And since London was the very audience whom he had to gain if he were to ever win any at all, he set about working for it.

'In a motion picture,' he told the *New Statesman* magazine, 'everything goes out from you, nothing comes back. The camera absorbs mechnically all that you give; nothing comes to restimulate you. With an audience, it's like a sending and receiving set.' It was a remarkably inarticulate form of words for Danny Kaye, but one knew what he meant. Perhaps that, too, was a sign of the insecurity his London opening had created in him.

Once more, he used his London trip as a chance to see something of British culture, something he had missed out on on his previous trips. He even sampled that mystery of all mysteries for an American, a cricket match.

Danny went to the Oval. It was a time when the public at cricket

[188]

matches were extraordinarily well behaved, people who clapped politely at the end of an innings. All so different from the audience at a baseball game, as much a Kaye passion in his rich days of 1955 as ever it was when he was a poor kid in Brooklyn. He didn't enjoy the British game one little bit, although he tried to be as well behaved about it as the crowds behind the Oval wickets.

The frustrated doctor in Danny Kaye had its opportunities to come to the fore during the trip. A boy dancer knocked on his door, saying he didn't think he could go on stage that night because he had a migraine. 'Come here,' said Danny. 'Lay your head next to my body'. While he did so, Danny went to work on him, gently massaging the young man's scalp with one hand while with the other he administered his own make-up. It wasn't long before the dancer said he felt a lot better.

Danny was pleased to hear it. 'Only let me know a bit earlier next time.'

The one man who didn't have to let Danny know in time for anything was his manager Eddie Dukoff. Everywhere that Danny went, Mr Dukoff went too. He was his agent, his organiser, his confessor, his fairy godmother.

He also knew what it took to make Danny happy. The man who would still retire into a corner with a miserable look on his face was happier with a crowd that he could dominate than being on one-to-one terms with a guest in his dressing room. That was why the dressing room was full every night. Eddie Dukoff made sure it was. There were the English stars, the English businessmen, accountants and doctors whose company he enjoyed – in bulk – as much as any in California.

The only people with whom he spent any time alone were the members of the Royal Family. Princess Margaret was the most devoted caller of all. At a time when the Princess was in the midst of a sad love affair with the divorced Group Capt. Peter Townsend, a romance outlawed by Queen and Government, the princess seemed to find consolation in Danny's company.

The friendship blossomed. They seemed to have an enchantment for each other. The Princess for Danny's talent, Danny for all that the royal lady represented. They didn't have women like her in America, or so he believed. Sylvia made no outward sign of resenting the relationship, but then it had been a long time since – to quote a line from the *Sisters* song in *White Christmas* – they had thought and acted as one.

Other members of the Royal Family enchanted Danny some-what less. Kaye was telling nothing more than the truth when he spoke of his continuing unwillingness to wear his Jewishness on his showman's sleeve. That didn't mean that his pulse didn't quicken when he heard about Jews either succeeding or in trouble or when he suddenly found a co-religionist in the most unexpected places, like in the salon of M. Balmain in Paris. He resented anti-Semitism as much as he objected to any kind of racism, but somehow it had a particular distaste for him, probably because it represented a personal affront.

It was at this time that he was introduced to a particularly august royal personnage, not known for her love of his people. The lady in question knew who he was, so he didn't need to be introduced. Just in case, the theatrical mogul introducing them thought it necessary to identify him, however, Danny decided to get in first. As the lady approached him, Danny bowed his head. 'David Daniel Kaminsky, ma'am,' he said. The royal lady wasn't really sure what he meant, but David Daniel Kaminsky felt particularly happy that he had had a point to make and had, in fact, made it.

That introduction represented a part of London he didn't like. But there were still other parts of the London story that made the city special for him.

The behaviour of London drivers, for instance, never ceased to amaze him – which is further evidence of how long 30 years can seem in a person's life.

He had been worried the night the chauffeur assigned to him by the Palladium management had trouble negotiating the jamming traffic between the theatre and the Dorchester Hotel where he stayed. There was practically a collision between the car and a man on a bicycle – bicycles were not an unfamiliar sight on London's crowded roads at the time. The cyclist admitted it was all his mistake. 'Sorry, guv,' he said. 'S'all right,' said the chauffeur. Danny Kaye sat in the back of his limousine not really knowing what had almost hit him. They didn't speak like that back home when people were on the verge of being knocked off the road.

He enjoyed the English under-statement – like the comments from his valet whom Danny himself greeted like a long-lost friend who had suddenly brought him a side of smoked salmon. Danny almost fell into the valet's arms. The man was no less happy to see his old boss. But the way he said it didn't seem to give that impression.

'And how are you today, sir?' asked the valet. 'You're looking very fit.'

Danny enjoyed that. Without wanting in any way to make fun of the Englishman, that comment was repeated everywhere he went and formed part of the private act Danny provided for his closer friends. It became an extension of his Walter Mitty RAF pilot officer routine.

Not that everything about everyday London was good. He

raised a point that was not exactly original but which seemed to sum up the way most visiting Americans felt about some of the English dietary habits.

'I go out to a meal in New York or Los Angeles,' he told reporters 'and I fancy myself eating again in one of those cosy little London restaurants.

'Then I taste that coffee! Boy! That coffee! No wonder, the English are a nation of tea drinkers! Their coffee is still about as good as American tea and believe me that can be bad.' That, too, is a demonstration of how long ago all that was. Both American tea and English coffee have improved somewhat since 1955.

The bills for his English restaurant trips were usually paid by Mr Dukoff. Danny was no better at looking after his own exchequer in 1955 than he had been at the dawn of his superstar career in 1945 – or so he and Mr Dukoff (and Sylvia, when given the opportunity) liked to pretend.

That created a nice image with his public.

So did the notion that he was entirely in their hands, and that if they let him down, he would be unhappy, he didn't know what he would do.

He asked his audience if they would like to join in a number. 'Yes,' a couple of voices were heard to say.

A couple of voices in a Danny Kaye show? Just a couple of voices? Danny made it all seem like a personal insult – a very old vaudeville technique that, it came straight out of the two-a-day when the cello player would call to the customers to join in *The Banks of the Wabash* and when they failed to respond he would tell them that he was doing them a big favour; when they sang, their lungs filled with oxygen, they got roses on their cheeks.

Danny's answer was to say that he was heartbroken. No, worse, 'I've been deceived,' he told them – and promptly burst into tears. Between sobs he stammered: 'I thought . . . if . . . I asked you a straight . . . question . . . you'd give me a straight . . . answer.' Those tears seemed so real, his audience felt guilty – and once more was his.

The biggest star the British knew was just a little boy at heart. It went down very well, particularly with the men and women who bought their children *Tubby the Tuba*, *Popo The Puppet*, *The Little White Duck* and all the other children's records which, as Danny so rightly pointed out, adults liked quite as much.

He went through his children's repertoire at the Palladium, too, and he also reprised sufficient of the old material to please audiences who, despite all they had read, just knew he was going to be sensational – and as the season progressed, more and more sensational he got.

[191]

Danny sang *Tchaikovsky* and his litany of other composers. Britain still had National Service with young men of 18 being called into the Armed Forces for two years. These youngsters, their girl friends and their parents enjoyed *Melody In 4-F* quite as much as the Americans had ten years and more before.

Once the early performances were over, the old enthusiasm of both entertainer and entertained seemed to have returned. On stage, Danny was now the personification of the artist people had come to expect to see. In the regulation dark brown trousers and fawn jacket, he cast a silhouette on stage of an elegant bird, light of wing, firm of foot.

There were no recipes for the chemistry he wrought from that Palladium stage. Danny Kaye called out, 'Let's have fun' and no one out front wanted to do anything else. He added, as if by an afterthought, though that was an integral part of it all, 'It's going to be crazy tonight'. If it wasn't, the people who had queued and paid outrageous prices just like in the old days would have demanded their money back. But they were willing him to enchant them and each and every one of them knew that he would, just as he had done in the old days.

Naturally, he had his own chemical formula for that reaction. He fixed his eyes on a little girl in the audience and asked her name, and then her age. She told him she was eight.

'That's exactly the same age as my daughter,' he said. 'Let me tell you about her. . . .'

Now that might have been incredible luck. No one believed the child had been planted in her seat in the stalls. And yet . . . What would have happened if she hadn't have given him a perfect cue for a wonderful routine? But it was Danny Kaye and you had to expect that he would have found something equally appropriate. And he would have found a way of talking about Dena at the slightest opportunity.

Dena was the one vacant spot in his life when he went to London or, indeed, anywhere else. He gave no outward impression of missing Sylvia. There were many of his followers on who would say that yes he did give that impression – he was much happier without the pressure of Sylvia being in the wings every night, telling him he wasn't performing the numbers she had written for him the way she had written them.

But Dena was a different matter. He missed her enormously. Every trip was a tug away from Dena, every ticket in his pocket for Los Angeles International Airport was a passport back to Dena. Every children's song he sang was a paean to Dena, whether he was eyeball-to-eyeball with a little black girl in Nigeria or standing on the Palladium stage a few feet away from the eight-year-old in the audience that night.

[192]

Above: Discussing the act with Sylvia
– at the Savoy, London, just before the
1948 Royal Command Performance.
BBC HULTON PICTURE LIBRARY

Left: At the front in Korea. He's
broadcasting home – and prescribing
medical treatment for a wounded GI.
BBC HULTON PICTURE LIBRARY

Opposite left: His most comfortable role – playing with children. This time in everyone's favourite children's movie, *Hans Christian Andersen*. NATIONAL FILM ARCHIVE, LONDON

Below left: The top hat and tails weren't typical. But the face could only be pulled by Danny Kaye. With Bing Crosby and Rosemary Clooney in *White Christmas*. NATIONAL FILM ARCHIVE, LONDON

Left: For a time golf seemed as important to Danny Kaye as his acting or his music – or his Chinese cookery or his flying. Practising on the set of *White Christmas*. NATIONAL FILM ARCHIVE, LONDON

Below: Three Teddy Boys: Sir John Mills, Sir Laurence Olivier and (centre) Danny Kaye. In London, 1955. BBC HULTON PICTURE LIBRARY

Left: He learned to juggle for *Merry Andrew* – and as everyone who knows him might have expected, he did it better than anyone else. NATIONAL FILM ARCHIVE, LONDON

Below: Sylvia and Danny greeting Prince Philip at the London premiere of *The Five Pennies* in January 1960. BBC HULTON PICTURE LIBRARY

Right: Popo the Puppet, one of the best parts of *On The Riviera*. NATIONAL FILM ARCHIVE, LONDON

Above: Louis 'Satchmo' Armstrong and Danny 'digging each other the most' in *The Five Pennies*. NATIONAL FILM ARCHIVE, LONDON

Left: Greetings on the set of *Madwoman Of Chaillot*. Unlike the photographer or anyone else, Danny Kaye can see that the lady in trousers is Katharine Hepburn. NATIONAL FILM ARCHIVE, LONDON

Above right: Every appearance in public is a performance. He's never happier than when fronting an orchestra. This time the London Philharmonic in 1966. BBC HULTON PICTURE LIBRARY

Right: In Japan for UNICEF. He had probably told the youngster about Myer the Cryer. BBC HULTON PICTURE LIBRARY

Left: Danny contemplating. He was 62 years old – and taking time off from conducting the London Symphony Orchestra. BBC HULTON PICTURE LIBRARY

Below: Danny the charmer – with Miss Piggy of the Muppets in 1978. BBC HULTON PICTURE LIBRARY

British show business was as enthusiastic as ever and one charitable group, the Variety Club decided it had yet another opportunity to honour him. They invited Danny to come along to talk to them about UNICEF, which seemed to be up both their streets.

After the traditional salmon and lamb lunch, the club had a special showing of *Assignment Children* at the Dorchester.

It was a moving experience with even Dame Margot Fonteyn on hand to make an appeal for needy children, which was always the club's favourite charity. The members responded in the way they might have been expected to do – by handing over a $150,000 cheque to Danny for UNICEF.

Dame Margot was just the sort of company Danny wanted at the lunch. She was the exponent of a different sort of art, one he had only really played at himself in *Knock On Wood* and he was as fascinated by her work as she undoubtedly was by his. It was a case of a mutual admiration society suddenly finding itself with a couple of new members.

She wanted to know his advice on making a speech. 'Easy,' said Danny. 'Just think of all those you have inspired to bend themselves into knots and to tie up their legs.'

Sir Winston Churchill, who had once told Danny Kaye a thing or two about mesmerising an audience, was now in retirement. His successor, the boyishly-handsome Sir Anthony Eden, still with no sniff of the Suez calamity that was to end his career a year later, entertained Danny at 10 Downing Street and was as impressed as his predecessor – even if Danny found Churchill a somewhat warmer personality to deal with.

Eden invited him to Number 10 to tell him how impressed he had been with his UNICEF work. The Prime Minister said he thought that Danny himself wasn't like any other man he'd met. In fact, he said, he was more like a nation. Others had been known to note that – except that Danny Kaye could usually be relied upon to get more laughs than most other great powers.

London was his as always. But he wouldn't appear at the Palladium again for another 25 years, and then only for one night.

It was an astonishing fact, however, that he only had to land at London Airport for him to find an assortment of greetings from the highest in the land. Few other Americans – and practically no other entertainer – ever had that treatment. It had been the same in France, where the President of the Republic immediately made it known that he would love M. Kaye to visit him at the Elysée Palace.

There were some world leaders, however, who shunned him and his work.

In Jordan, Saad Jummah, the country's Interior Under Secretary, with due formality resembling the excommunication of a Catholic in Rome, announced that henceforth every motion picture featuring Danny Kaye would be banned from the cinemas there. The decision hardly represented enough of a financial blow to even dent the income of any company with which Danny was connected but the Jordanians considered it worth making a stand. Kaye, they declared, was an 'enthusiastic Zionist propagandist'. Again, Danny didn't have to wear his heart on his sleeve to agree with that, although he studiously avoided saying anything on those lines on the stage, even when he could know that the audience he was playing too was largely Jewish.

But not all Arabs felt that way. In the summer of 1956, Danny was back on the UNICEF trail. In Zagora, Morocco, he set up shop in the tiny hamlet and invited the entire population to come and see his act. All 667 of them turned up. Kaye was like that other tradition of American show business, the medicine man.

He got them to come to him by waving his wand and telling them he had a song to sing. He walked peculiarly, he moved his mouth strangely, and the local population thought he was a mad American and laughed at the idea that those people from far away over the ocean were the supermen everyone had said. Once having convinced them he was their intellectual inferior, he started preaching the UNICEF gospel. Take your children to be innoculated. Give them more milk. Take the treatment the youngsters are going to be offered for trachoma.

Over the years, working the UNICEF route, Danny was beginning to reassess his role as an adult in a world of children. Previously, he had thought about himself as knowing everything there was to know about children simply because of his being a father.

Now, he had begun to see things differently. He even saw that position of being a parent in a changed way. 'I think my whole relationship with Dena has become different,' he said at the time.

'During such an experience as mine you are removed emotionally from being a father and you begin to deal with children as little human beings. Your whole relationship as a parent changes. You begin to look on your own child as a human being with a separate personality. I went a long way to find this out.'

When he came back, Danny not only talked about the kids to whom he played, but about the doctors, too – like a young Frenchman called Luc Dullière, who so dedicated himself to the anti-trachoma campaign that he caught the disease himself.

He told the story constantly, as he did about the woman who came up to dance with him, a woman with a lovely smile and a torn, broken body. She was a leper.

Wherever he went, Danny was asked to lecture on his experiences. The number-one entertainer was now a number-one celebrity on the talk circuit. In Philadelphia he was asked to take part in a forum on young people. On the surface, it didn't seem terribly exciting for someone of Kaye's calibre, but his other panelists made it a notable occasion. One of them was the then Vice-President, Richard M. Nixon. Another was Mrs Eleanor Roosevelt, widow of the late President.

Danny was less impressed when the questions came in. They didn't seem to want to know much about UNICEF or about the cruel diseases he saw on his tours. They thought that he, with all that experience he had had in Brooklyn, would be able to give plenty of evidence about drug addicts and pedlars. A whole succession of questioners sitting in the well-heeled audience wanted to know about juvenile delinquency.

Danny shocked them with his answer. He wasn't at all interested in juvenile delinquency. In fact, he said, he had come along to discuss something entirely different.

'It is called adult delinquency. Because if we didn't have adult delinquency we wouldn't be here discussing juvenile delinquency.'

'I believe we're to blame every time a kid goes wrong. I believe we've scored a failure every time a young hooligan hits someone over the head or goes out spoiling for trouble. Why should we adults be so critical? When we improve our own pattern of behaviour, the kids of London and New York and Moscow and Berlin are going to start copying us. So let's put our own house in order before we tear out our hair and moan that times have changed.'

Once more, he was invited to Congress to talk about his trips. It wasn't clever, he seemed to be saying, to make such a big deal out of it all. 'Any adult can communicate with a child,' he told the nation's legislators.

All he had to do, he repeated yet again, was to make a fool of himself. 'Stick out your tongue and there's no barrier at all,' he said.

Nobody else was saying that what Danny Kaye had done was just nothing. The American International College celebrated its 70th anniversary by awarding him an honorary degree of Doctor of Humanities. The citation this time read: 'For his contribution to the children of Asia in connection with his work for UNICEF.'

Those honours, those degrees seemed to come as frequently as letters delivered by the local mail man. In February 1957, President Eisenhower presented him with a scroll honouring the 'Big Brother of 1956', awarded by the Big Brother Movement, which supplies volunteer advisers for youngsters and fatherless children in trouble with the law. This award, it was said, was for his 'unselfish contribution of time and talent in bringing hope for a better future to children all over the world'. The President also made Danny a member of the National Committee for the White House Conference on Children and Youth.

In November that year, he was given the annual $1,000 Bryant Award for his UNICEF work 'for using his comic talents to bring love and laughter to children throughout the world'.

American children – and later those in Britain too – offered him a different kind of award. All over the country, youngsters marked Hallowe'en by a new kind of trick or treat. Instead of collecting sweets for themselves, they asked for money, which went off to UNICEF.

For Danny, it was magic time. His next project was going to be devoted to magic. The jester was going to court.

MANIC DEPRESSIVE PRESENTS

IMAGINE DANNY KAYE WEARING CAP AND BELLS HAVING TO OUTFOX the fox and becoming highly confused about which vessel contained the poison.

The chalice from the palace, as everyone now knows, or should know, was the one that held the potion with the poison and was the vessel with the pestle.

Panama and Frank, now on their third Kaye epic as part of their contract with Danny and Dena, *The Court Jester*, slaved over the tongue twister to beat any other tangle Kaye had ever been involved with. 'We gave it to Danny,' Mel Frank now recalls. 'And he seemed to get it in one go. Second time round, he had memorised it.'

'There was nothing that ever seemed difficult,' said Norman Panama. 'We had a terrible time trying to find a collection of medieval words that we could use in this case. But Danny didn't find it hard at all. Danny's just like that – with a marvellous sense of improvisation. He stuck to the words but he could improvise gestures and sometimes dialogue, too. He's quite remarkable.'

The two writers were unnerved at how easy he found the routine that should have tied any decent human being into instant knots. Their answer was to give him another: 'But the flaggon with the dragon contains the brew that is true.' That was too easy.

The story was roughly that Danny posed as a court jester in the course of being with a band of Robin Hood-type outlaws at a time when knights gathered at round tables, rescuing maidens so slender they would have slithered down any dragon's throat.

It was far away from any of the places he visited for UNICEF and pretty far from Brooklyn, too. But it was not too far from Danny Kaye. When he dressed as a seedy old man brought up to do nothing more exacting than chew on a piece of straw, it was the character who had scared Sylvia in her home and frightened off all the hired help a few years before.

There were opportunities for fooling, for feuding, for fencing – and for the kind of patter people paid to hear, including a brilliant spate of Kaye German at its bitterest.

If *The Court Jester* wasn't too easy to make, no one who saw it would have guessed. 'What a delightful film,' Norman Panama now says. It made up for all the angst he and his partner had suffered over *White Christmas*.

At least that is how Panama remembers it. 'He always took direction. He was very helpful if he had to be, very considerate to the director. Of course, we had a kind of special relationship with each other. He was like a third member of our team.'

Now they had an original story about the meek and mild court jester who looks after the king's baby and breaks the news about an attempt to overthrow the monarchy. Sylvia wrote the songs and Danny in cap and bells performed them as freshly and vividly as though he were standing on the set at the Goldwyn studios ready to make his first test for *Up In Arms*.

Glynis Johns, Cecil Parker and Basil Rathbone made the picture a medieval frolic, into which few might have imagined Danny would venture.

The most surprised of all was Basil Rathbone, who had long before hid away the deer-stalker and pipe he wore as Sherlock Holmes, but hadn't yet forgotten the fun he had had as Sir Guy of Gisbourne opposite Errol Flynn in *The Adventures of Robin Hood* 17 years earlier.

The jester was meant to fence with Rathbone in the new movie. Obviously, Panama and Frank thought, they would get a double. 'Naturally,' said the men at Paramount. 'You have no choice,' said the insurance underwriters.

'Oh no,' said Danny Kaye, who looked as if he were to import the chalice from the palace – the one that was the vessel with the pestle – and from it administer severe doses of the potion with the poison to anyone who dared make such a suggestion. So he took fencing lessons from the master. Basil Rathbone was paid an extra fee as a fencing instructor.

'I've never seen anything like it,' Michael Kidd, who spent a lot of time with Danny at the time told me. 'Within a day, he gave the impression of being a first-class, experienced fencer. He was brilliant.'

Ralph Gardner, who also taught fencing to Errol Flynn and a veritable army of swashbuckling actors, was brought in, too. 'None of the others,' he said, 'had Kaye's precision.'

He used a real sword – in one scene fighting with one hand, while he took a drink with the other.

Danny thrust and parried as well as Flynn and Rathbone at their best. It wasn't just professionalism for Danny Kaye. It was yet another example of seeing new worlds to conquer.

Norman Panama remembers Danny with mixed feelings at this

[198]

time. 'He is a man who is a comic genius. There isn't a thing he can't do. His sense of timing, his sense of puckishness, rhythm, sense of satire . . . it's all impeccable. What is probably lacking is an inner quality, which I suppose can be called, for want of a better term, heart. And yet he manages to convey this – because he's so brilliant.

'Nobody in the world has Danny's charm when he wants to be charming. Part of the problem for people outside of his inner circle – and we were right in that circle at the time – is when he just doesn't want to be charming. It isn't anything deliberate. Probably part of the neurotic compulsion to be very private.'

He was so very different from the other comedian Panama and Frank were working with at this time, Bob Hope.

'Say the two men got on an aeroplane. Danny would huddle in the corner in his overcoat wearing dark glasses. He doesn't want to be disturbed. Bob would go into the cockpit and end up giving a show.' But it all seemed to come together in *The Court Jester*.

Sammy Cahn worked with Sylvia on some of the tunes for *The Court Jester*. His memory of the experience isn't one of unmitigated delight, and he doesn't like talking about it today.

Mel Frank, who was at the apex of his long relationship with Kaye, might have been working on a totally different film from the one that Norman Panama was engaged on. He has no happy memories of it all despite the outcome on the screen.

'Making *The Court Jester* was pure hell,' Frank told me. Danny was in another one of his nothing-can-make-me-feel-good moods.

'He was in a deep, deep depression,' he said. 'It was not a simple depression. It was a serious, deep depression. We had not experienced anything like it before. *White Christmas* had been OK as far as that was concerned, and everything had gone beautifully on *Knock On Wood*. But this was something else.

'When *The Court Jester* came along, everything seemed to be wrong for him.'

And those things started going wrong the moment he put on his cap and bells gear. Danny who looked marvellous in that brown sports jacket and trousers ensemble and could be the epitome of elegance in a dinner jacket, didn't look so good in tights. In fact, the Kaye legs bared to public gaze were almost as laughable as the songs he sang.

'But he had to look like John Barrymore,' said Frank, savouring the memory. So he was given a pair of what were euphemistically called 'symmetricals' – in effect, leg 'falsies' that gave the impression he had the shapliest pair of male calves ever to grace a Hollywood sound stage.

Well, they may have been funny to Mel Frank, but they were

dreadfully uncomfortable to Danny Kaye. He sweated getting into them and sweated wearing them. The jester was inwardly a very unfunny man indeed.

On top of the symmetricals went the tights. One couldn't be removed before the other.

'I can't take a piss till three o'clock in the afternoon,' Danny said to his amused coterie. 'Can you imagine what that means!'

Frank was 'nominally the director' on the picture. Actually, Frank and Panama shared the responsibility. Mel on the sound stage, giving the instructions to the actors and the camera and lighting people, Norman in the cutting room. This time it was Mel Frank who had the daily confrontations with Kaye the actor. 'I really was in torture during this time, mainly through Danny's depressions,' he said.

Immediately after the film was finished, Danny went into analysis. 'He was so fascinated by this and by the man who was treating him – a psychiatrist of German descent who made comedians like Danny his speciality – that he told me about it. He was so interested in the things he learned during his analysis and what he discovered about the profession of psychiatry.'

To him it was immediately another subject on which he was about to become an expert. So expert was he at selling the idea, that he persuaded Mel Frank to join the queue and take his own turn on the couch too.

Frank came to some interesting conclusions about Kaye himself – for it soon becomes obvious that there is nothing so infectious as being a psychiatric study to make one turn into an amateur analyst oneself.

'It's like a seduction,' Danny told him. 'They have to be yours within a minute.'

Mel's analysis of Danny Kaye goes like this: 'If you listen to the patois of the vaudevillian, you'll find there's a tremendous amount of sadism in it. "Laugh? I killed 'em. I murdered 'em last night. There wasn't a dry seat in the house." What they are really saying was that they gain such control over an audience that they lose control of their normal, natural functions.'

And he added: 'I have to admit that it was a very exciting thing to realise that here was something that gave me a fascinating insight into the sadism that is part of the essential make up of every great comedian.'

In Danny it seemed very obvious to him, he maintains. 'Oh, look at his marriage. It's a born dream, a Freudian heaven. Danny is a total sadist as far as his marriage is concerned, Sylvia is a total masochist.

'We had the impression of Danny knowing that he is not a nice

[200]

guy and without wanting to hurt Sylvia, while Sylvia seemed to just want to be hurt.

'But I think that Danny would awfully like to be a nice human being. Nevertheless, from this experience I gained a lot of useful experience about how to deal with comedy actors. Danny, for instance, had a genius at this time for finding out what it is about you that is away from normality – and he will make it seem so funny that other people will die laughing. But it will be at your expense.'

But Danny, on the other hand, had among seemingly a thousand other faces, and other sides, one endearing quality. Unlike other comedians who take their comedy so seriously they barely do as much as smile at a suggested funny joke or routine, Danny goes overboard with his enthusiasm.

'On *The Court Jester* when Danny laughed, he didn't *just* laugh, he cried. He positively wept – like a fountain. He couldn't stand up straight. Water seemed to come out of his eyes, out of his nose, out of his ears.'

It was in a way, Danny himself appearing to have 'caught' something from the sick children on his UNICEF tour – this time the innocence of laughter. Mel Frank thought about that suggestion. 'Yes,' he said, 'I've always thought that it is no coincidence that actors and children use the same word for what they do. They both play. There are good children and naughty children. In both cases what they do comes from their unconscious minds.'

And both take it very seriously.

One of the problems with *The Court Jester* was waiting for Sylvia's songs. Just as in their first picture together, Sylvia was late delivering the songs that had to be knitted into the picture.

The film was previewed and produced a somewhat mixed reaction – partly due to the music. It didn't seem to fit into the finished product.

Walter Scharf, who had worked with Danny on the *Andersen* film was brought in for advice. 'We rescored the film completely,' he recalls. 'I think it cost $300,000. Danny, out of loyalty to his wife and his business partners kept totally stone-faced about it. Paramount weren't at all happy.'

And again there had been the problems of making Danny's not-always-so-natural warmth show. As Norman Panama told me:

'Once more, we spent the entire first reel building up his credibility as a nice guy. We made him the baby sitter to the baby king while Glynnis Johns was out there whooping it up as a kind of female Robin Hood. We were afraid to let him loose and let the coldness come through as it had in some of his early pictures.'

Before Panama and Frank had gone to work on *Knock On Wood*, they had prepared a whole set of routines and 'schticks' which they thought would suit a Danny Kaye character. 'We didn't use them all. What we didn't use in *Knock On Wood* we saved for *The Court Jester*,' Panama now remembers.

Sylvia didn't. Her songs were written specially for the film. The other writers would indicate where they wanted, say, an 'entertainment' number. Sylvia, one of the four partners in Dena Productions, came up with 'A Jester Is Nobody's Fool'.

When the picture was finished, Danny and his partners exchanged presents with each other. But Norman Panama doesn't recall his being particularly generous at this time.

The critics, however, were.

In London *The Times* headed its review: 'Mr Danny Kaye Set Free' and went on: 'A Danny Kaye film is an event. Perhaps things are not quite what they were when Mr Kaye took the London Palladium and the cinemas of the world by storm with a combination of engaging personality and immense technical skill. Glad, confident morning has seen a cloud or two form in the sky; Mr Kaye's own confidence has seemed at times to be acquiring a quality which rendered it less endearing, while the films in which he has appeared have cabin'd and confined the volatile excesses of his spirit, have curbed his gift for spontaneity and improvisation.

'*The Court Jester*, however, written, produced and directed by Messrs Norman Panama and Melvin Frank, has at least the right sound. For Mr Kaye is at bottom, a court jester. . . .'

The film, said the paper, 'is above all to be commended for liberating the incomparable entertainer Danny Kaye who so glories in entertaining.'

The Sunday Times meanwhile contrasted the picture with an amiable enough comedy made in Britain starring Frankie Howerd and called *Jumping for Joy*. That was amateurish compared with the American product. *The Court Jester*, on the other hand was highly professional.

It was, 'like all ambitious American musical films . . . made for audiences critical with the range. Nothing is slipshod; the most sophisticated spectator, if he happens to like clowning of the kind, can enjoy it. I don't myself think Mr Kaye is at his best; I prefer him in satire and parody rather than in the bangabout fun with royalties and tournaments and battlements in which, with his usual virtuosity, he indulges here. But if we must have films about horses in nightshirts, I am all for their being clowned. Anyhow, *The Court Jester* has one or two excellent gags, a couple of goodish tunes and, in addition to Mr Kaye, nicely ironic performances from Angela Lansbury and Cecil Parker.'

That was enough for Danny. What that last judgement proved was that his own theories about film making had been judged to be as on the mark as his sense of comedy and what he himself could do with it. There was no difficulty about either Angela Lansbury – who in recent years has become much, much more of a star than she was at this time – or Cecil Parker getting a good review. Danny's policy, never spoken but always understood, was that he needed to be the only really top star in any of his products. There was no way in which anybody would be allowed to deflect public attention from his own face and his own personality. *The Court Jester* proved that it worked.

He still did the occasional live performance in America. At the Ziegfeld Theatre on Broadway, he followed his friend Jack Benny – and did considerably better than the older man had done.

Poor Jack had been crippled by a newspaper strike. There was no publicity and so no seats sold. At least that was the story that Jack was told. It wasn't quite like that.

Irving Fein, Jack's manager, told me: 'About two weeks before we closed – I had had to give away tickets so that Jack wouldn't see we were playing to empty houses – the box office opened for Danny Kaye. He was an absolute smash, despite the newspaper strike. They were selling ten Danny Kaye tickets for every Jack Benny one. That was a real heartbreaker.'

With some people, that sort of thing could breed a jealousy so strong that it turns into enmity. Not between Jack and Danny. They played golf together. Once, Danny was playing badly. He decided he had to be quiet. He asked Jack not to speak. They played for half an hour. Then Jack, an enthusiastic golfer himself, could take no more of it. 'Please talk,' said Benny. 'It's so boring.' So Danny talked – and didn't stop. Finally, Jack shouted: 'Oh shut up.'

Their friendship, Fein told me, was very firm and fast. Benny, who had said he stood in awe of Danny, was one of those who shared Kaye's Caplan stories. In fact, after a time, all Danny had to do was to say the name Caplan for Jack to go into a state of near collapse.

Once Jack was in hospital after having had a nose operation. Danny phoned to see how he was, but was told that he couldn't speak to him. His nose was packed tightly with cotton wool swabs, 'OK,' said Danny, 'just tell Mr Benny, Mr Caplan phoned.'

The message was passed on and Jack laughed so much, an emergency team was called up to his room to replace the swabs which exploded on the impact of the call.

Jack called him 'Dammy'. 'Dammy' was a great talent.

Danny's policy about himself, however, was that he had a whole net of talent that needed to be spread ever wider. Appearing before the cameras was fine, but he had, after all, been doing that now for more than a decade. There were still more fields to plough and to conquer.

ON THE RIVIERA

IN MARCH 1958, DANNY KAYE CONDUCTED THE NEW YORK Philharmonic. By that time, the news didn't cause any great shock waves in the American music community. He had been known to do that sort of thing ever since he faced the Israel Philharmonic in Tel Aviv. Close friends had known about his fascination with the podium for years. Some who were very close indeed, would have been no more surprised had he actually taken up a scalpel in an operating theatre and finally performed an apendectomy. His desire to control an orchestra was so much part of him that by that time they took it for granted.

Two years earlier, Danny returned to London, this time to conduct the London Philharmonic within the near sacred portals of the Royal Albert Hall. His last experience there had been a lot safer. He had gone to talk about UNICEF. This time, it was Danny Kaye the musician's musician.

No one could pretend that there weren't apprehensions on the part of the orchestra. None of the consummate professionals sitting behind a music stand had ever found himself before being instructed by a conductor who couldn't read a note of music. That was one art Danny Kaye had not yet perfected. He figured he didn't need to.

Danny, of course, never pretended to be like any other conductor, but what he did, he achieved perfectly using those Svengali-like hands which had mesmerised countless live audiences to whom he had played all his life.

Conducting an orchestra was part of the Kaye road to power. What he could do for and to those musicians in front of him, each and every one of whom he admired for his or her considerable talent, was little short of intoxicating. For him on occasions like this, that sense of power was greater than anything he had felt in front of a huge theatre full of people. Those folk he had had to persuade, to cajole, to love him. It had been a seduction that was practically carnal. The orchestra was different. Here was a large number of men and women who were *compelled* to do what he told them.

The musicians in London had known what to expect from the moment he entered their presence. He didn't merely instruct. He used a stock of Italian phrases which he convinced the orchestra he knew and a mass of other Italian-sounding words that they were expected to believe were in the music lexicon. The fact that they weren't gave some slight indication of what was in store. So did the dozen or so batons he brought for the occasion, and the fly swats which they believed were much more up his street.

If they came to doubt, they ended enjoying this unique kind of Danny Kaye performance.

He didn't merely tell them what he wanted them to play, he sang it for them. Sometimes, it was a mere 'pom-pom-pom'. Occasionally, it was a 'dee-dee-da-dee'. Often, it was a Danny Kaye impersonation of the actual instruments before him.

The music he played was very much part of a Danny Kaye repertoire: *The Flight of the Bumble Bee, The Thieving Magpie, Fiddle Faddle*.

'By tomorrow,' he told the rehearsing musicians, 'we are going to do this at break-neck tempo. If you can play it as fast as I can sing it, it will be a . . . great shame.'

He agreed that it was 'absolutely immoral' that a musical illiterate like he should be allowed on to the conductor's platform. 'Terrible'. But he wasn't going to allow that to worry him. 'And I don't think I've ever permanently damaged an orchestra.'

A year later, he looked as if he might permanently damage the Boston Symphony. He not only laughed in the middle of a performance, he screamed at his players, he leaped about from one part of the platform to the other, he slouched on the podium and at one stage there were those who swore he fell asleep.

The result was that he had a standing ovation and the orchestra, like the London Philharmonic, the one in Tel Aviv and the other ensembles he had been not too reluctantly persuaded to front, were applauding most of all – and not simply because it was all over.

Charles Munch, the orchestra's permanent conductor, said it was all 'most unusual'. Indeed it was. But it didn't totally appal the serious music people.

'A strange and fitful genius,' was how one of the long-haired critics described his performance. 'Passionate – if erratic.' A genius? That was not the word Danny would have expected to hear after the performance. He might have reasoned that he would be received with the same kind of gentle indulgence afforded to Jack Benny who would play his Stradivarius violin with equal passion, but a lot less talent – if only because he had spent his formative years honing his act as one of the world's great comedians.

Danny, who couldn't play a single instrument any more than he could read a note of music, had done that, too. Yet still a professional critic who had seen and heard them all, could call him a genius.

At one time, three violinists were so convulsed by his performance that they had to stop playing. Another time, Danny turned away from the orchestra, faced the audience, lit a cigarette and explained: 'It sounds better that way.'

When it came to playing a Strauss waltz, Danny suddenly spoke to the orchestra in what sounded like Russian turning to German and then becoming Italian. It was, needless to say, none of these things, but that wasn't going to be allowed to matter. When it was made to seem that a musician or two did think it mattered, he ordered them out, crying 'Insubordination'.

As someone said, the only serious part of the whole evening was Danny's arrival in white tie and tails. The rest was sheer mayhem out of which, for some magic reason, came the sound of real and beautiful music.

It was all made to seem only a little bit easier than playing to small children.

Danny's friendship with people like Eugene Ormandy helped. It was he who, in 1954, had helped him lead the Philadelphia Orchestra through a performance that ranged from *The Stars and Stripes Forever* to the *Tritch, Tratch Polka*. (*The New York Times* commended 'Mr Kaye's semi-serious presentation in which the orchestra joined with vigour.')

Now, four years later, a concert by Danny Kaye was known to be something that would appeal to music lovers as much as to those who loved everything he did at the Palladium or the Palace.

In addition to the Boston, the New York, the Israel and the London orchestras, Danny had by that time had his way, too, with the Stockholm Radio Symphony Orchestra and the Dallas Symphony.

Harold C. Schonberg in *The New York Times* used that word about him again – 'genius'. 'This is a conductor,' he said, 'whose Press notices have burned a hole in any newsprint in which they have appeared and who has given the whole orchestral world a new and different standard of accomplishment.'

Danny himself would have no truck with anyone who dared criticise his standard of conducting. What he did was a totally serious business, despite all the clowning. Making jokes, insulting his musicians and delving into dictionaries in which he couldn't find the right words (which he then proceeded to make up) were simply his style.

As he said at the slightest opportunity: 'Ormandy, Stokowski and I are among the few left who don't use a baton.'

[206]

What no one was allowed to believe was that he didn't study his music and know it quite as well as anyone else who had ever stood in front of an orchestra.

Before he conducted a piece, he had memorised it totally. It was as if his mind was a 36-track tape recorder. He had not only memorised his music, he had analysed it. He knew not just what every single instrument sounded like, but where it came in. That 36-track mind heard, when it wanted to, only that instrument. When he had heard enough, he sat in his study, hat on back of head, sports shirt over shorts and impersonated every one of those instruments. Stokowski or Ormandy going over a score couldn't have done it any more thoroughly. Like them, he knew what he heard and did *not* like. So it was never a case of his merely copying the recordings he heard at home. He was going to give it all his own interpretation – just like any of the others. What was so remarkable was that that Kaye interpretation would be so respected by people who might have been expected to know the music even better than he did himself.

He analysed the music 'live', too. Before he played with the Boston Symphony, he attended a performance under Charles Munch. He decided to focus on one particular musician. He chose Gino Cioffi, the orchestra's principal clarinetist.

What Sig. Cioffi didn't realise was that Danny Kaye had chosen him as a new one-man audience. What went on from that moment was hilarious – unless you happened to think the way Mel Frank thought on seeing what happened to the Hungarian lady scientist.

Because he expected Sig. Cioffi to speak Italian and sound Italian, Maestro Kaye decided to speak to him the way he thought he would appreciate – in an accent Toscanini would have loved, but which sounded just a little like a waiter serving a dish of spaghetti Napoli, or perhaps Al Capone having ordered another wreath for laying at a North Side funeral.

'Very good,' said Danny, and the musician smiled appreciatively.

'Yes-sa very good-a performance.' The smile grew wider.

'But-a,' the maestro went on. 'The last movement-a was – a little slow? You maybe use-a your breath-a a little wrong? When I play the Mozart, I take-a a deep breath, and then you have a legato.'

The musician was stammering the word 'but . . . but . . .' But Danny wasn't allowing him to get a word in edgeways-a.

'You using one of Benny Goodman's clarinets?'

It was a not a polite question, but it gave some idea of what the musicians had in store for them.

One of the orchestra members at Boston was reported to be playing with tears in his eyes. It couldn't readily be assessed whether the cause was the standard of Danny's conducting and his desecration of the music or because the musician couldn't control his laughter. Undoubtedly, there were some who considered that Danny Kaye, genius or no genius, was insulting the music by which they earned their bread and enjoyed their culture.

Others were known to be laughing so much that they were totally unable to sit down in their chairs. Tears rolled down some cheeks so violently that they actually bounced off the sheets of music and smudged the ink.

When, on another occasion, he tried to tell Eugene Ormandy that he thought he, too, had played a little slow – like Sig. Cioffi, the great conductor told him: 'My dear maestro, you attend to your conducting and I'll attend to mine.' What hearing the word 'maestro' from the lips of M. Ormandy did to Danny Kaye's ego is not difficult to imagine. It was the supreme compliment.

His repertoire had improved and matured since he first started this extension to his performing career. For his New York Philharmonic performance, he was also featuring part of Tchaikovsky's *Nutcracker Suite*, and the Prelude to Act III of *Lohengrin*.

He felt strangely intimidated by this orchestra. It wasn't that he thought they were better than any he had 'worked with' before. But New York was a tough city and he had heard that the members of the New York Philharmonic could be pretty tough themselves.

So he met them playing tough, too. 'Who is Gomberg?' was his first question. Harold Gomberg was the first oboist in the orchestra and if the Philharmonic as a whole had a reputation for being difficult, then Gomberg was reputed to be the toughest of the lot.

Danny pointed his finger in his direction and for that moment he was a combination of Adolf Hitler and a traffic cop.

'Where's Goodman?' he demanded. He was talking about Saul Goodman, who played the timpany better than anyone else in the classical music world and always seemed to be threatening an erring conductor with a thrust similar to that with which he administered his drums.

He sized up Gomberg. 'Any s.o.b. who gives me trouble,' he said, 'I'll throw him off the stage.' The orchestra broke up. They were his.

As he always did before a new performance of any kind, he regaled his new subjects with stories of past activities, not all of which could exactly be described as triumphant. Sometimes, however, he turned adversity into a great success – like the time at Boston, the *Nutcracker* wasn't quite as brilliant as he expected it to be.

'I was fooling around with the overture,' he told them. 'And I was taking it at an awful tempo. They followed me, and when it was all over, I was so excited that I ran down and kissed the flautist.'

That was a sweet story. But it got sweeter. 'Their flautist is Doriot Anthony Dwyer – and she is much more kissable than the Philharmonic's Mr Wummer.' He planned it that way, but after that story, told in the usual insouciant Kaye style, that orchestra was his, too, hook, line and clarinet.

The idea of playing with the New York Philharmonic was not merely a natural follow on to all the other concerts he had headed. Dimitri Mitropoulos was the musical director of the orchestra and Danny told him it would be a brilliant idea.

Mitropoulos was like Queen Victoria. Not amused. 'It wasn't funny,' said the maestro. 'You are an amateur.'

For once, the smile on Danny's face faded. For the first time, he was visibly offended. Not only was he taking the whole exercise extremely seriously – despite the clowning about – but every time he conducted an orchestra, he was raising money for its funds, usually helping pension schemes.

But then Mitropoulos explained that he admired Danny more than he had been letting on. He still thought he was an amateur. 'And yet you get a better sound from the orchestra than I get. You have a natural talent.'

It was a natural talent that has, just the same, never lost the *ta-pocket-ta-pocket* excitement of a Walter Mitty in his glory. It was that bit about power that thrilled him most of all. As Danny said: 'Get a baton in your hand and you're a tyrant!'

But he knew his limitations. 'Anybody can beat time,' he said. 'Not that many can make music.'

And although every time he made an orchestra laugh to the point that some parts of their instruments were in danger of getting rusty from over exposure to watering eyes, it can't be pretended that every music man either liked what he was doing or appreciated the great talent that went into it.

Walter Scharf, for instance. The film music director who at the time Danny was making his début on the concert platform was conducting an album of Kaye children's songs – *Hooray, I'm Five* – has always been less than enthusiastic.

The record had been waxed by Decca taking up Danny's own suggestion that it was worth making. Scharf only wishes that he had stuck to that kind of music making.

'All he does really is just beat time. All he does is a 1–20 metronome beat. It's like milking a cow, up and down. The graciousness of the thing is in the flourishes. All the pieces are ones that the orchestras know well – like the *Sabre Dance*, one beat all the way through. The orchestra follows the first beat and after that, they're on their way. He has the intelligence not to go in for something that is beyond him, above his head. He wouldn't allow that to happen to himself.'

Others are more charitable.

To some, of course, seeing Danny Kaye the conductor is above all a chance of watching Danny Kaye the comedian, if in a supposedly different guise.

Michael Kidd watched Danny conducting a benefit performance of the Los Angeles Symphony on television.

'I am seldom moved by anything I watch on television,' he told me. 'Yet by this I was – as well as I know Danny, as often as I have seen him perform – absolutely doubled over on the floor with laughter.

'His absolutely startling lack of reverence for the occasion is one of the things, of course, that makes people laugh so much. A total incredulity on our part that anyone would dare to do such an outlandish thing at a normally staid symphony orchestra perform- ance. He is not only not inhibited, but he realises the great relief that people feel at seeing someone discard the normal reserve that we bring to an occasion like a symphony concert – and behaves totally freely in bringing out different foibles.'

Over the years, naturally enough because we *are* talking about Danny Kaye, he has developed and perfected his conducting act – which is also why he is so funny to people like Michael Kidd for whom it had seemed unlikely that anything new could possibly be discovered.

Recently, he has taken, as part of that act, to impersonating various different conductors and seeing the music through their various interpretations. Few are funnier than the ageing conductor who really should have retired at least ten years before.

He performs not only the man's tried and familiar style, but the difficulties it produces – including the problem of simply finding the energy to climb on to that podium.

As Kidd said: 'The very idea of a man being so disrespectful, the audacity of it . . . not only was the audience doubled up, but the musicians could barely play.'

None of this could happen if Danny himself was not such an ardent music lover.

'He adores music – and his tastes are extremely catholic,' said John Green.

Green it was who arranged the first concert held to inaugurate the very idea of the Los Angeles Music Centre in 1959.

The concert was held at the Ambassador Hotel in the city, based on 'an improbable idea – an evening of improbability'.

Green told the jokes while Jack Benny played his violin. And

Danny Kaye conducted the Los Angeles Philharmonic – even though its principal conductor Alfred Wallenstein, too was not amused. 'Danny conducted and Wallenstein was not laughing,' Green recalled for me.

'He was not your show business type. He was a serious, serious maestro from a to z. Alfred Wallenstein playing straight man for Jack Benny was of itself improbable. Dinah Shore was at the peak of her television superstardom. She came with her entire television troupe – her whole show.

'We put on a fashion show that night. We had every leading fashion designer from all over the world there with their top models.'

It was John Green who put the idea of this show to Danny. Not simply because he had done so much of it recently, but more because Green had known of his long-standing ambition to take over a podium long before anyone else had heard about it.

'From the first day I met him, I knew Danny wanted to conduct. He was always talking about how he wanted to be a conductor if he had ever studied music. His favourite pastime was standing in front of what you people would call the gramophone conducting.'

Elmer Bernstein and John Green had both been brought in on this occasion to school Danny in rehearsal through the *Thieving Magpie* score. 'Danny,' recalled Green confirming what others, too had noted, 'is one of the world's great rehearsers.'

On this day, he rehearsed in front of a giant tailor's mirror, the kind he had used in *The Inspector General*. 'He rehearsed it till he got it perfect.'

'By the time we had got through,' he remembers, 'Danny knew *The Thieving Magpie* better than Rossini knew it, let alone better than I knew it or Toscanini knew it – and we had used Toscanini's recording for Danny to learn the piece by. And he knew it by heart – every note of the piece. He was also absolutely set in the tempo.

'If he had been a metronome, he couldn't have hit that tempo better. Elmer and I thought we'd both have to call in the rescue squad when he stopped the orchestra. He didn't call out rehearsal bar numbers. He sang everything. He was telling the Los Angeles Philharmonic how to play – musically. I expected him to be letter perfect and that he would use his foot instead of a baton, all in perfect rhythm. But he was talking to the horns . . . "Tongue it more precisely," he told the first horn player. "It's too legato".

'And he spoke to the violins, too. "Give me longer strings, gentleman." It wasn't just for fun. He took it very seriously.'

But Green was a little sceptical, nevertheless. "I adore Danny. If he were my own kid brother I could not love him more. And yet when I heard people talking about him as though he were a fully qualified conductor, it galled me. It still galls me. Danny has to be one of the greatest minds who ever lived. So when he's a conductor he looks more like a conductor than Toscanini and Gelini put together.'

Green has been to concerts with Danny, sometimes sitting next to him, sometimes a seat or two away. 'And I don't always enjoy it, because it can be distracting. Danny studies the baton technique of the conductor that he's looking at, the real conductor down on the stage. Danny's gotten to the point that physically he looks just right in everything. He can look more like a boxer than Joe Louis.

'If Danny were doing, for example, *America* from *West Side Story* which is metrically predicated on a generic Mexican alternation of rhythm between 6–8 and 3–4, that doesn't bother Danny Kaye at all. You know how few people can do that, who aren't trained conductors as such?'

Get into conversation with Danny, Green recalls, it is as though one is talking to Zubin Mehta or Eugene Ormandy.

And yet, and yet. So, is Danny Kaye a good conductor? The answer one would expect from Green as a Kaye friend is that he is brilliant. The answer from Green as a professional conductor himself would be that he is lousy.

Green actually says neither of these things. Danny is very good – as an imitation conductor. 'No. He is a dazzling brilliant imitation conductor. A conductor is a man to whom someone comes with a score he has never seen before, hoping that that conductor will perform it. The conductor says, "Leave it to me and I'll let you know in a month." The conductor sits down and then says, "I like this piece and I'll see when I can find time to perform this piece." And he then calls the composer and says he will meet to ask some questions and tell him a few things he think should be improved or changed. Can Danny Kaye do that? Well, no . . . He can't do that any more than I could fly a 747 blind on instruments.'

That, incidentally, is something else Danny Kaye can do.

MERRY ANDREW

THE WORLD, IT SEEMED, WAS BECOMING DANNY KAYE'S OYSTER. IF that oyster sometimes appeared to others to need a little seasoning, it plainly was not affecting his own view on life. He had found that he liked spreading the God-given talents he had, even though it was becoming equally clear to a lot of devotees that there was less and less available of what he could do better than practically anyone else.

The change in the Kaye philosophy dated from his first UNICEF tour, which possibly also showed at that last trip to the Palladium. For a time, the magic of performing there had left him. He had found new fields to conquer.

His old fans were quietly begging him to go back to the old Kaye routine, but he was looking for those new pastures. Which possibly explains why *Me And The Colonel* came about. For in *Me And The Colonel* he played a Jew in what was a very different kind of comedy film.

The movie was based on a reasonably successful play by Franz Werfel called *Jacobowsky and the Colonel*. Danny, wearing a beautifully elegant moustache and an Anthony Eden homburg hat was Jacobowsky. Kurt Jurgens was the colonel.

The story of this 1958 movie was of two men fleeing the Nazis following the invasion of France in 1940. One was the Jew, Jacobowsky, running away for obvious reasons. The other was a member of the Polish officer class who, like most men of his kind, would probably have won a contest in anti-Semitism with any SS oberfuhrer.

The two men, so different in appearance and in motives, suddenly found themselves with common cause and, to neither's liking, on the road together. Both had come from Poland, although Jacobowsky was heard to say that he had 'spent most of my life trying to become a citizen of *some* country . . . in the technique of flight, you might say I'm an expert.'

For Kurt Jurgens the very fact that he wasn't himself playing a German was difference enough. For Danny it was much more than that. *Assignment Children* apart, it was his first non-musical role.

[213]

And although there were a number of jokes, it was also his first serious part.

If dear old Sam Goldwyn had complained about Danny's red hair, no one need have bothered about *Me And The Colonel*. To go with his moustache, specially grown and cultivated for the role, the hair was grey, and *très distingué* at that.

The film was selected for the autumn 1958 Royal Film Performance with the Queen as guest of honour for what was frequently said was her favourite star. Frank Sinatra came to London for the show, too.

Time magazine was quite ecstatic about it all. 'Not a prat in the whole picture falls, and not one double-talked song or double-sung talk issues from the silly putty that is Kaye's usual movie face. The result of this hold-down of his celebrated talents is the most appealing and one of the funniest films Danny Kaye has ever made.'

The reviewer liked everything about it, including the love interest in the shape of French actress Nicole Maurey.

'Less surely handled by director Peter Grenville or either of the principals, *Me And The Colonel* would tip over into maudlin sociology or an embarrassing joke. But Actor Kaye, in his first completely straight role, keeps such a clear grasp of Jacobowsky's innate strength that every sly remark creeps through with the force of wisdom as well as the bite of wit.'

What it wasn't was particularly Jewish. Hollywood had not yet escaped from its sensitive period. Still largely controlled by the moguls who were Jewish (Columbia was still in the hands of its iron dictator Harry Cohn who had brought the studio along the road from the narrow thoroughfare known as Poverty Row) the studios had a marked reluctance to give anyone the opportunity of thinking they were over-sympathetic to their roots.

The film was fun, but a standard bearer for Jews in trouble it wasn't. One almost had the feeling that S. N. Behrman could just as easily have made Jacobowsky Irish, if only the Nazis had conveniently organised a pogrom or two in Dublin.

Danny said he was grateful for what was a 'radical departure'. As he said: 'I'm not me in this picture.'

The *New York Times* agreed. The film offered, said Bosley Crowther, 'Danny Kaye in a role of surprising variation for this usually blithe comedian.'

Since the film had such opportunities for effect as a middle-aged adaptable Jewish refugee who acquires for his escape a car he can't drive, and a companion who is stupidly vain and prejudiced, one would have thought it could not go wrong.

It is a pity that not every reviewer saw the good things in it.

There were some beautiful lines, most of which went to Danny in the face of a companion-opponent who wouldn't have known what a dictionary was if given one with leather binding and gold inlay.

'You undoubtedly have one of the finest minds of the 12th century,' Jacobowsky tells the Colonel who didn't realise he was being insulted. All that the aristocrat, whose religion was devout snobbery, knew was that he was in the company of a man whom he would hesitate to allow to clean his boots – for fear of him discovering how many other people he had walked over. It was a very interesting departure indeed.

The *New York Times* wasn't so sure. The film, on the face of things, 'might seem as comically inviting and pure as was that of Charlie Chaplin in *The Gold Rush* when he was a little prospector snowed-in for the winter in a cabin with a mountainous moron who hated him. . . . However, along toward the middle of this tale of an incongruous escape – in which, incidentally, the colonel's mistress and his aide are also involved – one is likely to wonder, all of a sudden, what's so funny about what's going on? What's amusing or even gratifying about watching a patient Jew in desperate and outrageously insensate negotiation for his life with a fool?'

Danny, said the piece, played the role 'with affection and sympathy'. He gave the role, too, 'a lot of familiar sad-eyed poignancy'.

'Nevertheless,' Crowther wanted to know, 'how can anti-Semitism be fun?'

That critic was not alone in being unable at all times to understand everything that Danny did. At about this time, a group of dancers from the Moscow Moiseyev Dance Company were treated to a private showing of, not *Me And The Colonel*, but *Knock On Wood*. Danny thought he would like them to see how the ballet could be made fun. They couldn't make out a single word of the dialogue but said – through an interpreter – that they had never laughed as much in their lives as they had at Kaye the ballet dancer. The Soviet Cultural Attaché made immediate arrangements to buy that picture for the Soviet Union. *Me And The Colonel* might have had more value, however.

Merry Andrew wasn't old-style Kaye either. But it was a little closer to it. The setting was an English public school and Danny was a teacher – searching for an old statue, even though it was shot on the MGM lot which had seen some of the greatest moments in movie history. It was, however, Danny Kaye's début there.

It was meant to be set in a tepid English summer, but was filmed in a Californian heatwave in August.

Leslie Halliwell, the critic who has become known as the cinema buff's guru, is not terribly excited about it. The movie, he says 'plumps too firmly for whimsy and, despite its professionalism, provokes barely a smile, let alone a laugh.'

That may be just a little bit hard. *The New York Times* this time ran a double-page magazine spread on the picture. 'What is Kaye's universal appeal?' asked Seymour Peck.

'His artistry lies partly in his marvellously expressive face; in an age when many comedians stand still before a mike shooting wisecracks into it, Kaye is a master of the vanishing art of panto-mime. He doesn't have to be heard to be enjoyed; across his face comes a rapid varied flow of emotions, funny, poignant, puckish but always clear and brilliant. Yet, when Kaye opens his mouth, the effect can be equally dazzling; his tongue races over scat song, his mouth twists through the labyrinth of a double-talk lyric; his voice trembles and breaks wildly on a high note. Even if the words are incomprehensible, the sounds are wonderful.'

Saul Chaplin, the musical director and associate producer of the film, wrote the score with Johnny Mercer. Chaplin remembers the dexterity with which Danny joined two dancers in a particular routine and made these highly professional 'hoofers' seem like a couple of amateurs. 'It was extraordinary what happened. All eyes left the other dancers and were suddenly focused on him.'

Michael Kidd directed the picture which cannot go down as one of the greatest of MGM musicals – as much because, according to Chaplin, it had to be finished two weeks before anyone was ready to complete the film. The money had run out.

'Michael had to adjust the script and rearrange the shooting schedules to make some sense of it without the last two weeks of filming. We had four songs ready for use which had to be abandoned. It's a shame. The picture was OK. But it offered no problem to the man who had 'simply' listed a collection of Russian composers.

There was also Danny's own version of *Colonel Bogey*, which by then was better known as *The Bridge On The River Kwai* theme, *Another Day* and *Peachy Creamy Day* which fit the lyrical Kaye voice beautifully.

(It was a good opportunity to sell records; his *Merry Andrew* songs were recorded and then released, as was an album of old Kaye hits – from *Jenny* to *Anatole of Paris* – at a knock-down price of $1.98. One music critic commented: 'The backward glance also reveals that good as he was then, he is even better now.')

At one point in the film he joins Italian opera singer Salvatore Baccolini in a duet – in a number called *Salut*. It was too good an opportunity for Danny to miss. He just had to engage in a conversation with the old gentleman in his own language. Of course, it was nonsense. The Italian couldn't understand a word of it, but he knew that he *should*. While the veteran singer literally scratched his head wondering what had gone wrong with his own brainpower, Danny was talking away as merrily as the title role in the movie suggested. It hadn't been in the script but it was kept in the film.

Danny wrote the music and lyrics as he went on – and Salvatore followed him, verse by verse. It was so good, it was retained. The trouble came when it was time to record the piece – and Danny and the singer had to remember what they sang so that it could all be lip-sync'd.

As Danny has since said: 'I speak eleven languages. Is it my fault no one else understands them?'

Much of the film turns on the teacher's change of profession – when he goes to work in a circus. He unwittingly climbs into a lion's cage. He learns to juggle.

'I've never seen anything quite like it,' recalled Michael Kidd. 'He had to juggle on camera, three balls in the air at one time. He had never done any juggling in his life. So he said: "Someone come and show me how to do it." We had an expert come in. I tried it at the same time but I couldn't manage it. So I didn't stick with it and quit. But at the end of the day, Danny said, "Here watch this!" He was talking and juggling at the same time without any interruption in his speech. He had no trouble stopping everything, so that it didn't affect his other mental processes. When it came to shooting the scene, we did it and he was perfect. He picked up the balls and continued with the scene as though he had been doing it all his life.'

He found it as easy as conducting a symphony orchestra. Well almost. What he did find a little more challenging was flying an aeroplane – although, as he was to say, if he could do it then anyone could.

LIFE COULD NOT BETTER BE

MICHAEL KIDD WAS THE MAN WHO GOT DANNY HOOKED ON FLYING. At first all he ever thought he could learn from the pint-sized New York East Side dancer was how to do a pirouette in mid-air, certainly not to bring a plane out of a dive.

But Kidd, the man whom Danny at one time swore never to accompany in a car because he thought his driving presented a distinct challenge to the nearest hospital emergency centre, got a pilot's licence and the Kaye psyche demanded one too.

It happened at around about the time both were working on *Merry Andrew*.

Danny had to go to New York after filming and there met Kidd's assistant Sheila Hackett – soon to become Mrs Michael Kidd – with whom he had also worked on *Merry Andrew*. 'You know that Michael's become a flyer,' she said. 'He's just got his pilot's licence.'

Kaye couldn't understand it. 'Let's call him up,' Danny ordered. Sheila put through a call.

'Mike?' he said 'This is Danny. What's this about you having a pilot's licence? When did you do this?'

Kidd told him. Danny's reaction was immediate. 'I want one too.' But he didn't leave it at that. Because Danny Kaye was Danny Kaye he wanted instant answers – to very detailed questions.

'Did you have to take an exam?' Yes, he was told. He had to take an exam. 'Was it a written exam?' Yes, it was a written exam. 'Is there a lot of arithmetic, math in it?' That was the crunch question, because a fellow like David Kaminsky who had left school before arithmetic questions started getting difficult and who relied on his manager to add up his restaurant bill was beginning to get daunted.

'Yes,' his friend replied. 'But there's nothing too complicated, Danny.'

'You're sure?' The dancer comforted him that it was easy. The assurance was almost enough. 'But then Danny, who is – as in everything else – a superb driver, thought that if a terrible driver like I could pass the test, then he could, too.'

[218]

The difference was that Michael Kidd was content enough to fly small private propeller-powered aircraft. Danny Kaye was already looking ahead to the time when – providing they could be invented within his life span – he would fly 747 jets.

'He was so determined not to let me get away with it,' Kidd told me, 'that he did everything in his power to get that licence.' Dena gave him some updated mathematics lessons.

He even took the big step of agreeing to go flying with Mike himself – which was extraordinary bravery in the face of danger, considering his intense reluctance to allow him to be ferried around in his car. Kidd picked him up and took him in the direction of Van Nuys Airport.

What he did was to immediately engage an instructor. But, naturally enough, not any ordinary instructor, not the kind of man who was doing very nicely thank you training people to pass exams at the nearest neighbourhood flying school.

He engaged the man who ran a ground school – where the fundamentals of flying were taught before people got up in the air, how to compute winds, to relate compass readings, to calculate weight, position, how to read maps, charts, work out your air speed.

None of that had given Michael Kidd, who had had a scientific background, much trouble. He at one time had been studying to be an engineer.

George Budde, the school owner, was paid to come to Danny's house to give him private instruction. 'After a few lessons, he was furious with me,' Kidd recalled. 'He said, "Just a few simple problems, huh?" He worked at it for months to the exclusion of everything else. He took his private ground school lessons, took his exams, passed them and went in the air – and took his licence.'

Before long, Danny also had a commercial pilot's licence. 'He had this extraordinary determination to do this and nothing was going to defeat him.' Nothing of course ever did.

Later, Danny himself would say: 'I *had* to find out about Mike's flying. Curiosity gets the best of all of us sometimes.'

But he was a man who went up in his first aeroplane in 1933 in a Ford tri-engine craft that owed more to goodwill than good design.

'Somewhere in my uninformed mind, I had the vague idea that if I ever flew an aeroplane I'd hop in and yell, "Hey fellows, this is Danny and I'm going flying."' He didn't mention anything about the engines going *ta-pocket, ta-pocket, ta-pocket,* but that must have been part of the general idea.

As much as anything, Danny was impressed by the way Mike got the plane ready to fly that first time; how he talked to ground control. As he said: 'This was the most beautiful combination of

[219]

Greek, Japanese and native Aleutian I'd ever heard in my life. It sounded like, "Roger, neaw-whupempup, altimeter razzmatazz, wind wheepkipperedherring."' Sylvia couldn't have written a better line and James Thurber couldn't have imagined a better scenario for him.

He worried about the things anyone else who has ever controlled a plane worries about the first time he gets into the pilot's seat. What if the craft just stops?

'Like this?' asked his instructor. 'This,' was to turn off the engine. 'Now there's no engine,' said the instructor blithely. He pointed out that glider pilots fly quite safely without an engine. That was quite a stunt and not one to be copied too slavishly.

He studied on the ground every morning and in the air every afternoon – which, for the average person would knock up quite a bill. But money was no more an object for Danny Kaye than was the consideration that he might not go through with it all.

Mike Kidd wasn't sure that Danny would go through with it, especially the written exam for which Kaye had primed his strength with the aid of a liverwurst sandwich by his side as he contemplated the questions. 'That did it,' Danny recalled. 'I'd get my ticket or else.'

Unlike most people, Danny Kaye got himself a licence to fly two-engined planes before he got one enabling him to fly single-motored craft. Then he got an instrument-rating licence. Finally, there was his commercial licence and the one that said he could fly jets.

CANDY KISSES

WHAT ONE COULD NEVER SAY ABOUT DANNY KAYE WAS THAT HE WAS content with his lot. Flying was always more than a means to an end with him. It became a consuming passion, but like his golf and conducting symphony orchestras it was one that was in a neatly packaged file which he drew out when he either needed it or when the desire stirred within him. There was always room for something else.

That 'something else' in the late '50s and early '60s and which has never left him was cooking. Not ordinary cooking. Not barbecue cooking. But the real thing – and particularly cooking Chinese style.

Danny always liked Chinese food. Ever since that first trip to Shanghai, it had represented more than just a kind of eating, but an art form. Setting out the dishes was as important as preparing them. As far as he was concerned, it was much, but much more important than eating them. Danny would invite close friends in for a meal that he had cooked and then barely nibble at the results himself. Usually, he just sat and watched the assembled company eat a feast prepared in a special Chinese kitchen, designed by a chef from San Francisco whom Danny regarded as the greatest in the land.

That same chef would also say that the meals Danny serves are finer than he himself could serve. If you want to know how that could be possible, Kaye has a fast-order answer: 'No restaurant could possibly afford the ingredients I use.' So there are the finest ingredients – operated on in the finest equipped private kitchen in the world. The word 'operated' is deliberate.

But both the kitchen and the ingredients were merely the start to it all. Danny decided that the gas pressure being fed to San Ysidro Drive was insufficient and persuaded – instructed is possibly a more appropriate term – the city gas undertaking to increase it to a level that allowed him to cook the best Chinese dishes in the country.

And not just Chinese. His Italian cooking is superb, too. He doesn't eat that either, but those privileged to share it report that it is the greatest they have ever tasted. As for his pastry – real experts in the field say that there is not a better patisseur in America.

The passion that was merely warming up in the '50s has been more than a little consuming in the years that have followed.

Marlene Sorosky who teaches cookery in Los Angeles dedicated a cookery book to Danny – because, she says, he is 'the best.' The best? 'He is better than master chefs like James Beard, Jacques Petia and Julia Child. He is better than them all.' But what makes him so special? She has no doubt about the answer: 'His sensitivity,' she said. 'It's the same as when he conducts an orchestra. It's his fine tuning.'

Every party for which Danny cooks the food is a gourmet event, with gourmet conversation to go with it. Afterwards, he leads the guests in a series of comedy routines, with the others repeating lines *Minnie the Moocher* style. 'They are some of the filthiest lines you could think of,' says Saul Chaplin who is still regularly invited to the Kaye home. Sometimes, after a meal cooked to perfection, Danny himself entertains, bringing out the Yiddish accent which could be cut with one of the knives in his kitchen – but which is never used to cut a traditional Jewish-style meal. 'Much too heavy for his tastes,' said Chaplin.

A meal cooked by Danny is a favourite present to people he particularly likes. He gave one to the new Mr and Mrs Michael Kidd to celebrate their wedding.

'His idea of a wonderful evening is to invite a few friends down and cook for them. The dinner he cooked for us was just superb. He did it with all the flourishes you could imagine. It was a Chinese dinner you could probably not get in any Chinese restaurant, even the very best. He bought the finest ingredients, prided himself on doing it perfectly.'

Two days later, he called the Kidds: 'Come down and I'll cook you an Italian dinner.'

Isaac Stern came that night. 'Again it was absolutely superb – although he didn't touch any of the food.

'It was another show for him. Done with great expertise. He whisked the wok out, brought the food in, and tossed it. If we tried to take it too early, he'd shout: "Wait a minute . . . not yet." And the food just kept coming and coming.'

A rapid-fire conversation accompanied it all. 'Now you would expect, 'said Kidd, 'that since cooks are very busy people, they need to concentrate on what they're doing. Well Danny concentrated, but could talk and play at the same time.'

Sometimes, he even allowed taste and discretion to get the better of him and switched his patter from Yiddish to the kind of Chinese only he would understand – and then only when he recited it.

[222]

'Every once in a while, he would serve the food and assume that Chinese accent.'

He had help making the food, cutting up the vegetables and meat and so on, giving the necessary instructions, like any master chef, and did the final flourishes himself. Every course was cooked individually. 'You had to finish that before he would serve the next one.'

On more than one occasion, he would go to his friend's Chinese restaurant in San Francisco – give the chef the night off and take over the kitchen himself.

For the moment, none of this was interfering with his career, although he was staying at home more now and he and Sylvia were seen together more than they had been. His one-man-show theatrical appearances were a great deal fewer, but he was still making films. They weren't the Goldwyn-type movies any more, although there were a number of people who wished they had been.

Danny, however, was on the whole looking for something new in the kind of films he made, too, even if there were those who still would have preferred to see the old *Wonder Man* suddenly start to mesmerise them, from the screen in a motion-picture theatre.

The Five Pennies was again a new departure. It was the first time he had played a living person on the screen.

It was the story of Red Nichols, a musician who would have had the term 'legendary' in front of his name, if only enough people had been prepared to make him a legend. In fact, although he had in the late '40s deputised for John Scott Trotter as musical accompanist for Bing Crosby, he was virtually forgotten by all but a handful of afficianados of the big band era. He had, however, deserved better. Not only had he played on platforms with the likes of Louis Armstrong; Glenn Miller, Bob Crosby and Benny Goodman had all played with him – and for him.

World War II had really marked the end of what the musical world knew as Red Nichols and His Five Pennies. His daughter was crippled with polio and he had to find work in a shipyard.

Well, that was the part of the story that appealed to Mel Shavelson and Jack Rose, one of Hollywood's most accomplished and sought-after comedy writing teams who had worked for both Warner Brothers and Sam Goldwyn and who had written material for a host of some of the funniest men in town, not least of whom had been Bob Hope.

It was their idea to take the guts of the Red Nichols story, slightly sanitise some of the less happy parts of his relationships with musicians, and make it partly, at least, a comedy picture. They thought Danny – with, Sam Goldwyn take note, his natural red hair – would be a natural for the role. Since to Danny it represented

[223]

something else that was new and different, like discovering perhaps Romanian cookery, he was keen to proceed.

'We thought it would be a good venture for Danny, an intimate family story, which we had done fairly successfully with Danny Thomas and Doris Day,' Jack Rose told me.

Because Sylvia and Danny were involved together, this became something of a family production, too – with not altogether satisfactory results. 'The fact that they were both there tended to slow the juices of creation,' recalled Rose.

In fact those juices were threatened with drying up altogether during the weeks before a screenplay acceptable to both Danny and Sylvia could be achieved. 'It was pretty exasperating,' he told me.

'It would have been easier if Danny had worked by himself. On the other hand, it might not have been as good.

'When it was done, it turned into a pleasant experience.'

Red Nichols himself was technical adviser on the picture. And he played the trumpet while Danny mimed the action.

'Unless it worked, Danny wasn't going to do it,' Rose recalled. 'Nichols was just a plain ordinary trumpet player. We added to it the funny things that Danny did so well. You create these things from necessity. You put a quite boring man into situations, like needing money, and let your imagination go from there – even if it wasn't true in fact, in spirit it was.'

They wrote the script, Sylvia produced the songs and Danny was left to put it all together. One item in the movie represented the finest, sweetest example of how comedy writers and Danny Kaye could merge into a finished product. We had seen a hospital ward. Not all the children were bright and sunny as they were usually depicted on movie screens. Some were crying. Now, back at Nichols's home and for the benefit of his sick daughter, Shavelson and Rose devised a routine in which Danny would demonstrate different kinds of cries, much as other writers and comedians had planned different kinds of, say, snores. Kaye fans cherish the memory of one of the children Danny introduced to the youngsters – Myer the Cryer. He didn't just cry, he sucked in air and exploded.

That was what Shavelson and Rose wrote. (Like Panama and Frank, they shared the production and direction duties between them. Rose produced the film and Shavelson directed.) What Danny Kaye did was to demonstrate it all, complete with blows, sucks, heaves, sighs, desperate searches for air – the lot. They couldn't have *told* him how to do it. That was why they had Danny Kaye. The tears literally rolled down Danny's cheeks as he told the story of Myer the Cryer. Real tears. The audience's faces weren't wholly dry either, and not just from crying at the pathos of the scene.

'But that's what writing a comedy routine is all about,' Mel

Shavelson told me. 'It's what we do. We just wrote "Danny cries", and left the rest to him.'

Another reason they had Danny Kaye was because they knew he *couldn't* play the trumpet – yet. So, as they knew he would and as he had previously learned to juggle or play golf – to say nothing of those other activities which will not be repeated now – he learnt. It was never intended that it would be Danny's own trumpeting audiences would hear from behind the screen. That would be asking too much even of Danny Kaye. He was, after all playing a virtuoso cornet player, who was prepared to record the music himself.

But Danny did learn how to finger the trumpet, so that his movements corresponded perfectly with the sounds made by Nichols.

'It was the most incredible thing,' his friend Saul Chaplin remembers. 'Do you know, there isn't a single thing that man can't do.'

'The only trouble we had with Danny,' Shavelson told me, 'was that Danny would only want to do one take because otherwise he'd lose the spontaneity. If he had to do more than one, he'd start ad-libbing and everyone else would blow their lines.' It would be a continuing problem.

In the end, the pair called in Sylvia to try to mount a rescue operation. She told him: 'Danny, both of us are trying to make some money out of this, so we've got to try to get going. It's fine for you, but look what's happening to the other people.'

As Mel told me: 'We left him plenty of opportunity to go into a routine which required Danny. That was nothing to do with us. It was like turning on a steam engine and letting it go.'

The most famous number in the picture also became one of the most popular of all Danny Kaye songs – and was one of the first soundtrack items to be released as a record single (as distinct from having it re-recorded specially for disc).

It was the tune he recorded in a smoke-filled speakeasy at the time of Prohibition – the duet with Louis Armstrong of *When The Saints Go Marching In*, the traditional fiery Black spiritual with some very spirited additional lines supplied by Danny with Sylvia's help.

Danny loved the scene so much that long after it had first been shown in the rushes, he would take visitors into the projection room just to see it again.

(Shavelson told me that he and Kaye discussed that time fairly recently. Danny told him, 'Those were the good old days.' The reason is easy to understand: 'Danny was just getting bigger and bigger and it seemed that it was going to stay going on that way.')

But there were the occasional problems on the set, even when that scene was being shot.

At their first meeting on camera, Danny called 'Satchmo', *'Mister Armstrong.'*

The world-renowned black musician interrupted him while the camera was still turning. 'Do you want this film to play in the South?' 'Satchmo' asked him. 'If you do, you'd better call me, "Louis".'

The fact that Louis did take such a commanding part in the film, even though it was really in just one scene – but what a scene! – helped the whole project to hold up. For days, people would find excuses to get on to the set just to watch the two men working together.

Jack Rose is convinced that Danny liked the whole project mainly because it was his first movie playing a real live character. 'It tended to extend his acting muscles. It was really astonishing how a man was able to do all the things that trumpet players are able to do, with their lips and their fingers and everything else.'

In this film, as Rose hinted, it was Sylvia who judged the sort of material he would do in the movie.

'She was also tough,' recalls Shavelson. 'Particularly with the music. She drove the music people crazy and I had screaming battles with her.'

She had rows with arrangers. Sometimes, they had to tell her that not only was she wrong, but she really didn't know what she was talking about. 'She was going for effects and instruments that would never be heard. When it happened that she was right, and things were done over, the differences were so slight they couldn't be detected.

'But she had control over the music and the studio had to listen to her – because if they didn't she would be unhappy.

'She was protective for herself.' Since she wrote the score for the picture, she doubtless felt she had to be. One thing she wrote, however, landed her in trouble. It was the title song for the movie, *The Five Pennies*. Soon after the picture was premiered, an Italian publisher made it known that it was an old number and he held the rights. Sylvia apologised, saying it was one of those coincidences that many another music person would recognise.

There didn't appear to be too much in the way of tantrums between Danny and Sylvia while the film was being made, although Shavelson's wife Lucille says that she remembers a number of them. 'Danny was wonderful when he was wonderful but when he was bad, he was horrid. You know he was like the little girl with the curl in the centre of her forehead.'

'But Danny seemed to be enjoying life very much. He had all those other interests,' Mel himself told me.

[226]

'He was, however, always much happier doing his musical numbers than he was when acting. You could always separate the stage person in Danny Kaye from the others.'

What you couldn't separate was the perfectionist. As always, the music played by Nichols (and mimed by Danny) and Armstrong had to be added afterwards. Danny bet Louis that he would get the fingering right – but that 'Satchmo' himself would get it wrong and out of synchronisation. Danny, as one might expect, won his bet.

'Louis could never remember because it was all ad-lib,' recalls Mel Shavelson. 'Danny who had never played the trumpet in his life memorised it all and could do it in one take.'

One of the comedy scenes added for the movie that were purely out of the Rose–Shavelson inventory was a series of radio commercials in a montage early in the film. It was while doing this that Danny decided he was fed up with the perfection insisted upon by the continuity girl. She spotted everything. But Danny had a bet with himself. In one scene, as a Mountie on horseback, he switched to playing his cornet with his left hand instead of the right he used in the rest of the movie. He was sure no one would notice.

No one did. Danny said nothing about it till the picture was completed. 'We decided to leave it in,' says Shavelson.

'We wouldn't have written the film the way we did if Danny Kaye wasn't going to be our star. They don't do that sort of thing any more. In those days it was quite common to write a film around a star and what he could do best, with block comedy routines like Myer the Cryer, block comedy music like *The Saints* – and the rest was the story.'

Red Nichols and his wife (played on screen by Barbara Bel Geddes, then best known as the daughter of an eminent Broadway actor but in recent years much more as the original 'Miss Elly' in the *Dallas* TV soap opera) liked the film. In fact, they both loved Danny.

When the film was shown for the first time in a Paramount projection theatre, *Life* magazine joined them to photograph their reactions, using infra-red. They caught Red Nichols crying. He wanted his story told – even with the necessary changes and additions – and he liked the way that it was.

I wondered whether Danny Kaye was the kind of man who appreciated material written for him. 'I don't know if he did,' Mel Shavelson told me. 'But he laughed. That was enough.'

ON THE DOUBLE

THE 1960S WERE GOING TO BE THE START OF THE TOUGH DECADES FOR Danny. The man who had done it all looked out for new perspectives to survey, new fields to conquer and came back with no real answers.

For a time he became a fanatic about table tennis and before long was generally regarded as the ping-pong champion of Beverly Hills – well, could he be anything else? But it didn't have the same satisfaction about it which had been afforded by conducting a symphony orchestra or making a Chinese meal or even allowing the Walter Mitty syndrome in the frustrated surgeon to take root.

Occasionally, he was able to merge those Mitty-like dreams – like the time he was flying his own aircraft and felt a stabbing pain in his side. He directed himself towards a field close to the Mayo Clinic in Rochester, which he knew would be able to deal with the case he had already diagnosed as acute appendicitis.

Of course he knew about the Mayo Clinic, and not just because it was famous or because he had met its founder all those years before. He had mentally filed away details about every hospital in the United States, these he approved of, those he hoped he wouldn't be seen dead in – and arranged to be driven by ambulance. The hospital confirmed his diagnosis and performed an operation. On another occasion, he was a mere passenger in a passenger jet when a fellow traveller appeared to suffer a heart attack. Danny immediately put himself in charge of the man's condition; he administered artificial respiration and talked over the aircraft radio to the hospital.

He still booked himself into the Mayo Clinic for a total check-up lasting two or three days every year, and admitted he was heavily into analysis, although even he found it too expensive, he said.

He was still something of an ambassador – and when not for the United Nations, for the State Department in Washington. In 1959, he had gone to Moscow for the annual film festival in the Soviet capital and attended the Fourth of July celebrations at the US embassy.

It was a time and a stage in his life when others were making new assessments of him and his contribution to the business he had all but mastered – and that 'but' was beginning to worry people; why hadn't he really taken total control of an industry which just ten years earlier had been willing to make him its king? The reason is now clear to see; by deciding that there were so many facets to his life, he was spreading himself too thin. *The Five Pennies* had been visible proof of it all. Apart from *When The Saints Come Marching In* and the Myer the Cryer routine, there was just too little of the old Wonder Man in view.

Time magazine said it all: 'The basic trouble with movie biographies of famed jazz musicians is that the camera is not a horn. What matters about the average music man is the music he makes. . . . Comedian Kaye, whenever the script gives him a chance, does mimic wonders to fatten up a part that is really from hunger.'

Nobody denied he was special. The trouble was he wasn't allowing himself to show just how special he could be.

If Jack Benny said he 'stood in awe' of Danny Kaye, plenty of others were doing that, too. In Israel, the Ben Gurion University in the Negev presented him with their second Lifetime Achievement Award.

And to his own child he was still king, never to be toppled from a throne that would have seemed grand enough if it were no more than a chair in her nursery. Despite his love for his daughter and the equal amount of affection and devotion of Sylvia, Dena hadn't been spoilt. Danny had given her a weekly allowance which began at a nickel a week and didn't rise to any heady heights even when her own adolescence and the growth of inflation seemed to indicate it. She was now at Stanford University and was giving every impression of inheriting a number of her parents' intelligence chromosomes.

People couldn't understand why Danny was not grabbing at the new medium of television which by 1960 had already proved itself to be bigger than anything that had ever gone before it in the world of entertainment.

At 47, however, Danny was playing cautious and announcing he was in a 'kind of self-imposed semi-retirement.'

But then he decided to take a stab at the small box. Sylvia explained why: there just didn't seem anywhere else to go.

In October 1960 he did a spectacular for CBS, a good portion of it live. 'I can tell you some people aren't going to like the show,' he said in an amazingly revealing prognosis of a kind he would never have dared in previous years. 'And I may just look at this tape and decide I don't like it myself – so I'll do it live.'

That's how the show went, and well received it was, too. He did new numbers and routines and old ones – 'because it would be silly not to do the ones people know'. And expect.

General Motors was his sponsor for three shows, for which he received an undisclosed six-figure sum.

He said he liked to please people. But none of that should give the impression that he was always now a benign example of Danny Kaye at his most charming. In November 1960, Danny entertained at Las Vegas, which was only just really thinking of becoming the gambling and show centre of America. He met columnist Lyn Tornabene for an interview for *Cosmopolitan* magazine and proceeded to be insufferable.

'Put away your notebook,' he told her over lunch. 'Don't you have any manners?' The lunch may have had something to do with his own manners. It was seven o'clock in the evening, but then playing in Las Vegas is like working in another part of the world – which it really is. With no clocks on view in any of the hotels – they might encourage people to stop playing the machines or the tables – it is a time zone all of its own.

'Don't write about me,' he instructed. 'Write about my periphery.' Whether she understood that any better than her readers the polite Ms Tornabene decided not to reveal, although she did note: 'Danny Kaye is a sullen man.'

He himself would have put it all down to the way he was treated by reporters, who from my own research seem to have given him a pretty good deal over the years. No, said Kaye, 'journalists with no brains interview me for an hour, analyse me and then go tell the world what they've uncovered.'

He wasn't going into the business of revealing himself – he should have realised he was doing just that very effectively indeed – because, he pointed out, 'if I woke up feeling exactly the same way every day, I'd shoot myself. Wouldn't you?'

The *Cosmo* lady's experience was potentially to be repeated every time he met a journalist, although others would say that he treated them differently. I interviewed him myself and found him extremely pleasant. Nancy Wise, a BBC interviewer with a fine record, said she thought he was particularly charming – even if he did play games with her name.

Lesley Salisbury, a Los Angeles-based writer for London magazines, on the other hand, says he treated her abominably – saying that he couldn't understand why she was working and not sitting at home raising a family. That sort of taunt didn't endear Mr Kaye to members of the Press, although very few were either prepared to show it or to remove him from the pedestal they had helped create for him.

Danny Kaye could still have been the world's greatest entertainer, but going into semi-retirement at 47 wasn't helping. And to be fair, he wasn't seeking that title. He gave every impression of being very happy with the way things were going for him professionally. He had an opportunity to do anything that took his fancy. It was his fans, that very large devoted band of people on two or even three continents, who would have liked more.

There were some reporters who would have liked Danny to relate his UN work to the world political scene. He wasn't having any of that at all. 'Look fellows,' he told them, 'I made a deal with the State Department. I don't discuss politics and they don't make movies. And we're getting along just fine.'

In 1960, he was on his travels again for UNICEF, seeing more children, entertaining more children, being filmed talking to children and playing to children, and coming back home afterwards telling his listeners yet again that children were generally a hell of a lot brighter than most adults. They had heard it all before, but it was as true and as valuable a job as it had been before.

UNICEF proclaimed that he had been appointed their Regional Director – for the World. The organisation held a special meeting in June 1961 to celebrate his seven years working for them.

Danny knew that the proceedings were being translated in various languages simultaneously, so he kept his speech serious but simple. He asked for contributions and his fellow delegates applauded warmly. He went on to talk about his trips. His audience listened intently and the interpreters did their work brilliantly in true United Nations fashion. Without any warning or change of pace, he then declared: 'Insofar as the consequential elements have not but can be, there must be perturbing facts to the contrary. . . . Let's see what the interpreters do with that.'

What they were doing at that stage was coughing, stammering and wiping brows in their glass booths. They were also seen to be laughing. His UNICEF work kept him very busy indeed.

It meant that he and Sylvia weren't seeing any more of each other while they weren't working together – television had brought them closer, but then he was off on his travels again.

And when he was home, she would have liked to have him behave a little more like a man of his station. 'It takes an Act of Congress,' she said, 'to get him to eat at the dining room table.'

He would even say that he didn't know how many rooms he had at San Ysidro Drive. 'Let's see,' he said, 'we have a dining room, a study, a music room and a couple of bedrooms.' And that was all he was prepared to reveal – or admit to. On his study door was a brass plate presented to him after a season in London. It said: 'Elder Statesman, I.N.T. Club. London Palladium.' 'That's just the sort of thing Danny will display,' said Sylvia. 'I.N.T.' stood for

'International No-Talent' which was a suggestion no one at all had ever dared make about Danny Kaye. The more justifiable complaint was that he was not using the talent that he did have.

'I am a performer,' he told *The American Weekly* in November 1962, 'and I'm intensely proud of my profession. I get a great sense of pleasure, of satisfaction, of fulfilment from it. If my profession were ever denied me, I don't know what I'd do. Worse, I don't think I'd even know who I was. It gives me great joy to walk out on a stage and entertain people – to feel their joy coming back across the footlights. But I'd be less than honest if I did not admit I wish I could turn more of that happiness inward to myself.' That was also a kind of honesty one had not yet heard a great deal about in public.

Meanwhile, there were those taking their happiness from seeing another Danny Kaye film, again with the help of Rose and Shavelson.

On The Double brought Walter Mitty back into the film business – with Danny again playing a British officer; this time in the Army and this time for the length of the film. Of course, he wasn't called Mitty and neither was he supposed to be dreaming, except that for Danny it seemed to represent a dream part and his fans were pleased to hear him doing another crazy accent and dressed to kill in British Army uniform. It wasn't a brilliant movie but there was plenty in it to have fun with.

It was based on the film made four years earlier, entirely seriously and recalling a real incident, called *I Was Monty's Double*, which told the story of how an actor who bore a passing resemblance to Field Marshal Montgomery impersonated him as a ruse to upset the Germans.

This time Danny, an Army private looking somewhat old for his rank and stationed in Britain during World War II, enjoys impersonating the British general to whom he bears an uncanny resemblance. Apart from the fact that he constantly forgets which eye to cover with a patch and doesn't know his flank from his front, he looks a dead ringer for the 'old man'. And as for his accent. . . .

To cut a not outstandingly wonderful storyline short, the British think it would be a very good idea to protect their general by using a double who, of course, gets to go to bed with the man's beautiful wife (Dana Wynter) who can't understand how her unbearably selfish and unfeeling husband has become so tender. His mistress (Diana Dors) finds him strange, too. He also mystifies his battle axe of an aunt (a delightful-as-usual cameo from Margaret Rutherford) as to how he has forgotten the old clan's Scottish war dance.

'Danny got on with everyone on the film beautifully,' Rose remembers.

In a way it was as much like *Wonder Man* as *Walter Mitty* – with two Danny Kayes talking to each other in the same film.

Mel Shavelson directed the picture and Rose produced. Sylvia asked Jack Rose why he never directed. 'I don't like to talk to people, let alone actors,' he answered.

There were those who said similar things about Kaye.

Relations between Danny and Sylvia were, even for them, at their most fraught during the making of *On The Double*. There were reports of blows being exchanged between them. 'I could hear the rows between them all the time,' Allan Cuthbertson told me.

Cuthbertson played the villain of the piece, a German spy intent on killing the general for whom Danny was substituting – and who gradually suspects that he is, in fact, a phoney. His role fitted in with most of the plausible features of the film. The archetypal British officer was supposed to be a member of the 'McGregor Highlanders' who could wear a kilt one moment and say two German words the next.

Cuthbertson had a caravan next to the Kayes. 'I could hear the noise coming from their caravan. They were rowing like blazes. I remember on one occasion either Danny threw Sylvia out of the caravan or Sylvia threw Danny out. One of them left with feathers ruffled.'

As on many of Danny's projects, it was Sylvia who made many of the decisions on *On The Double*. This time, it was she who decided to make the movie in the first place.

'I remember handing her the script,' recalls Shavelson. 'Sylvia said, "Right, we'll do it." Just like that. I asked her whether perhaps she didn't need more time or that Danny ought to have his say and she just said, "good is good", which is very flattering for any writer, but it meant that she was in charge.'

Wasn't that self assurance something of a pain? 'I wouldn't describe her as a pain,' says Jack Rose. 'She was just a wife looking after her husband's best interests.

'Danny was pleased to go along with it. It was more to his taste than *Five Pennies*. He had given that one a shot but he wasn't going to make a career out of sentimental stories.'

The accent Danny used in *On The Double* was, of course, perfect – as perfect as his *Five Pennies* trumpet.

As Rose told me: 'He is so perfect with accents that he can't be ordinary. So he has to look for things that are almost science fiction as far as a comedian is concerned.'

'Danny was a somewhat self-conscious performer,' says Shavelson. 'He always felt more comfortable as a singer than as an actor. He seemed to enjoy himself more than most people because he did all the things he did, but he was happiest of all while performing.

'The pictures I made with Danny seem in retrospect to have been happy pictures.'

Kaye made *On The Double* work the way he had made *Wonder Man* work. He seemed to thrive on playing a double part. 'Maybe that's because he was a split personality,' said Shavelson, only partly joking.

In one scene, Danny as the General sits behind a desk talking to Danny, the American private. He then moves to the front and bangs the American on the back with his stick. 'I've been trying to remember how we did that,' said the director 'because I want to use it in another film. And I can't remember how it was done.'

Judging how Danny behaved on the set of *On The Double* depends on who one speaks to. Wilfrid Hyde White has no doubt that he was nothing less than perfect at this time, and to him in particular.

'Oh, he was marvellous,' Hyde White told me. 'Not only was he a brilliant comedian, but a great friend to me.'

The actor, who soon afterwards would be best known as Col. Pickering in the film of *My Fair Lady*, played the head of the British intelligence unit who put the whole 'double' idea to Danny following his impromptu impersonation – which would otherwise have landed him in the guardhouse.

'He went out of his way to be kind and considerate to me,' he recalled. 'I couldn't be fonder of the fellow or think of him more kindly.'

There were reasons for this, of course. Part of the film was shot on location in Britain. The rest was made in Paramount's Hollywood studios. It was while filming there that the British actor had an offer from MGM that he did not want to refuse.

The MGM people asked the English actor to have lunch with them. But the Metro studios at Culver City were too far away from Paramount for this to be practicable. So the MGM men were persuaded to come to see Hyde White. He booked a table in the executive commissary.

'I was just going over there when someone came over to me and said that lunch was ready. I didn't understand what he meant, but then he told me. Danny had given me his dressing room and insisted we had our meeting there. What a lovely fellow!'

Allan Cuthbertson said that Danny was nice enough to him, too. 'But I could see that he wasn't a happy gent. And,' he said, 'he made life very difficult for a lot of the people on the movie.'

'His trouble was that he didn't want to rehearse,' the actor said – a symptom which others might recognise. The big problem came with the dance scene. 'They had five Technicolor cameras trained on him during the dance, which Danny really didn't do very well.

[234]

But he refused to do it again. They brought in eight dancing boys from New York to make up the rest of the guests and Danny just said, "Shoot it". The first thing Danny did was to grab the dancing boy who was teaching me and send him off the film. So I had to do it without help.

'It really wasn't good enough. Morecambe and Wise used to do scenes like that, but they'd rehearse them again and again. In one shot in that dance scene, I was supposed to hand Danny a sword, but he refused to take it – so I just disappeared out of camera range and he had no alternative. He only came to one rehearsal. He turned up, said "Hi, kids" and then disappeared. He thought it would just happen.'

Danny himself has never denied his reluctance to join the perfectionist bandwagon and spend his time rehearsing.

'Anyone who claims to be a perfectionist is displaying an inflated ego,' he wrote in that *American Weekly* piece soon after making *On The Double*.

'I prepare for my work with a great deal of fervour. But I don't want ever to repeat a scene over and over, striving for the impossible, perfection. I'd far rather have the spirit of spontaneity with technical imperfections. Sometimes in that you achieve a sense of perfection.'

Even Margaret Rutherford had problems with him. 'She was totally batty, of course,' Cuthbertson remembers. 'She wanted to speak in the broadest Scottish accent you could imagine, but Danny told her no one could understand what she was saying. She didn't like that.'

But the late Diana Dors told me she regarded Danny Kaye as 'one of the very few geniuses I have ever met'.

One of Danny's problems at this time was that he was not allowed to go flying. The film's insurers wouldn't consider it. But then he discovered that Cuthbertson had flown during the war. 'He was constantly trying to persuade me to take him up. I wouldn't do it. I'd done enough flying in the war to last me. Finally, he persuaded me to do so when I found it was a way to see the Grand Canyon. But for some reason or other, it didn't happen. In the end, I don't even think Danny and I said goodbye to each other.'

Which is not a happy memory of a film that perhaps now deserves a better memory than the one afforded it by most movie buffs. It was to prove to be the last Kaye movie in the old semi-Goldwyn tradition.

But there were still people who thought that everything Danny did was marvellous, and it did still look that way from a seat in the theatre. Certainly, it seemed that the Kayes would have to move house if they were going to find room for all the awards he was chalking up.

In April 1963, he was presented with the March of Dimes Humanitarian Award, marking the charity's 75th anniversary. He was acclaimed 'one of the greatest ambassadors of America to the world today'. Meanwhile, other Arab states were taking exception to him – and the occasional comments he was known to make in favour of Israel, most of it privately because he was still as willing as before to go wherever UNICEF sent him, in the Middle East or anywhere else. He and actor Jeff Chandler were blacklisted alongside 12 American and European companies on the orders of the Arab League Boycott of Israel office.

At the same time, UNICEF asked him to observe the condition of children in Russia. His report was glowing. He told reporters that he regarded his work in that regard as complementary to his life on stage. 'I need both . . . to express myself. Either would be meaningless without the other.'

The Moscow kids were no different from those anywhere else. 'We didn't speak the same language, but I found, as I've found everywhere, that if an adult behaves like a child with a child, communication is a simple thing.'

He went to children's wards and he attended children's concerts. At one he led the audience in singing a Russian youth song. The visit coincided with the third International Moscow Film Festival. At the Rossma Theatre in the city, which had been showing *West Side Story*, he sang this paean to young Socialism and brought the house down.

Observers of the scene still wondered how either he or Sylvia had not yet brought the house down in San Ysidro Drive. She would joke about a pact they made long before – 'I'll tell you nothing and you give me no advice'. But they seemed pious words.

In 1963, he made his last comedy film to date, although not even he at the time would claim it offered anything to either his audience or the Kaye mystique. *The Man From the Diners Club* bore all the signs of being a pot-boiler, except there seemed little in the pot to boil.

It was an attempt to revive the *Wonder Man – Kid From Brooklyn schlemeil* with none of the patter or comedy music to go with it. Danny was 50 years old, plainly too old to play the role of a clerk trying to retrieve a card that went to a gangster – without making himself seem ridiculous. There were the predictable moments – his tie getting caught in a machine, cards flying everywhere. He went through something like 850,000 cards in that scene.

The only people who seemed pleased were the men from the Diners Club – for understandable commercial reasons. The club featured him on the cover of their magazine. Why they would feel that way in an artistic sense, of course, defies comprehension. Danny Kaye was not doing their reputation a whole lot of good.

Probably the best comedy scene of all was one when he hides behind a shower curtain – only to be revealed by the gangster he is chasing.

'What you doin' here buster?' asks the mobster.

'Oh nothin',' says Danny. 'It's election day and I'm voting.' The line was entirely Danny's, ad-libbed in best unrehearsed Kaye style.

Martha Hyer was one of his co-stars in that movie:

'He was much more serious than I could have imagined,' she told me. 'Like all great comedians he seemed to have that streak of melancholy.'

She had known the Kayes socially for some time but it was working with Danny when she says she really became aware of this. 'It was the first time I saw the melancholia in him, just sitting and talking. He only seemed to be happy when the camera was rolling. It was like being with Phil Silvers. You always expect them to be the same funny people off screen as on. But they're not. It's as though life is merely a stage wait to get on. But I must say I learnt a lot from him – especially when it came to timing.'

Timing wasn't always a perfect quality with Danny – or involving Danny. For instance, he found it difficult to synchronise movements with his old partners Panama and Frank. It was then that they planned together to make a new Kaye film, called this time *Knock on Silk*.

A deal was set up to follow the *Knock On Wood* pattern with a film shot in the Far East. Columbia Pictures commissioned the movie, Danny agreed to star in it, and the two writers went to Hong Kong and Japan to survey the film industry in countries not known for making films (making cameras yes, but what came out of them was a different matter).

'The very first thing we found out was that it was impossible to do the picture till the spring,' Frank told me.

With that thought in mind, the two decided they would get on with another picture in the meantime, one for which they had already been paid. Danny read about this in a trade paper while on an aircraft. 'He and Sylvia thought we had double-crossed them. They didn't stop to realise that we couldn't make that picture for six months or more. So they cancelled it. We had no chance to talk to them about it. I was furious and for months we didn't talk. After all, we had done three pictures with the guy.'

But then they decided on another venture, which was called this time, *Five Pieces of Maria*, in which Danny would co-star with Sophia Loren.

'We had originally planned it as a vehicle for Sinatra and Dean Martin,' Frank told me. 'Well, Danny said that if we got rid of Sinatra and Martin, combined their two roles into one for him, we had a commitment right then. Commitments were very hard to get in those days, so we said yes immediately.' But the commitment didn't remain.

'To this day, I don't know why he pulled out,' said Norman Panama. 'I think his ego was bruised when Loren decided not to do the film. He also thought it was going to be too much the woman's picture.' The movie was to have been shot in Europe, probably France.

Why Loren decided to give up the film part was summed up by the two words *Two Women*. She delayed the making of the movie to do a black-and-white film for Vittorio de Sica – which just happened to win her an Oscar and make her immediately the hottest property in Hollywood. 'By then,' said Panama, 'she had decided that after *Two Women*, she wouldn't want to play with a comedian.'

As Frank said: 'We were getting her for $300,000, but after her Academy Award, she could demand $1,500,000.'

The two writers-cum-producers sued her – and lost. Their contract said that they had to submit scripts to her, which gave the connotation of her approving them. 'We had no intention of giving her approval at all. We intended by the word to mean "deliver" but the French courts ruled against us – in two different hearings.'

With Sophia gone, they had to think of someone else. She was replaced, temporarily, by Melina Mercouri. The film was now going to be shot, instead, in Greece. But it still didn't work out.

'He and Mercouri seemed to get on very well – which I don't think pleased her husband Jules Dassin very much,' said Panama.

His partner recalled: 'Yes, we had two huge female stars, both of them ruled in different ways by their husbands. Sophia's husband, Carlo Ponti, made the decisions because he was a businessman; Dassin because of his artistic temperament and he wouldn't let Melina go.'

Danny was equally difficult, too. 'He was never satisfied with the script, which was rewritten four or five times – and then another writer was brought in. Finally, it was abandoned. It wasn't going to give anyone cancer and our first script was probably better than the last. But it soured our relationship. We wasted a hell of a lot of time.'

After that, the writers' relationship with Kaye became non-existent – although they had planned in the meantime another project. Danny was asked to play the role of Fagin in a screen version of *Oliver*. They went to London together to see the show, starring Ron Moody, and decided that this was not a part for Danny Kaye.

'We all thought it was much too anti-Semitic,' Norman Panama

[238]

told me. Besides, after the *Knock on Silk* fiasco, Panama and Frank were distinctly anti-Kaye.

Mel Frank and Danny would see each other regularly at the Tamerisk country club in Palm Springs – Kaye together with men like Hal Wallis and Walter Scharf had founded the club in protest against the anti-Semitism of other clubs in the region.

'We would drive right past each other in our golf cars, one totally ignoring the other,' Mel told me. 'In the end, I felt such a horse's ass that I went up to him and he put his arms around me. But it took a very long time to get that far.'

By then, Danny felt he had to find yet another challenge. The one he chose was called television.

THE DANNY KAYE SHOW

DANNY KAYE HAD ALWAYS STEERED CLEAR OF TELEVISION AS A regular weekly occupation. He had done his annual special for General Motors and the occasional UNICEF-inspired feature, but that was all.

He had been right to avoid it. He was an intelligent visual comedian, whose style demanded a great deal of him, and whose audiences expected certain degrees of perfection, no matter what he said publicly about the word or what his fellow actors sometimes thought of his work.

Bob Hope succeeded on TV because he had that joke factory working to a set formula. He was devastatingly topical and since the news changed every minute of every day, his writers had more and more material with which to deal. Danny was different. His work entailed a great deal of thought. When he began his shows in 1963, it proved to be a monster that was ready to consume him – whole.

The Danny Kaye Show on CBS started with a 20 million audience which Danny accepted willingly because, as he put it, 'television is the number-one entertainment medium'.

He was convinced he had the answer to keeping those millions. 'You can't be on televison each week, unless you can talk to people and make them like you.'

He was sure he could do that. On the whole, people did like him. At first Sylvia was not going to be in attendance, which sparked new rumours of a rift between them. 'Oh hell,' said Danny, 'there's been gossip for 23 years and it's been just that – gossip.'

But she then wrote his material, woke up in the middle of the night if she worried about it fitting the required time slot and, just as in the old days, worked and harried her husband to the degree of perfection she considered he had still to attain.

'There are a great many people who appreciate what Danny does,' she said at the time 'but they do not have the faintest idea what makes it come out that way. I resent it when people say to me, "Oh, do you write the music too?" I wonder where they think it is coming from.'

[240]

With occasional help from Hal Kanter, Sylvia wrote the show, formulated the music and decided where the jokes had to go.

She agreed that their working relationship wasn't always easy. 'Because I'm a creative person myself, I believe in letting other creative people have their way. They can yell at me. I have no sense of protocol. Usually, I just like to give advice. I hate to put the hammer down. But somebody's judgement has to prevail in the show.'

She left no doubt that, as before, the judgement that would prevail would be hers.

Whatever the outcome of the show, it was something Danny needed to do. 'I found in the last seven years or so,' he said at the time, 'that I was falling into a pattern. There was a kind of sameness to everything I did; one picture a year, then play theatres for six or eight weeks, then travel for the UN. I was kind of lingering . . . I felt I had drained all my creativity doing what I had been doing.'

TV was one answer. 'I had to do it because I wasn't alive enough for my own good. It was not a haphazard decision. I do not make haphazard decisions. . . . Some say I've got nothing to prove any more. But it's like a guy playing the violin. He finds he knows how to play, but he practises every day so he can play better.'

There were a number of bright ideas – like singing a song called *What Is A Woman?* while in the background the beautifully busty Gwen Verdon, star of *Damn Yankees* – and later of the original version of *Sweet Charity* – provided generous illustrations.

He also used all the old skit-scat routines that he knew people would like and sat on a stool, feeling – and looking sometimes – as though he were back on stage at the London Palladium.

'Kaye is so good,' wrote *Newsweek* magazine, 'that his show can be frustrating. The flying feet, the magic hands, the rubber face and the vaulting voice are generally put to work one at a time and they have not yet gotten together for the sort of madcap masterwork that shows Kaye at the very top of his form. Too many of his comedy skits have been pointless. Sometimes he tends to peddle his own cuteness, which is inappropriate for a man of 50.'

The show was entirely in his control as chief producer – 'My writers say I'm the best writer without a pencil.' And, he said, 'I *couldn't* sit down and write a skit out, but I can draw it in the air.'

Mike Dann, the network's programme chief, was given an early indication of how much control Danny would take. The first time they met, Dann arrived in his own office late. He found Danny sitting in his chair, drinking his whisky and answering his mail. The Kaye chutzpah hadn't changed any in the new medium either.

Mel Shavelson was producing his film about Israel, *Cast A Giant*

[241]

Shadow, at this time. As a request to his old friend and partner, Shavelson asked Danny to find a way to plug the movie for him. Kaye agreed and invited Chaim Topol, just four years away from his triumph in *Fiddler on the Roof*, to appear as a guest.

'Chaim kept complaining,' said Shavelson 'that Danny was taking away all his best lines so that he would appear to be the funny one. Chaim was left with nothing.' It didn't stop Topol's revering Danny as a superb entertainer.

The show was sponsored not by GM this time, but by the rival giant, American Motors.

The show was to prove something of a nursery for other entertainers who became TV giants on their own – and would eclipse Danny himself on the medium. Dick Van Dyke and Mary Tyler Moore became regulars with Van Dyke frequently playing Danny's stooge.

Every Saturday night, the show was taped in front of an audience and aired the following Wednesday. Preparing the final script was rather like one of the operations Danny still doted on one day performing. He attacked the script with not just a scalpel but with a suction device. He poured an antiseptic douche over anything that he didn't think was right for him.

He went through songs the way he attacked sketches. The words had to fit the music, the music had to be in accord with the tempo he fancied. What Kaye wanted went, but other people had to help it along its journey.

He studied camera angles. He didn't like the idea of talking straight into the camera.

There were publicity stories and pictures of Danny welcoming children to the CBS studios as he had welcomed them to hospital stations in the African jungle.

Julius Epstein, the eminent Hollywood writer – among his trophies is the Oscar he and his brother Philip won for *Casablanca* – phoned Danny one day and asked if he could bring his then young children to the show. 'Fine,' said Danny, 'and take them around to my dressing room afterwards.'

He did. 'I was doing my own television show at the time. My children were thrilled at the prospect of going to see him.

'We went up to him, but he said absolutely nothing. Completely ignored the children, who were very upset, and he ignored me. He just looked and turned his head away. I said, "To hell with it" and took the children away. They were very disappointed.

'Terry-Thomas who was on the same show was very nice to them. Nobody was terribly fond of Kaye.'

One of them who wasn't was Lucille Ball, then at the very peak of her *I Love Lucy* fame. They had a scrape – or so it seemed to everyone around – when both were hosting the 1964 Emmy Awards at Los Angeles's Coconut Grove.

As always happened on these occasions, the programme over-ran.

Lucy suggested to Danny that he speed up his reading of the various citations. But she didn't exactly whisper the advice. It was heard all over the hall, which failed to put Kaye in a perfect frame of mind. He, nevertheless, did what she said – at breakneck speed, so fast that it would have fitted beautifully into the lyrics of *Tchaikovsky*. Kaye fans loved it. But the award nominees did not. And nor did Miss Ball who thought he was taking the rise out of her.

Despite this, Lucy fulfilled an obligation she had made previously to appear on Danny's show a month later.

She wasn't happy with it. In fact, only her husband persuaded her to stay to complete the show. She complained that Danny was being 'high-handed.'

Kaye himself was heard to say – in a voice quite as loud as the one used by Lucy at the awards ceremony – 'Get this red-headed dame off the set'.

When the show was over, the two stars went their separate ways – without exchanging goodbyes. Danny later taped an interview for newsmen in which he said it was all a big joke. 'I didn't really mean it,' he added when asked about the 'red-headed dame' bit.

The series was bought by the BBC for the opening of their BBC 2 Channel in 1964 and ran for another three years. But it can't be recorded as one of Danny's triumphs.

By that time, the ratings had slumped and both Danny and CBS decided that it was not worth continuing for the 1967–68 season. (In November 1966, it had fallen to 79th place with a rating of 14.6.)

In any case, by then he was already looking for something new again. The trouble this time was that he couldn't really find it. And probably never would again.

But he tried. In 1965 at what then seemed the height of the Vietnam War he flew to 'Nam to entertain troops. It proved almost as heady an experience as Korea had been.

He was there for two and a half weeks. He told the Press that despite all they may have read, the troops were totally committed to the war – even more than they had been to the conflict in Korea.

It hadn't been easy for him. In Saigon he actually saw a hotel filled with American officers blown sky high. When he was sent to the battle front, he found that all but a handful of men had moved off elsewhere.

But what about Danny himself? Did he approve of the war? *The New York Times* seemed to think he had lost patience by then. 'I was there for 14 days,' he shouted. 'I don't think that's enough time to get well informed.' He realised that Vietnam was fast becoming the most unpopular fight America had ever involved itself in.

Danny probably wouldn't have liked to call it that, but it would come under the heading of his good works. Another was raising money for charity. Soon after the Vietnam war, he was one of the principals behind raising $40,000 for the New York Philharmonic – conducting the orchestra of course.

That same year when UNICEF was awarded the Nobel Peace Prize Danny was among the distinguished guests at the ceremony in Oslo.

Which was no more than one would expect of the man who in November 1966 was named 'Splendid American' and was presented with the award of the Thomas A. Dooley Foundation.

In June 1967, the Middle East was in ferment again: with the Six Day War between Israel and the Arab States. The war not only affected the parties concerned, but much of the world besides, including the man born David Daniel Kaminsky.

Danny was playing at Las Vegas at the time of the war. Straight after the night-club season he was due to go to England. Not to appear again at the London Palladium – that was now behind him like the Goldwyn films. Nor was he making a new movie of any kind. He was to have a serious role in *A Servant of Two Masters*, one of the plays to be put on as part of that year's Chichester Festival.

Much to everybody's surprise, Danny made a decision that caused little pleasure to the people at Las Vegas or the organisers of the Festival.

Kaye, the Jewish entertainer who had always decided that his religion and his ancestral heritage were no reasons to affect his career, cancelled both seasons and flew off to Israel.

He was caught up in a bug that affected Jews everywhere. In America and in England, there were those who cancelled the building of houses or the buying of cars so that the money, instead, could go to Israel. Some gave away their businesses. Danny was giving his most precious asset – his talent. It was not a thing that would have been expected of him.

He entertained troops throughout the country and in the newly-occupied territories. He opened his tour at a military base outside Ramallah.

He sang Israeli songs, dipped into his Jewish joke book, dropped the occasional Yiddish phrase – which at the time was considered less than good taste; the young Israeli 'sabra' liked to think that Jewish history began with the establishment of the State in 1948 and was somewhat ashamed of the image of the cowering Jew – and introduced local entertainers like Chaim Topol.

It was a perfect opportunity for Danny to dress the way he felt

[244]

most comfortable – the most brilliant military victory of recent history was accomplished by soldiers who regarded the discipline of smart uniforms to be a frippery with which they held no truck at all. He wore an Army drill jacket over his favourite open shirt and slacks. And the ubiquitous floppy white golf hat, which was precisely what was being worn in every well-dressed kibbutz in the land.

Danny was in Israel for six weeks and was seemingly dividing the shows between pure entertaining and congratulating the troops on their recent feat.

He said he loved Israel. 'Even if I were not tied to it by heritage or by culture, merely the fact that it is an incredible country and has achieved so much in the last 20 years would be enough to excite anyone. I feel very much at home there, and have many friends there and feel deeply about its future.'

He and Topol were sitting in the Israeli's London apartment on the day Danny was due to fly back to New York. 'You know,' he told him, 'why don't we go have some humus?' So instead of flying to New York, they both flew to Israel, had their humus and then flew back again the next afternoon. 'Great fun it was,' Danny said.

So was leading the Israel National Youth Symphony Orchestra on a fund-raising tour that literally went around the world.

In October 1969, he toured Army hospital wards.

It was all part of a two-way thing for him. 'Sure I go to entertain,' he said in an interview with *The Guardian*'s Catherine Stott in London. 'Though not in the formal sense of the word. I go visit the troops and we sing together. It isn't entertaining so much as their knowing that somebody cares enough to visit them. Morale boosting if you like.'

Meanwhile, Danny's breach of contract with Chichester meant that he would be liable for the losses he had caused. He had told Sir John Clements, the festival's director, that he would personally make up for any way in which the festival was out of pocket. No one thought it would be – because the substitute production, *An Italian Straw Hat*, was a virtual sell out. But as it turned out, the theatre was going to be £7,500 in the red, thanks to Danny's breach of contract. He apologised and immediately wrote a cheque for the amount which was sent off to Sir John.

It wasn't the most startling development in the Kaye career at this time. General Motors was reported as having ordered an inquiry into Danny's 'morals and political beliefs' as well as one on Ralph Nader, the man who had set out to prove that the cars made in America were unsafe. Why Danny should have become subject to the investigation – by private detectives – was never explained. What was revealed was that Kaye got a 'favourable report'.

Meanwhile, Danny thought he had found that new interest he had been looking for. He combined his passion for flying with the idea of becoming a businessman – and a top businessman at that. He was invited by the Lear Jet corporation to become one of their vice-presidents. It was an offer that was plainly too good to refuse. His responsibility, it was said at the time, was to 'participate actively in the international business for all Lear Jet aircraft.'

Danny was busy doing commercials for the plane. 'This is such an incredible airplane . . . [it] exceeds everything that you hear or expect,' he told *Popular Science* magazine. 'It's alive. It wants to fly. You go to level out and you're still climbing. The airplane is that "clean". Do you know how I fly this airplane once I've got it to 41,000 feet and flying straight and level? I pull my knees up and rest my hands on them, and just use finger movements. It's that easy. Of course, you can put it on autopilot and do crossword puzzles if you want to.'

That was obviously something to please the aircraft industry, but may not have done very much for the other kids from Brooklyn with whom Danny grew up. Yet they were not kept out of his act either. The Brooklyn Chamber of Commerce decided that Danny had a very important part to play in the history of their borough. The Chamber gave a ball at the Brooklyn Museum with Danny as guest of honour. He was also the first to be honoured in a 'Gallery of Great Brooklynites' which was being established at the museum, featuring people who had been brought up in the district and attained national prominence as 'outstanding citizens'. His sculptured bust was put on display. But it was his work for UNICEF and 'other humanitarian activities' which earned him the honour, not his entertaining.

No one quarrelled with that. But the citizenry of New Orleans in 1969 were less enamoured with him. For the first time, it was not a New Orleansian but Danny Kaye who was picked to be 'king' at the Mardi Gras carnival. He was enthroned as 'King Bacchus God of Wine' for the parade and was seen drinking – supposedly – wine from a ram's horn, surrounded by a jazz band.

But what about 'real' entertaining? In October 1969, Danny announced he was dealing with that. Years after he first thought about it, he was going to play Don Quixote in a new film. His Sancho Panza would be his friend Topol. A good idea, but like so much in show biz, it didn't happen.

What a shame! As Danny said, he and that 'other lunatic' Topol had been talking about the idea in Jerusalem. They were going to film it in South America, because that seemed an easier destination than Spain. But the story would be pure. It had everything to commend it. The story was, he said, more than just about a madman who charged at windmills. 'It's about an idealist in a materialist world.'

What did happen was a film that it would have been much better to have left alone. *The Madwoman of Chaillot* starred Katharine Hepburn, the sort of actress whom he, naturally enough, greatly admired. Danny played the ragpicker. Many critics said Danny's role was just about the best in the film, but that didn't say a great deal for him. The picture was practically disastrous, came, went and disappeared from most people's memories.

It was beset with problems from the beginning. It was made in two segments because the movie had two directors. It all started off with John Huston directing a cast that included also Charles Boyer, Yul Brynner and Paul Henreid. But then Huston had a row with the producer Ely Landau and he was replaced by Bryan Forbes who didn't in the least bit endear himself to Mr Henreid, for one.

'I remember,' he told me, 'that Kate had Danny Kaye in deep conversation and there were few other characters in their section of the film. But when I saw their scenes on the screen, it was absolutely ridiculous. It was unspeakably bad. Because Danny Kaye and I were in two different parts of the film we didn't even meet very much. It was terrible.'

The film – about an eccentric millionairess who is convinced the entire city of Paris is about to be turned into a giant oil field and so asks all her friends to try to do something about it – was shot on location on the French Riviera. That was not a bad place to be, especially for someone like Danny Kaye who was seemingly a lot happier sampling – and providing – the cuisine of the area than he was making the movie.

He was particularly happy at the Voile d'Or in Nice. One day the entire kitchen staff of the restaurant visited Danny at the studio where *Madwoman* was being shot and presented him with the highest honour they – or probably he – could imagine. They gave him a hat, jacket and check trousers of a master chef – and inscribed it all: 'To our great chef, M. Kaye.'

If others had known Danny was a master chef, the gift confirmed it. 'And all I did,' he explained, 'was a bit of peasant cooking.' He needn't have added, but could have done, that that was regarded as the best cooking in the world.

If he didn't enjoy the film so much, this honour more than made up for it.

Danny would claim, however, that he enjoyed the picture very much indeed – just as he was going to enjoy making *Don Quixote*, given half the chance, which of course he would not be given. 'I have reached that delicious point in life where I am just going to do the things I want to do; I'm no longer compelled to do anything else.'

[247]

Madwoman had been one attempt at getting back to the medium in which he had once been so adept. Now, he thought he ought to return to another – the stage.

TWO BY TWO

IF DANNY HAD TAKEN THE ROLE AT CHICHESTER IN 1967, IT WOULD have been his first ever wholly legitimate part and his first stage role – as distinct from his variety and cabaret appearances – since *Let's Face It* more than a quarter of a century before.

He hadn't appeared in vaudeville since soon after the TV shows. Audiences had at that time decided they had seen enough Kaye and wouldn't buy the tickets.

Now he was ready to try again. In November 1970, he opened on Broadway in a new Richard Rodgers show about Noah and his Ark, called, inevitably, *Two By Two*. It might have worked, except that people who came to see a book show with a script that other actors had to follow as well as its star were put off by Danny turning it all into a kind of performance he gave at the Palladium. He fooled around when he should have been reciting semi-serious lines. He made Danny Kaye-type faces and did Danny Kaye-type business.

Then, in the midst of the run, he tore a ligament in his left leg during a performance. Two weeks later, he returned and appeared on stage in a wheelchair – Noah in a wheelchair? And at a time when wheels, let alone chairs on wheels, had not as far as anyone knows been invented? But he sat on that chair, and got angry with people – and showed it by waving his stick around.

In effect, Danny (even in a wheelchair) was a great deal better than the other vehicle in which he appeared, the show. Clive Barnes in *The New York Times* said: 'Danny Kaye is a great and a good man and last night at the Imperial Theatre he returned to the Broadway stage after an absence of nearly 30 years (obviously his stint at the Palace didn't count). You had better go and see him now, because at this rate, he won't be back until 1999. And even though he might then be in a better play, is it really worth the wait? Mr Kaye is so warm and lovable an entertainer, such a totally ingratiating actor that for me at least he can do no wrong. It need take no unduly critical mind to note the flaws in the musical itself. . . . There is too much rain, but then there is also a great deal of Mr Kaye as compensation.'

[249]

They all came to see Danny's first night, and to walk through a whole crop of policemen who cleared the way for the likes of Leonard Bernstein, Gina Lollobrigida and Arthur Schlesinger Jnr, who had come to see the new Danny Kaye. They came two by two as well, noted another *Times* writer.

He wasn't the sort of Noah people had expected. He didn't even have a beard, for God's sake. Danny himself saw it all as revelant as, well perhaps, Don Quixote. 'There was always a generation gap. There were revolutions in Noah's time. They had drugs.'

Part of the story was that Noah, opening the show as an old, old man, experiences in the middle of the play, a form of rejuvenation. Suddenly, age turns to apparent hail, hearty and hilarious middle age. Looking, said the *Times*, only 35, Danny brought the house down with his number *Ninety Again*. He was 57 at the time.

The show was so long, said Clive Barnes, it might have been called *Three By Three*, but Danny was still worth that little inconvenience. Barnes wasn't so thrilled to hear a four-letter word appear in the script and he wondered if Danny was either.

After the show the celebrities could be seen going, two by two, into Danny's dressing room. Dena was there to see her first Danny Kaye first night. She hadn't been born when he last starred in a show. She said she was very proud. Sylvia was there and this time there wasn't the slightest suggestion that she was anything but as enthusiastic for Danny's success as he was himself.

'A writer is always unhappy before the curtain, even if you had nothing to do with the writing,' she told a reporter. 'It always takes me about two seconds flat after Danny walks on the stage when I see his first steps, hear his first line, then I know, then I relax.'

There was a relaxed look on Sylvia's face all evening.

The *New York Times* sent a whole clutch of writers to record what they obviously assumed was going to be an important night in the history of the musical. None of the scribes appeared to be in the least bit disappointed with the star's performance.

The still respected and still feared Walter Kerr wrote: 'If you want to know why *Two By Two* works in spite of all that is wrong with it, just pay attention to a very tiny thing that happens somewhere early in the second act. It isn't much. It doesn't last. But it fills the house with magic and music and in a musical comedy what else is there? It's a walk. Nothing more. Danny Kaye as that Noah who had so much trouble with the weather, has for some time past been revelling in the fact that God had restored him to a very fit 90 even though he's actually 600 years old.' He did it all with a walk.

Danny tore the ligament in his left leg during the first act of the show in February 1971 and had to hobble off. He was out of *Two By Two* for almost two weeks. When he came back, he used it as an opportunity to slice the play into his own kind of product.

He was greeted by a roar of applause as he came on in the wheelchair, stood up, pointed to his plaster cast and hobbled along the stage using first two crutches and then one as somewhat difficult to manage balancing mechanisms, rather like a skier on the nursery slopes for the first time. He bumped into scenery and into other performers – who were totally thrown by both Danny's movements and the one-liners he kept delivering.

In one scene he was meant to talk to God, like Tevya in *Fiddler on the Roof*. Danny looked to heaven and pointed to his leg. 'Where were you when I needed you?' The audience thought it was marvellous.

It worked that first night, so Danny used it all the time he was in that cast.

Like Jolson dismissing the rest of his show companies in the midst of a performance – he'd call to his audiences, 'Do you want to see them or do you want me?' – Danny ad-libbed to the other performers. 'Shall I feed you the right line?' he said once to an embarrassed actor. Another time, he yelled to a singer: 'Don't back up or you'll be in *No, No Nanette*.'

There were those in the audience who didn't enjoy the spectacle quite as much as Danny might have hoped they would.

Not content with allowing its professional writers to have their say, the *Times* opened a special correspondence column on Kaye in a wheelchair – which gives a further idea to how important it was all considered.

'Recently I handed over the bargain basement price of $12 to the Imperial cashier because I thought it would be fun to see a musical conceived in the classic Broadway tradition, *Two By Two*,' wrote Mr Anthony W. Harris of Nashville, Tennessee.

'The curtain had not been up five minutes, however, before it was quite obvious that I along with a sizeable audience had paid our money to attend an entertainment that might be called The Danny Kaye Show or perhaps One By One.

'Kaye had his left leg in a cast, and it must be said he brought to bear all his considerable experience to, in effect, direct himself skilfully around that drawback. In fact, as his role was allegedly that of a patriarch, this handicap could easily have blended into his characterization and become almost unnoticed had he let it. But he didn't.'

Mr Harris complained of his 'terrorizing' the rest of the cast.

Mrs Richard Taussig of New York was equally unhappy. She said she and her husband watched the show with 'a sense of indignation amounting to outrage at the exhibition put on by Danny Kaye. It could not be dignified by the term "performance".

[251]

He mugged, grimaced, hammed and ad-libbed. . . . The producers should be required to make refunds and apologies to all playgoers who thought to see a musical and found themselves at a burlesque show.'

Meanwhile the theatrical profession thought more kindly of Danny and gave him yet another award – the Sam S. Shubert Foundation Award 'in recognition of his outstanding contributions to the American Theatre in 1970–71.'

When the show folded later in 1971, Danny had to find something else to do. He went back to UNICEF to make a new film for them which would emphasise 'the relevance of UNICEF's work on behalf of women and children in the long-term social and economic development plans of the individual countries.'

The experience of *Two By Two* was another in the Danny Kaye opus of trying to broaden horizons that seemed so stretched, they were in danger of becoming transparent.

To Kaye admirers, the show was what they wanted of the man who used to manipulate them with a twist of the tongue or of his hand. It didn't satisfy those who complained because they were after something totally different.

The message should have been that Danny ought to have gone back to vaudeville. But he had done that. Vaudeville and even the Palace were *passé*. He wasn't in the least bit interested in even going back to the Palladium, where a new generation would probably have given him all the love their mothers and fathers had offered and had accepted.

Kaye was in another restless mood. After all he had done, was anything else left?

There was, of course, opera. Danny, who had sung a great deal and recorded most of his repertoire, had never appeared in opera – at least not since the 'Me Scaredo, Me Fraido' aria at the end of *Wonder Man*. So why not? It happened in January 1973, at the Met in New York.

Well, to be fair, he didn't actually sing, not in any serious way, although the idea itself was serious enough to encourage children to like a branch of the arts which for them represented territory completely uncharted.

They had, of course, to like Danny Kaye first but that wasn't likely to be a problem. If he could get the kids of the Third World to like what he did, those coming from within a stone's throw of his own neck of the Brooklyn woods wouldn't find him too difficult.

Met star Regina Resnik called it 'the first opera laugh-in'. She wasn't entirely wrong. Danny was to be the host and compere of what were really opera *shows*, which said a great deal for what he was going to do.

[252]

Actually, the shows were called 'look-ins' – with schoolchildren aged between 10 and 14 going to the opera house at 11 o'clock in the morning and hearing about everything from making an opera set to getting together a mass chorus. They were then introduced to actual opera moments which were considered likely to be the most appealing – like the chorus from *Aida* and the shaving scene from *The Barber of Seville*.

For that the children would pay – or more likely have had the payment made on their behalf – no more than $2.50. As soon as the project was announced, the house was completely sold out for the first two shows, held at the end of the Christmas school holidays.

Somebody called it 'utter Kaye-os'. Well, nobody could have expected anything else. Danny didn't just turn it into a one-man show with the operas as a side line, he controlled the house of children as he had every audience over the previous 30 years.

He also controlled those on stage. To 500 professional opera singers he commanded: 'Say "aaahh".' They said 'aaahh' and with a sweep of his arms, Mr Kaye let it be known that behold it was good and he was satisfied.

Danny might have seen it all as an investment for the future. If the shows didn't convince the children from various parts of New York, New Jersey and Connecticut that they were going to like opera for ever and ever, it surely made them awfully fond of Danny Kaye.

Sets and backdrops appeared as if by magic – as indeed it was. The children were watching the Kaye magic of old, as if they had been snapped back in time to an era they never knew existed.

Who else could have inserted a scene from *Madam Butterfly* into the end of the first act of *La Bohème* and have even the purists sitting with the children laughing their heads off?

Danny explained it all, from the prompter's box to the way the flies worked – the kind in the theatre, that is. When for a moment the audience seemed to get restless, Mr Kaye the schoolmaster held up his hand just as he had all those years before at the Palladium. And 3,000 miles and a whole world and era away from the theatre in Argyle Street, the audience reacted precisely the same way. Svengali Kaye had wrought his will and the youngsters were suitably mesmerised.

Then he took the baton from the conductor James Levine and the rest was a Danny Kaye symphony concert. The orchestra didn't noticeably take much from him, but he took a great deal from them. An orchestra was always his favourite prop and he used it like a baggy-pants comedian used a jug of water or a slapstick.

The kids were entranced. The trouble was they were likely ever after to associate opera with Danny Kaye and it may have taken

[253]

them an awful long time to realise that it wasn't always as good fun as that.

Danny would have preferred to have seen it all as another one of his contributions to the arts of America – like being the first person to buy two $100 'patrons' seats for a gala performance at New York's City Center in aid of the Dance collection at the public library.

If you thought that it was time Danny got another award, Mrs Rose Kennedy should be thanked for putting the matter to rights. She presented him with the Variety Club's International Humanitarian Award. Then there was the Lions International Conference Special Award for his 20 years service to UNICEF and . . . even he by now must have lost count.

The Isrealis certainly thought he was worthy of one. In October 1973, Danny flew back to their country to entertain troops in another Middle East conflict, the Yom Kippur War. With Zubin Mehta and Isaac Stern, he visited the Syrian and Suez fronts and communed with the wounded in the wards of the Tel Hashomer Hospital in Tel Aviv.

Danny was the intimate of the great, the near-great and those who considered themselves perhaps only grand. Go to a party at San Ysidro Drive and you'd meet the Henry Kissingers – Danny was a guest at their wedding in June 1974 – and hear them repeating those outrageous lyrics. When Jack Benny died in December that year, Danny was, together with Governor Ronald Reagan, Frank Sinatra and George Burns, among the pallbearers.

There were other interests still to be fulfilled. And because they involved Danny Kaye, they had to be taken seriously. No one knew how rich he was, but he was accumulating a wide sweep of business ventures, including a number of real estate deals and the control of various radio stations.

Everybody who knew Danny Kaye knew about his passions and enthusiasms. They knew, too, that he liked baseball, or rather loved baseball. As an old Brooklyn kid, of course, he supported the Dodgers, now conveniently based in Los Angeles.

What no one had suspected was that he now decided he wanted to *own* a baseball team, which might or might not be called something like the Wonder Men – if only by writers marvelling at their prowess since Danny took over the helm. In December 1975, he put in a bid for the San Francisco Giants, but failed to pull off a deal.

Two months later, however, he was part of a group of businessmen who bought a team which would bring back Major League baseball to the city of Seattle after an absence of seven years. He was to part own the Seattle Mariners until 1984. Naturally enough, he became as fanatical about the interest as he was about anything else he touched.

Quite as fanatical as his music – the 300,000-member American Federation of Musicians gave him their Gold Card for 'making a significant contribution to music' and allowed him to join, in the Federation's archives, the names of Harry S. Truman, Jack Benny, Duke Ellington and Pablo Cassals. Almost as fanatical as medicine. He had now watched so many operations – mostly at the Mayo Clinic – that the American College of Surgeons made him an honorary member, too.

And then there was that session at the opera. The 1973 shows had been so successful that they were repeated the following year and televised as *Danny Kaye's Look At The Metropolitan Opera*. He won an Emmy for his performances.

He was doing more television now – but in specials; TV films that a few years before he would have turned into Hollywood spectaculars. The first was *Peter Pan*, in which he played Captain Hook. The second was *Pinocchio*. Both had been Disney films, *Peter Pan* after being a hallowed English children's story; *Pinocchio*, a lesser-known Italian children's story which became a Disney classic. In this, he played Gepetto, the lonely wood-carver who creates the puppet into which he breathes life.

'It's a genuine character role, in every sense of the word,' he said after completing the *Pinocchio* role. 'It was a wonderful part. It required almost the whole emotional spectrum, from the utter devastation when Gepetto finds himself abandoned, to the elation when Pinocchio becomes a real boy.'

That was Danny's story, too. He was always something of a Pinocchio who became a real boy. But a Peter Pan boy who didn't want to grow up.

PETER PAN

THE AWARDS CONTINUED TO SHOWER ON HIM TO THE EXTENT THAT HE might have been buried by them. Like the 1978 Philip Murry-William Green Humanitarian Award presented by the American Federation of Labour, the AFL-CIO. Two years later, the Cannes Film Festival honoured him with the order of *Officier Des Arts Et Lettres*, one of the highest honours that could be given a foreigner by the French Government.

At the age of 67, it was gratifying. He was, after all, now at a stage in life when people consider retirement. Danny was doing nothing of the kind. He was flying constantly in his Beechcroft jet from Los Angeles to Seattle to look after his baseball team or to the Mayo Clinic or to one or other of the destinations where he was going to conduct an orchestra. So he was busy.

But why was he not doing another Danny Kaye spectacular? It surely wasn't because he would find it too exacting. Those people sampling his Chinese and Italian cuisine knew that he could still twist heart strings the way he twisted tongues.

He gave the impression of being a lot happier simply doing more work for UNICEF. In January 1979, he took it upon himself to work for the International Year of the Child. He told how he got a great kick out of going back to former disaster areas and seeing how his child fans had grown into healthy, responsible adults. But what about that kick he could have given to audiences who just wanted to see a Danny Kaye show of old? He didn't seem interested.

Was it because he still felt there were new things to do? Probably. He still looked for fun. 'He's an elf,' says Melville Shavelson. 'I have an idea that when his personal life finished as far as Sylvia was concerned, his professional life finished, too.'

Certainly, there were no signs of he and Sylvia working together again. When Sylvia in the early '80s did a series of television shows on the musical, Danny went on the screen to give support. But, said a man who considers himself a friend, 'I think he did it somewhat ungraciously. He tried to take over.'

Danny could have taken over any show that he wanted. But

[256]

why didn't he want to do the kind of show that he and only he could perform? No one will ever really know.

Undoubtedly, he still had his status. He came to London and appeared on the radio chat shows. But whereas every other celebrity on these BBC programmes was given five or ten minutes, it was still taken for granted that Danny Kaye would command the whole show.

When, in March 1980, Disneyland celebrated its 25th anniversary, it was only sensible that Danny Kaye should host the celebratory TV show. Or was it? *The New York Times* did not think so.

He played Captain Hook again, sang the Disneyland anthem, *It's A Small World*, with the International Children's Choir and did a medley of other Disney songs. It wasn't up the *Times*'s critic John J. O'Connor's street at all. 'Depending on your tolerance level for Danny Kaye – mine has been persistently low over the years – *Disneyland's 25th Anniversary* on CBS TV can prove either charming or exasperating. As host, Mr Kaye is all over the place, getting into just about everybody's act.'

Much more significantly was that in 1980, he again did it when for the first time since 1955 he topped the bill at the London Palladium. This time, it was for the Royal Variety Show. Stars like Sammy Davis Jnr., Peggy Lee, Mary Martin and her son Larry Hagman (J.R. of *Dallas*) were on the bill, and James Cagney and Pat O'Brien walked on stage, too. But it was never beyond doubt that Kaye was the real headliner there.

He told the crowded theatre that some of the happiest moments of his life had been in that country, that city, and that theatre.

It looked a magnificent *tour-de-force*. The Queen Mother was in the Royal Box. It was all intended to be a tribute to her after her 80th birthday.

Danny came on, sounding just a little bit hoarse, and announced that he was 'a comparatively young man when I came here the other day' (to begin rehearsals).

He sang the gypsy song from *The Inspector General*, with all the marvellous domination of the audience of old. He divided the audience into three sections, just as he had in the film, and got them to repeat inane phrases like 'shtock, shtock' after him. He told some stories about London, sang *Ballin' The Jack* – and invited the audience to follow him in 'First you put your two knees right up tight. . . .' Then he led the entire cast in *Maybe It's Because I'm a Londoner*. It was a wonderful performance, the kind that would have had those Londoners eating out of his as-ever expressive hands if only he had done it for a Palladium season again. But he still said he wasn't interested.

The Danny Kaye who appeared on stage was not quite the

Danny Kaye who had arrived in London a few days earlier. Or indeed the one who had met the show's producer Lionel Blair in Beverly Hills a few months before.

'I had gone to his home to discuss the show,' Blair told me. 'We sat down in his den and a maid brought in coffee and biscuits. Danny helped himself and I was just left sitting, while he talked and ate.

'In the end, I asked him if he minded if I took myself some coffee too.'

That was nothing compared with what happened when he flew into London. 'We had sent a car to the airport to meet Danny when he arrived at Heathrow, but he didn't find the driver and the driver didn't recognise him. He had changed quite a bit from the days when we all knew him on the films. So he and his manager got themselves a taxi into London which made him hopping mad. When he came to the theatre after checking into the Savoy, he let go with a stream of four-letter words. He said: "If it wasn't for the Queen Mother, I'd go straight back." He was not a nice man that day.'

He also had the bright idea of wiring up the Queen Mother's box so that she could join him in *Ballin' The Jack*. Louis Benjamin, the Palladium's boss, turned the idea down flat – as he knew the Palace would, too. Danny then suggested that the audience should sing Happy Birthday to the Queen Mother. Since the show was in November and the birthday had been the previous August, this was turned down as well.

Harry Secombe was no more pleased with Danny – who immediately recognised him and shook his hand. Now that might seem like elementary courtesy and something that Sir Harry would appreciate. 'I didn't very much. I had first met Danny at a Royal show years before and he was just as friendly. Then, several years later, I saw him again, went up to him and got a very cold glare in return. I couldn't believe that he knew me again now, but not then. Funny man – but not in my sense of the word.'

But nobody could doubt that his talent was still there.

That same year, he was in another TV show. But this one was different. *Skokie* (shown in Britain, for some reason – probably because the title meant nothing to most Britons – as *They Marched Through A Thousand Towns*) was a highly dramatic play about the anger of the people in the town of Skokie, near Chicago, at the plan of American Nazis to hold a march in their midst. The story was true and struck Danny to the quick – the townspeople of Skokie were mostly Jewish survivors of Hitler's camps. Adopting a slight Polish-Jewish accent – with not a trace of the dialects that were most familiar to Kaye fans of old – he was quite brilliant.

In 1983, the Carnegie Foundation Peace Award went to Danny 'for the numerous and outstanding activities he has carried out in his capacity of goodwill ambassador'.

The citations all seemed to say the same thing. But each one was as deserved as the one before. Yet you always felt that he had a great need to do those good deeds – as much as he needed to do his cooking.

The really important citation was that he had contributed so much to American entertainment. He didn't deny it. Twenty odd years ago he was saying: 'I don't know what makes a person successful. I don't know how I became successful. I'm glad I am.'

Mr Kaminsky was always glad that he was, too. So would his mother have been. If she had only known *how* successful when she used to ask him to stand on a chair and 'make like Mary Pickford' or whoever it was.

Both of his parents might have simply been glad he didn't follow the two schoolmates of his whom he revealed years afterwards had ended up 'in the pen'. Danny was penned in only by the adoration of millions who still wanted a lot more.

Most people in the profession seem to think that if he starred in a new Broadway show, he would be a sensation – much more so than in *Two By Two*. Films are likely to be harder. One producer told me: 'I tried hard to find a project for him, but couldn't. And if I had found one, I doubt if I would have got it financed.'

People wanted to know about the future of his business. He wasn't sure where the new entertainers were going to come from. Not television. 'Television pushes them on too fast,' he said. It had, after all, taken *him* years to be that overnight sensation.

And yet Melvin Frank wasn't wrong when he said that despite all that he had achieved, 'you feel as if he has never given all he is capable of giving.' He has given prodigiously, but his talent is such that you know that, even now, there is a lot held in reserve.

'As an entertainer,' says Milton Sperling,' he was always non-pareil. He has great charm. And yet he is a child in a man's world.'

The hardest thing for him, seemingly, was conducting orches-tras. Not only did he have to learn the score by ear, he had to tone up at the office of the local chiropractor before going on. But it appeared worth it. Zubin Mehta who shared with him the respon-sibility of conducting the Los Angeles Philharmonic at a benefit concert, which was also televised, said: 'The difference between Danny's comedy with music and Jack Benny's is that Jack played the best he could and it was awful. Danny does the best he can and his best is very good. . . . As for the music itself, there's no distor-tion at all.' By the summer of 1981, it was estimated he had raised $5.5 million for orchestra charities.

He seemed to put an equal amount of effort into *going* to concerts, usually being seen at all the important events at the Los Angeles Music Center, frequently in the company of Mrs Dorothy Chandler or Olive Behran, the President of the Centre Foundation – the only woman with a licence to pilot a Venice gondola. Sylvia is rarely seen with him.

The unfortunate thing is that he is no longer mobbed. Those who remember worshipping at the Kaye shrine are now mature enough to allow him his privacy. The younger ones mostly don't know who he is.

Danny made friends and lost them. Sometimes, he didn't just make friends, he had love affairs with people – a-sexual affairs, bred from his charm. Just as easily and for no more apparent reason, the friendships cooled, the affairs died away.

He attracted highly emotional women, 'women with dark personalities' was how one friend put it. The dark affairs continued, although there were to be changes in his life style.

The depressions were still there. 'They hang over him like a deep cloud,' another friend told me.

In Los Angeles in February 1983, the enthusiastically healthy Danny Kaye was suddenly whisked into the Cedars-Sinai Hospital with an undisclosed illness.

Then it was revealed he had an irregular heart rhythm although how any Danny Kaye rhythm could be irregular defies imagination.

He had a quadruple by-pass operation, which distinctly slowed him down and put an end to a suggestion that he would come to London with Rock Hudson in a version of the top musical *Cage Aux Folles*.

The operation wasn't his only problem. Afterwards, he developed hepatitis. Friends who saw him in late 1984 reported they were shocked by his appearance. He was walking with a stick because he was awaiting a hip operation. His hair was unusually long. His face looked strained.

But as one would expect, he did come back, if not exactly bouncing, that December when – together with his friends Isaac Stern and Arthur Miller, Lena Horne and Gian Carlo Menotti, he was presented with the ribbon and medal of the Kennedy Center Honor. President Ronald Reagan made the presentation to Danny and his fellow honourees at the John F. Kennedy Center for the Performing Arts on December 2, 1984.

When he returned home to Los Angeles, he told radio show host Michael Jackson that it was his intention to keep his fingers in as many pies as possible. He wasn't going to give any of them up. Except, that is, the one his dearest friends and fans would have liked to have seen most: the old Danny Kaye act which no one could ever do the same way.

In the spring of 1985, the Jerusalem International Conference on Volunteering gave him another award – Prince Philip got one, too – for his work for UNICEF. But he still wasn't volunteering to perform.

He explained: 'I find I just cannot do anything less I am really excited about it.' As for doing the Palladium again or another TV series, that had to be cast back into history. There is just no point, he maintains, in doing something he had done before, 'quite pointless'.

He went on: 'All that was of a special time, a special era and a special place and it belongs there.'

But doesn't it also belong to his audiences, too? And his potential audiences who would like Danny Kaye at the age of 73 to once again be acclaimed the world's greatest living entertainer?

It's probably a dream. Just like Walter Mitty's.